I0812411

POSTCARD HISTORY SERIES

Aberdeen

IN VINTAGE POSTCARDS

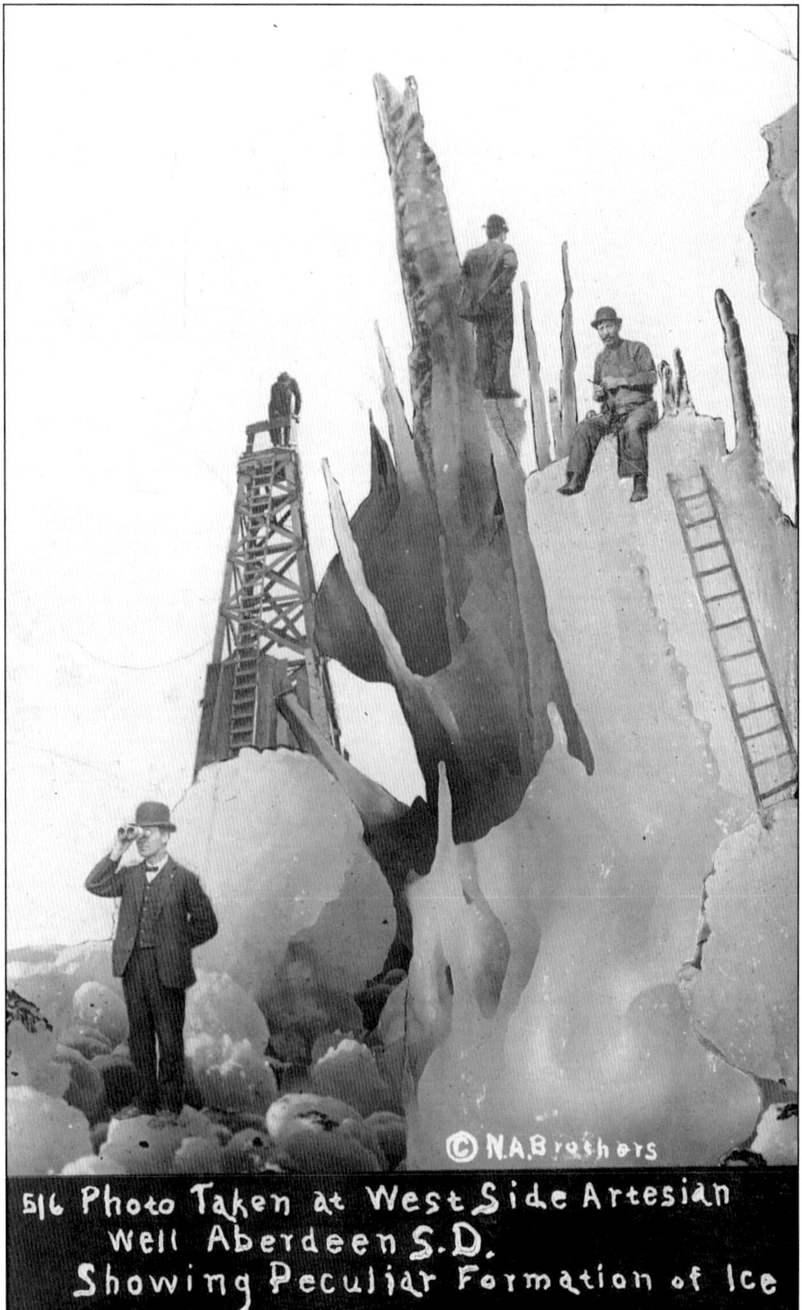

The Milwaukee Railroad drilled the first artesian well in Aberdeen in 1881, north of the present day courthouse. The well was so powerful that city fathers passed a bond issue to drill one for city use that was completed in 1884. The city's uncontrolled well shot water into the air for days with a flow estimated at four million gallons daily. Several other wells with equal pressure were drilled throughout the city in its early years. All of these wells were a great source of pride, attracting tourists to the city to view them. The photographer obviously decided to have a little fun with this image.

POSTCARD HISTORY SERIES

Aberdeen

IN VINTAGE POSTCARDS

Tom Hayes and Mike Wiese

ARCADIA PUBLISHING

ISBN 978-0-7385-2308-8

Published by Arcadia Publishing
Charleston, South Carolina

Printed in the United States of America

Library of Congress Catalog Card Number: 2002116526

For all general information contact Arcadia Publishing at:
Telephone 843-853-2070
Fax 843-853-0044
E-Mail sales@arcadiapublishing.com
For customer service and orders:
Toll-Free 1-888-313-2665

Visit us on the Internet at www.arcadiapublishing.com

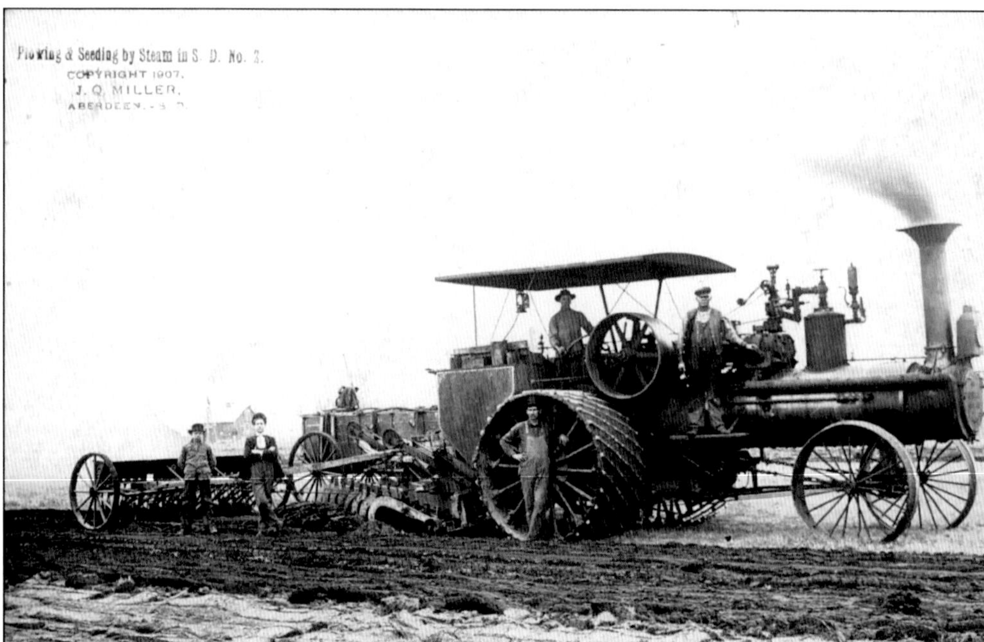

Steam driven plows and threshing machines first appeared on the prairies, taking the burden of fieldwork from oxen and horses. Most steam engines used for agricultural tasks used straw for fuel, some used wood or coal. These huge machines were equipped with driving wheels, which enabled them to move under their own power while pulling an implement. These monstrous machines worked slowly but had the power to do 12 to 16 furrows at a time. The period from 1890 to 1915 marked the heyday of steam engines on the farm.

Contents

Acknowledgments

Postcards, to most of us, are used for one of two things—either as a quick and inexpensive way to keep in touch with family and friends, or in the case of picture postcards, a sure way to have a professional quality photograph of something we want to remember from our travels. Postcards, to others, are highly prized collectables sought either for their postal cancellations or their historic picture views of a particular area or location.

Most of us do not think of postcards in connection with history. However, the views in this book, selected from the massive postcard collections of two Aberdeen businessmen, Mike Wiese and Tom Hayes, do in fact present a brief history lesson about Aberdeen, South Dakota: its beginnings, its dreams, its successes, and even its failures. Some of the scenes document buildings, businesses, and a way of life that is forever gone; while others depict some of today's well-established institutions and neighborhoods as they looked in their earliest days of existence.

If you are a present or former resident of Aberdeen, it is our hope that these scenes will spur many "I remember this..." or "I didn't know that..." moments for you. Our hope for readers with no knowledge of Aberdeen is that these postcards will give you a better understanding of and appreciation for this prairie town we call home.

To all of you, we hope you enjoy our efforts to share some of Aberdeen's great stories with the help of a few of our favorite picture postcards. This would not have been possible without the patience and understanding of our wives while we were working on this book and their support of our collecting habits. A very special thanks to Sue Gates, executive director of the Dacotah Prairie Museum, for writing captions for some of the postcards using information gathered from the museum's archive collection.

INTRODUCTION

It has been 38 years since *Early History of Brown County South Dakota* was published in 1965, and 23 years since *Brown County History* was published in 1980. Both are excellent books with comprehensive historical content and a number of wonderful photographs. We are not intending to replace either book, but to show some of the history of Aberdeen through postcards and postal history. With the exception of the 1914 photograph of the new fire engine and the Ward Hotel door sign, all of the other items represented in this book were or could have been sent through the mail.

Postcard collecting was in its heyday from approximately 1907 to 1915. On March 1, 1907, the post office finally allowed messages to be written on the address side of a postcard. Before that, any message had to be written on the picture side, which defaced the picture and did not encourage the sending of postcards. It was better to be able to write a message when sending a postcard for the cost of a one cent stamp. If we think back to what everyday life must have been like from 1907 to 1915, we find that very few people had or could even afford a telephone. At that time, a three minute long distance phone call could cost up to $15, and that could be one or two weeks wages. Socializing was an important event (with no televisions), but could not be done everyday, as the homes lacked such modern conveniences as fast food, or microwave ovens. Doing the laundry and keeping the furnace going were some of the big chores. Families were lucky to have one automobile, and you will read in this book that in 1916 Aberdeen had *two* women drivers.

So people sent postcards, and they were easy to send in Aberdeen. The cost was one cent for a postcard and two cents for a letter. Conveniently, Aberdeen had twice a day home mail delivery and once on Saturdays. One could mail something in the morning and it would be delivered, even across town, that afternoon. Mail delivery was fast, and with the trains, mail would be delivered the next day—even as far as Minneapolis.

Postcard collecting and the exchanging of postcards became a major hobby during this period. Postcard "pals" would exchange postcards on a weekly basis, and this happened all over the country. Most of the postcard collectors were women. They would fill special albums for postcards. Any out of town trip, for business, family, or vacations would always result in postcards being mailed, and the true collectors would keep some for themselves. This collecting craze came to an end about 1914 or 1915. Up until this time, virtually all of the postcards were printed on the superior six-color printing presses in Germany and Hungry. Once World War I began in Europe, this entire supply of postcards stopped. One can tell the postcards printed in America after 1915 because they had a white border around them and the details were not normally as sharp.

From our personal Aberdeen postcard collections, we have picked out about 225 items for this book. With so many to choose from, it was difficult not to include them all. What we wanted was to give you, the reader, a glimpse of the early history of Aberdeen: its people, buildings, and events through postcards, with some historical context accompanying each. We wanted to use postcards instead of photographs because this is what we actively collect and it is a way of sharing our collections. This book is comprised mostly of real photo postcards. Many were done by "NAB" or N.A. Brothers, a very successful Aberdeen photography studio. Their pictures of the depot and furniture store fire are wonderful, and look as though they were taken for the newspaper or the evening news.

Aberdeen is the largest town in Brown County, a county that at one time or another has been comprised of 45 different towns. Today there are only 15 left. Aberdeen is the third largest town in South Dakota and we seem to be holding our own. The town has changed in the last 122 years, but many of the buildings, parks, and memories are still here.

The authors hope you will enjoy this book, its varied subject matter, and the captions for the pictures. In conducting research, one finds some disparity in the various printed histories. Some errors will go on repeating themselves with every new article. We hope that we have been accurate. We have chosen a period of Aberdeen's history where actual eyewitnesses are impossible to find. I have all of the Aberdeen City Directories except one, and even though they were published contemporaneously, they were not always correct. The older directories sometimes gave information one did not expect, such as listing someone the year after they died and even including the date of death. The history books mentioned above were excellent sources of material. And this couldn't have been done without the wonderful help of Sue Gates, curator of the Dacotah Prairie Museum, and her staff. We thank you and hope you enjoy this book.

One

Early Aberdeen

Aberdeen, Dakota Territory was planned and plotted out a good six months before the first settlers arrived in June of 1881. Aberdeen was envisioned to be a larger than normal town along the Milwaukee Railroad line. Planners hoped to get an early start on building the town before the railroad tracks reached Aberdeen in 1882. The post office was authorized and John H. Drake was appointed the first Postmaster on February 17, 1881. The Homestead Act provided a lot of cheap and free land for farming, and by 1887 every available quarter section of land in the county had been claimed. The town of Aberdeen was blessed with many men with a true pioneer spirit who had the foresight to build this town—men like Samuel H. Jumper, C.A. Bliss, Alonzo Ward and S.W. Narragang, to name a few. And grow we did. They not only built banks and businesses, but homes and churches, and government and organizations, and social events. Everything that reminded them of back home.

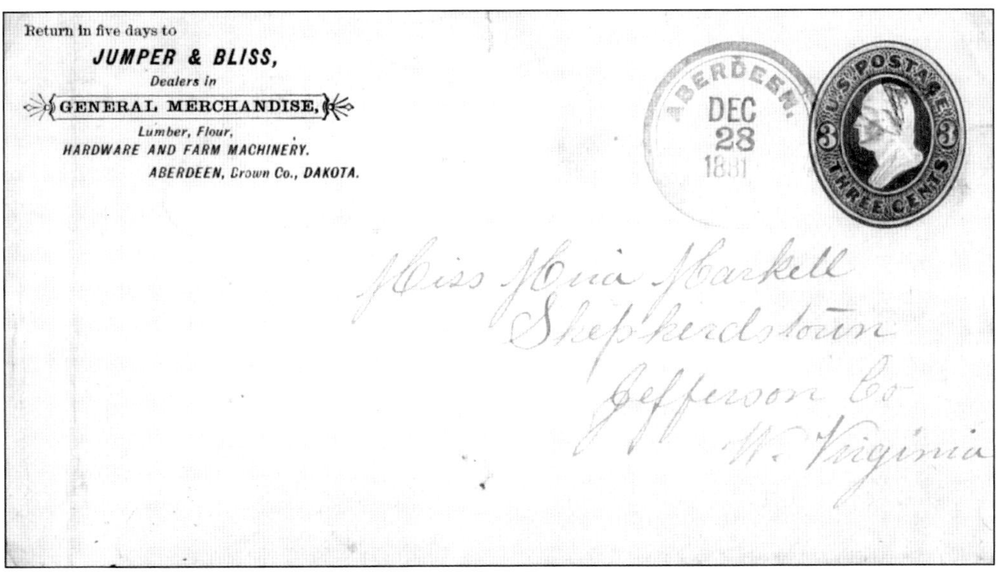

This is one of the earliest known postmarks from the new town of Aberdeen, Dakota Territory, from two of the pioneer merchants. In fact, Samuel H. Jumper was the very first person to arrive here on the empty prairie as the agent for C.H. Prior, the land agent for Milwaukee Railroad the owner of the town site.

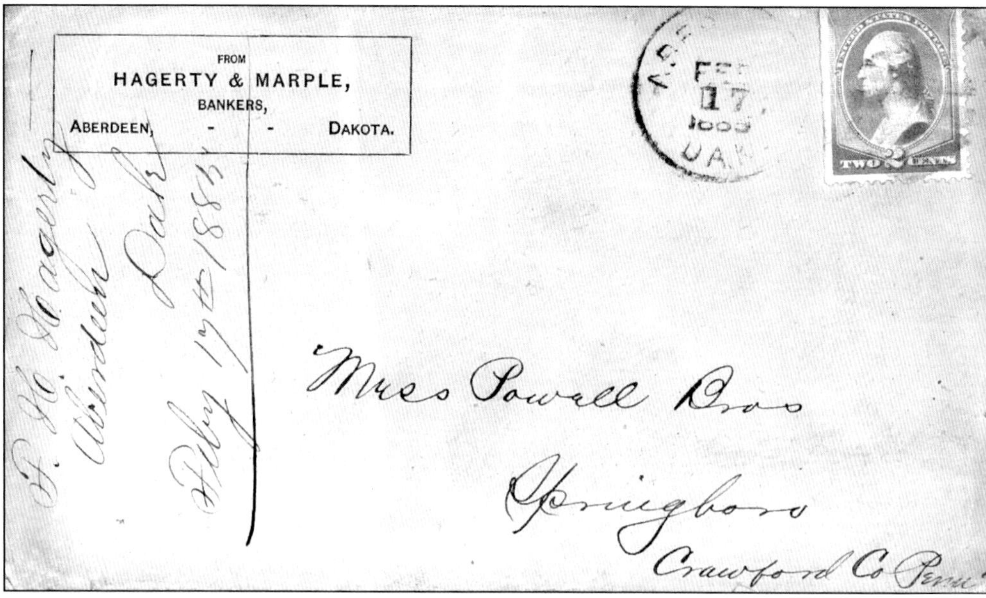

Frank H. Hagerty and his partner, Henry M. Marple, were both prominent territorial pioneer residents and businessmen. These bankers were located on the southwest corner of Main Street and Second Avenue. The Citizens Bank was built upon this location after their bank dissolved. This envelope is from 1885.

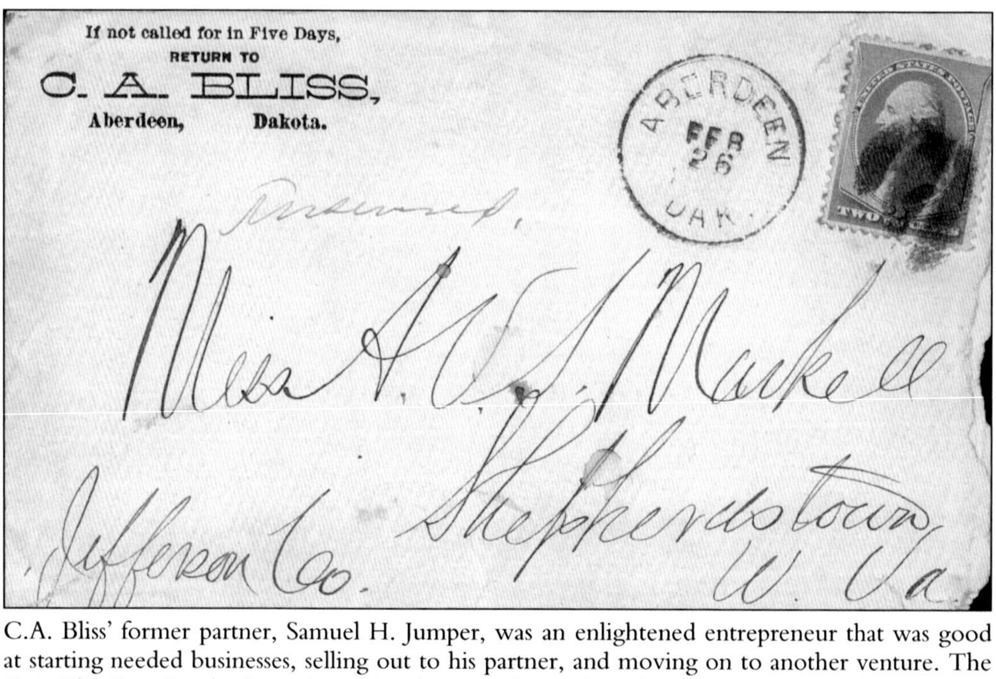

C.A. Bliss' former partner, Samuel H. Jumper, was an enlightened entrepreneur that was good at starting needed businesses, selling out to his partner, and moving on to another venture. The C.A. Bliss Dry Goods, Groceries & Crockery was located on the northeast corner of Main Street and First Avenue, on the present location of the Dacotah Prairie Museum. This envelope is from 1885.

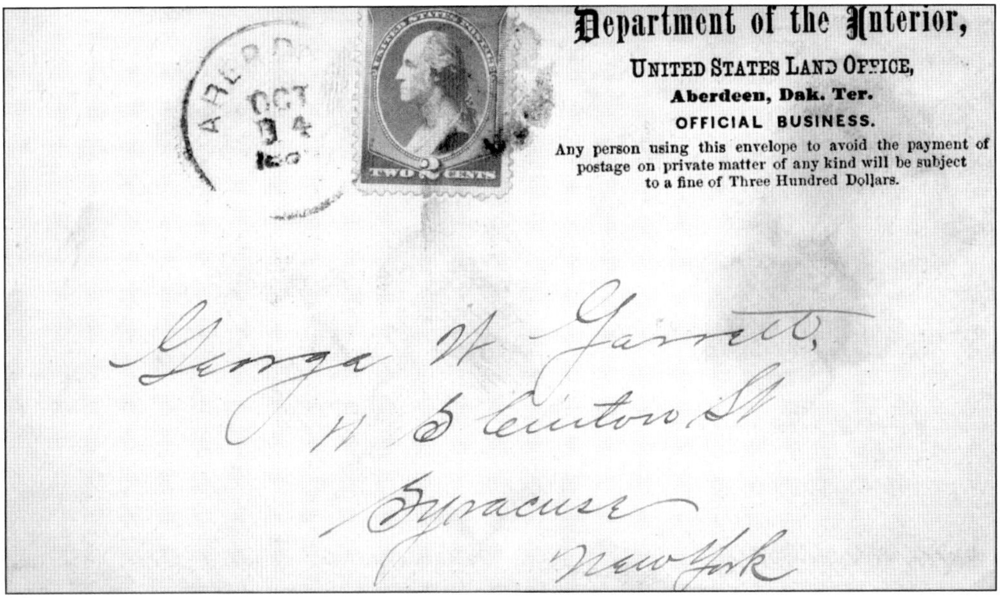

Horace Greeley was quoted as saying, "Go west, young man, go west." And to the west people came as more land was opened up for homesteading. Those who settled in the Aberdeen, Dakota Territory area in the early part of the 1880s had to walk or go by horse to the U.S. Land Office in Watertown to file their claim. And remember, there were no roads or bridges at that time. Finally, the Department of the Interior opened a land office in Aberdeen. This is an example from 1885.

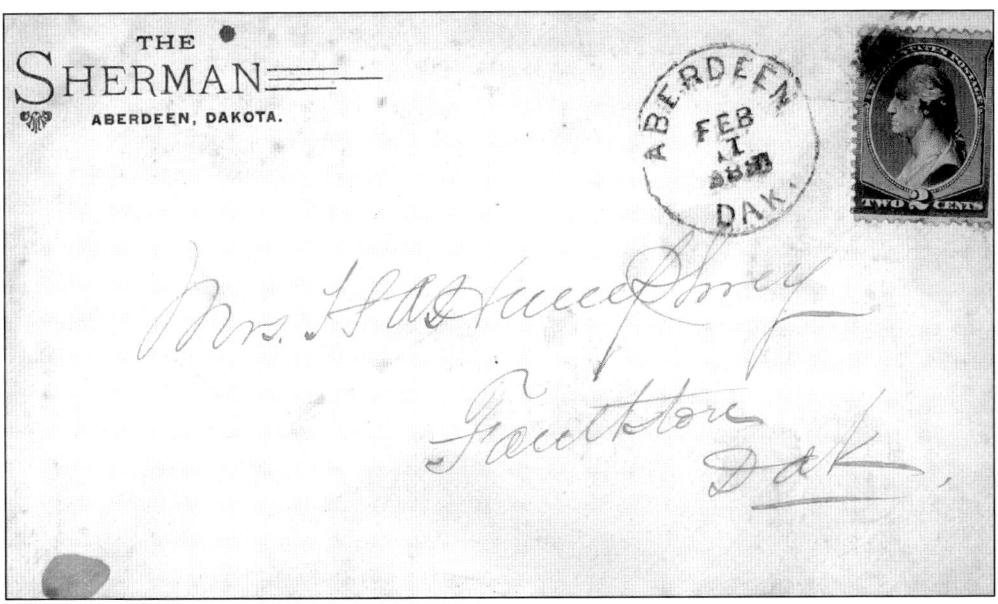

In the 1880s, the Sherman House Hotel was located on the northeast corner of Main Street and Third Avenue, the present location of the New Sherman Apartments. Before this and after the hotel was demolished in the 1970s, they built an albatross of a three-story parking garage that never lasted long as it proved unsafe and was demolished.

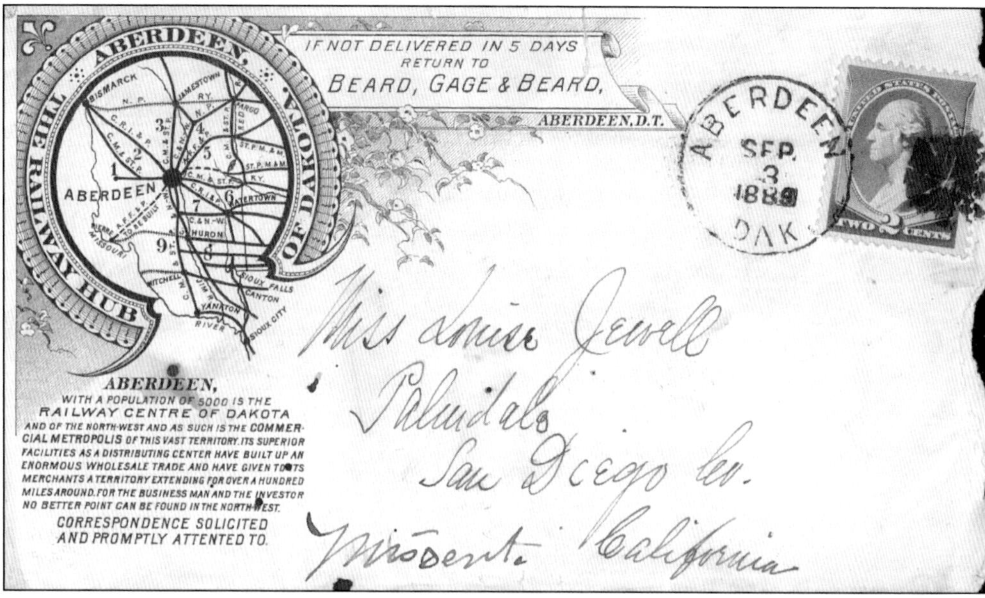

This advertising cover from Beard, Gage & Beard, a dry goods and grocery store located on the southeast corner of Main Street and Third Avenue, gave rise to the town's nickname. This nickname, "Aberdeen, the Railway Hub of Dakota," was shortened to "The Hub City." This map shows all the different railroads and tracks that came through Aberdeen, creating what looks like the spokes of a wheel with Aberdeen as the hub or hubcap. The postmark on this is from 1888.

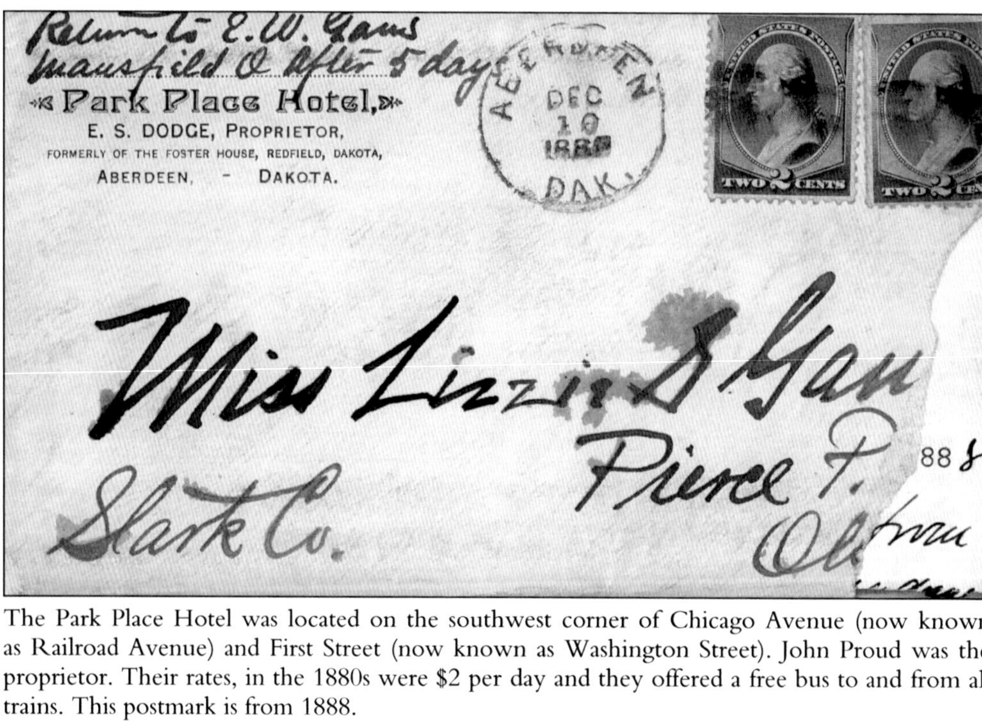

The Park Place Hotel was located on the southwest corner of Chicago Avenue (now known as Railroad Avenue) and First Street (now known as Washington Street). John Proud was the proprietor. Their rates, in the 1880s were $2 per day and they offered a free bus to and from all trains. This postmark is from 1888.

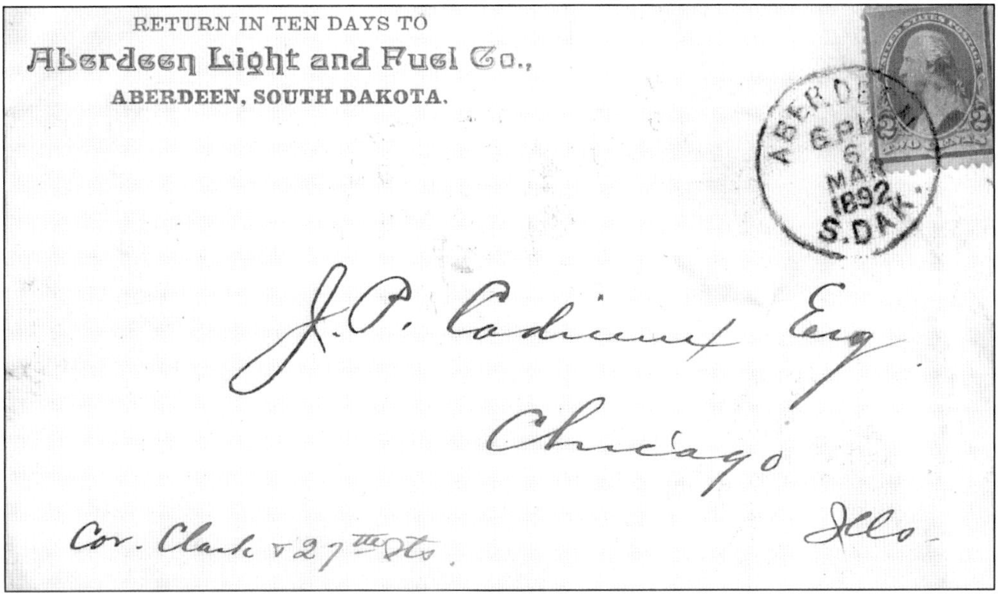

Aberdeen quickly became one of the larger towns in South Dakota and people in town wanted all the new inventions considered to be modern conveniences. These included indoor plumbing, telephone service, and electricity. Part of this was satisfied by the Aberdeen Light and Fuel Co. that later became known as the Aberdeen Gas and Electric Light Co. This envelope is dated 1892. Their offices were in the Northwestern National Bank Building, which is now the Dacotah Prairie Museum Building.

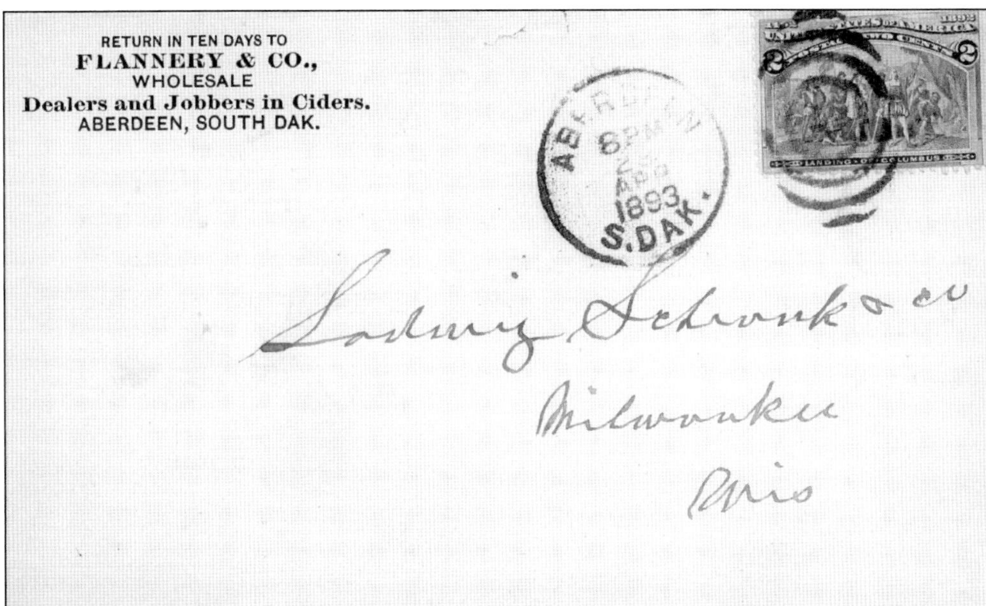

This 1893 envelope has one of the then-new Columbian Exposition stamps on it commemorating the 400th anniversary of Columbus' discovery of the Americas.

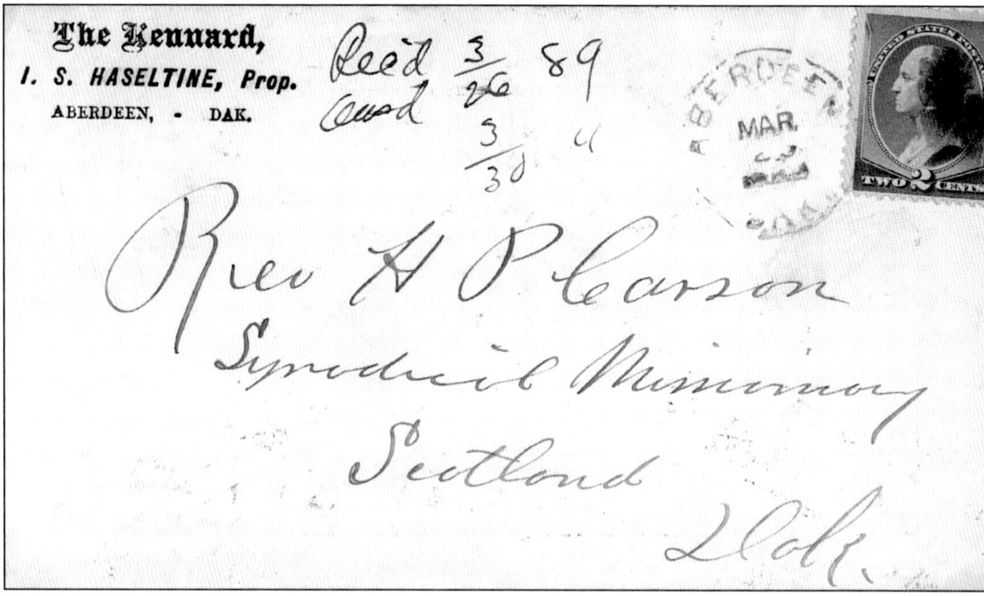

This is the front and back of an advertising envelope from 1889. The front is for the Kennard House, a hotel on the southwest corner of First Avenue and Second Street, now known as First Avenue and Lincoln Street. Ira S. Hazeltine was the proprietor. It became the Commercial Club and now is the location of the Bill Clark Building. The reverse is an all-over advertising for J.J. Petty Real Estate and Loans, located at 302 South Main. This was a partnership between Judson J. Petty and Clarence Dennis. There is also a scarce reference to the Northwestern National Bank, a bank that only lasted three years, from 1888 to 1891.

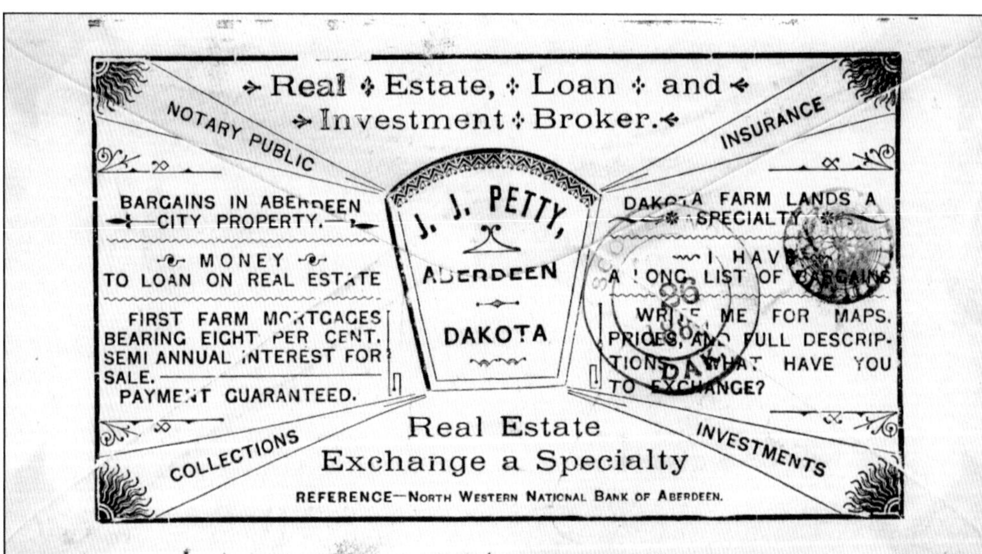

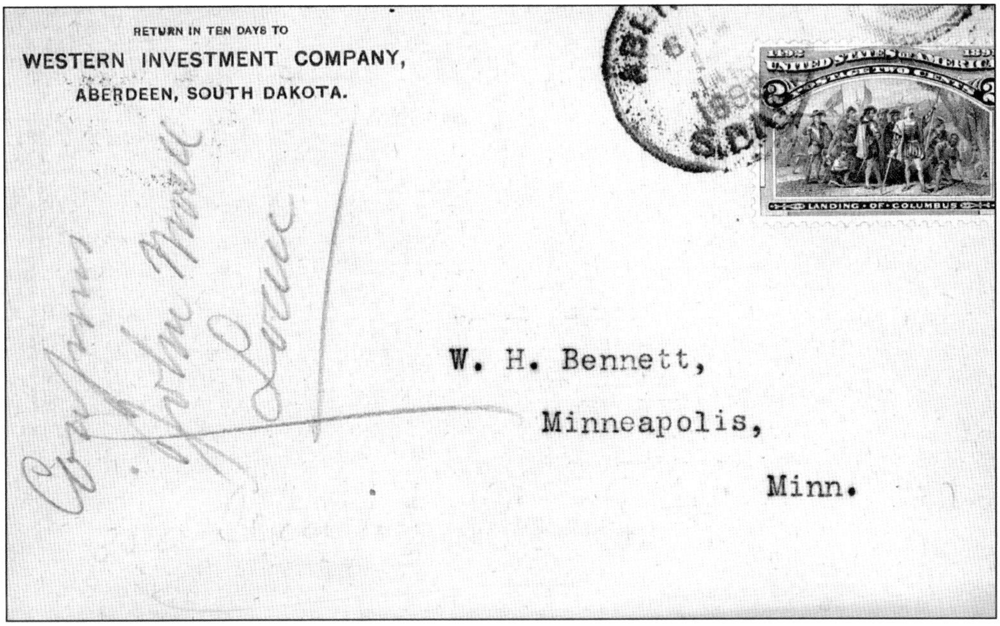

The Western Investment Company only lasted a few years from the late 1880s to the middle of the 1890s. It is important to know who the three officers were: Byron C. Lamont, later of Wells-Lamont fame; Charles A. Howard Sr., the Captain of the South Dakota Regiment in the Spanish American War and later of the firm of Howard & Hedger; and Samuel H. Jumper, Aberdeen's first resident who was involved in many, many businesses.

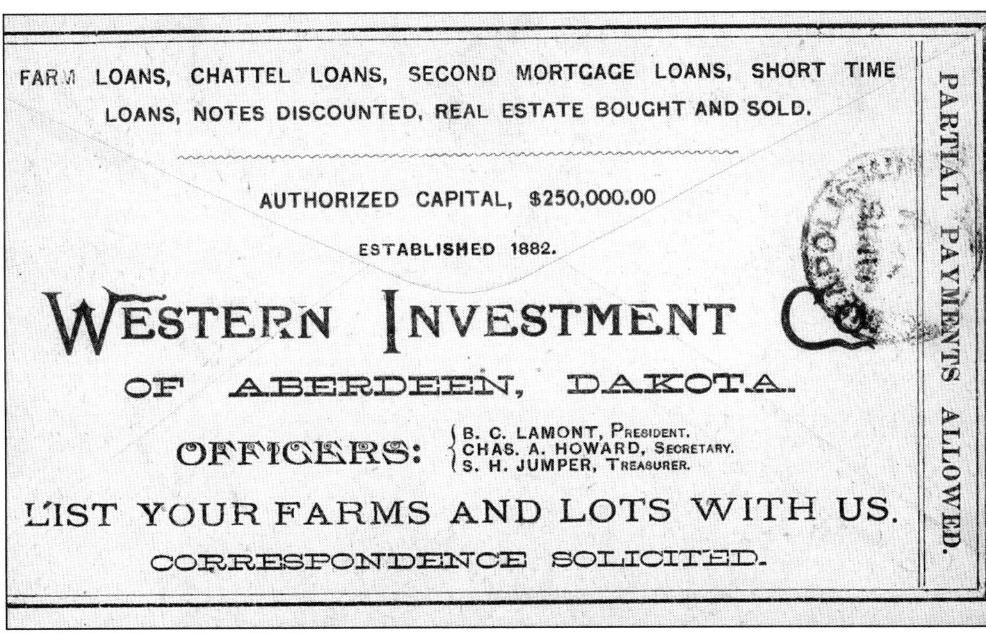

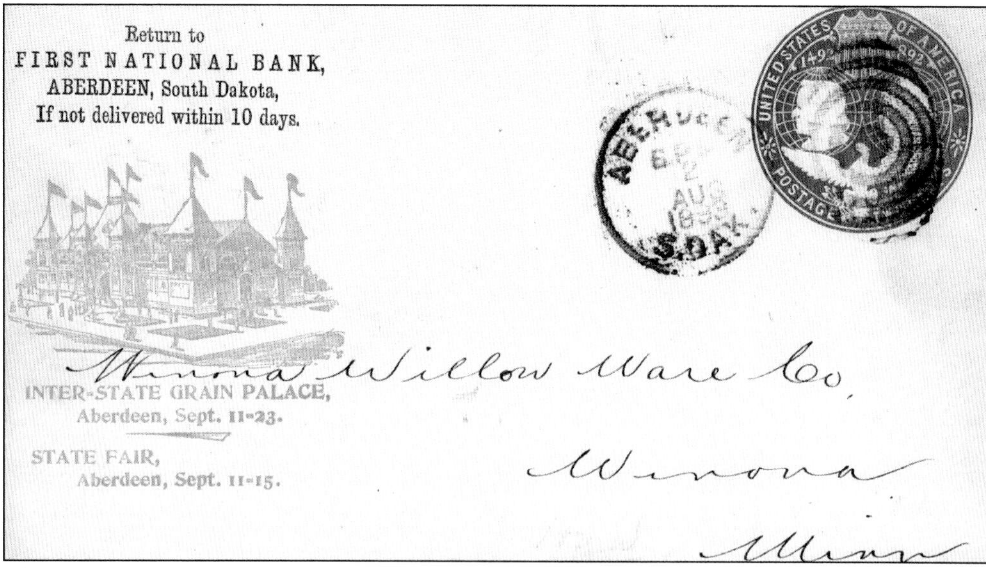

The South Dakota State Fair used to be held in different towns every year. In 1892, it was decided that to reduce costs, yet provide a community event, that different events would always be held in the same community. Huron would get the State Fair, Mitchell would have the Corn Palace, and Aberdeen would have a Grain Palace starting in 1893. This envelope from the First National Bank was mailed on Sept. 2, 1893, just before the first Grain Palace Expo, as an advertisement for the Expo.

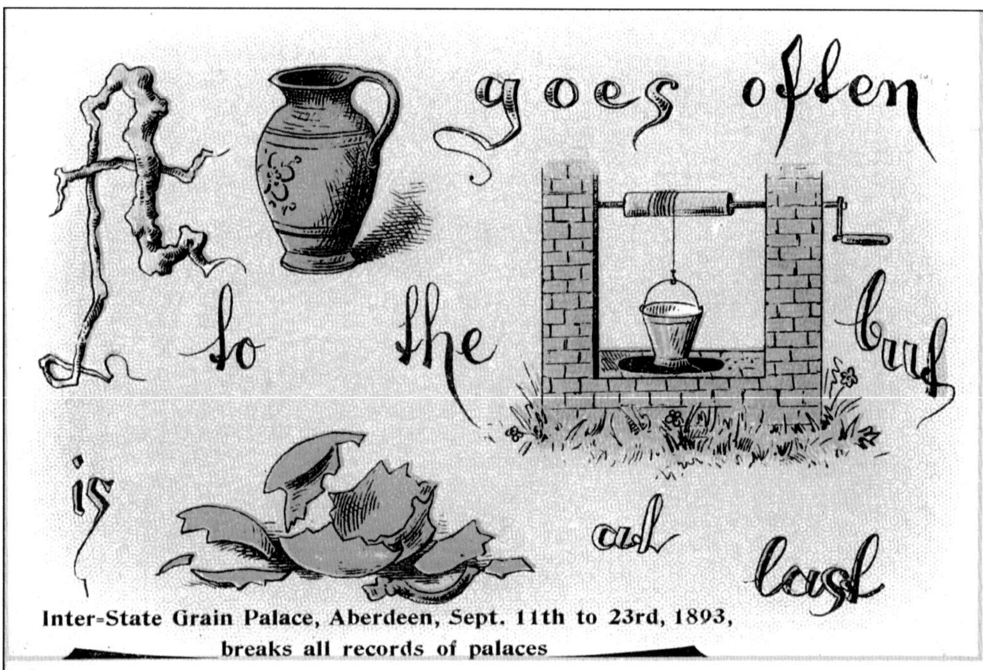

This Pictograph was distributed as an advertising item before the first Grain Palace Exposition in 1893. The Pictograph now seems to be a lost art form. Can you read what it says?

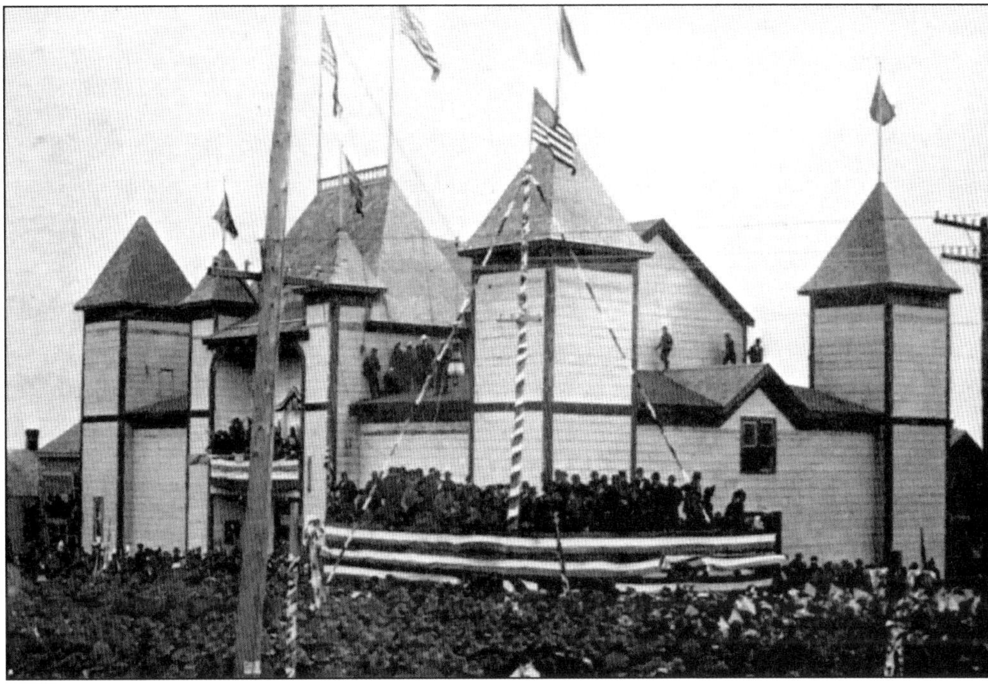

This is a copy of the only known photograph of the Grain Palace and unfortunately shows a lack of decorations. During its nine-year life before burning down on April 29, 1902, it was a popular and well-used convention and meeting hall. President McKinley spoke here in 1898 and U.S. Senator J.H. Kyle of Aberdeen had his funeral here. The decision not to rebuild was not a very popular decision.

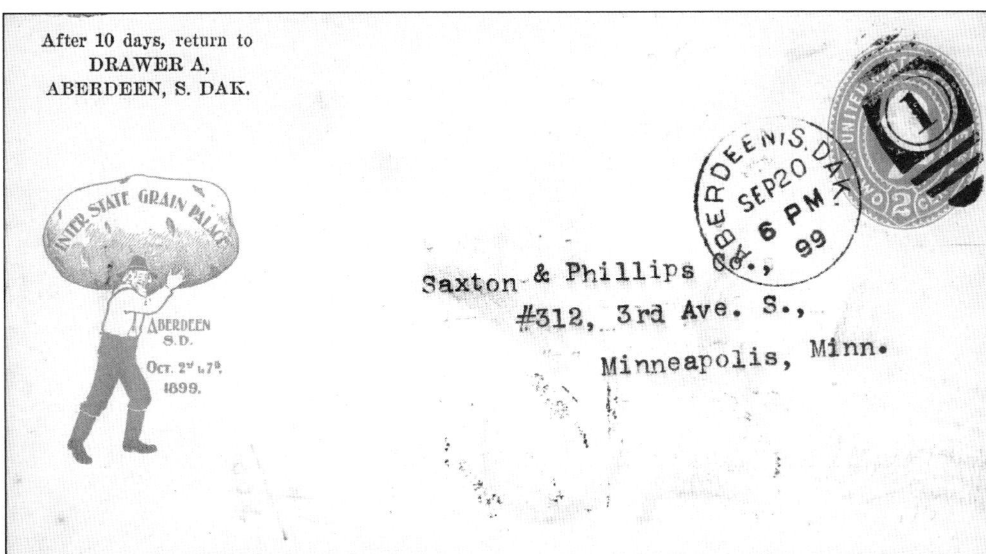

It was not uncommon for a business to advertise civic functions on their correspondence. This is for the 7th Annual Grain Palace Expo in 1899. It is speculated that the Drawer A return address was for B.C. Lamont.

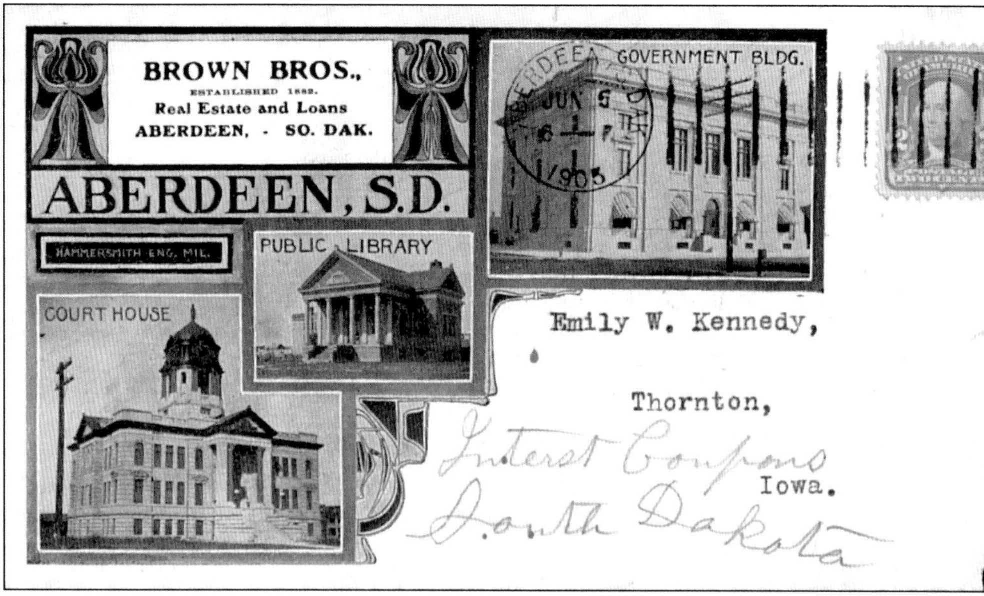

This is the front and back of a popular advertising envelope used by many different businesses in 1905 to promote Aberdeen. The city experienced a large population growth over the next 10 years. The Brown Brothers also became bankers of the only Aberdeen Bank that collapsed because of the panic of 1929. Citizens were so angry at the Browns that they even destroyed their family tombstones in Riverside Cemetery.

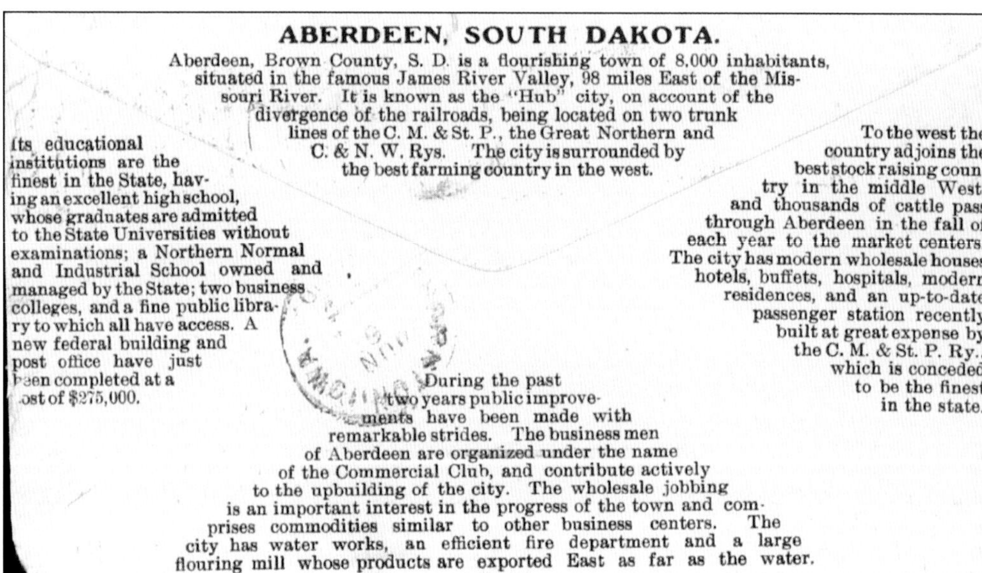

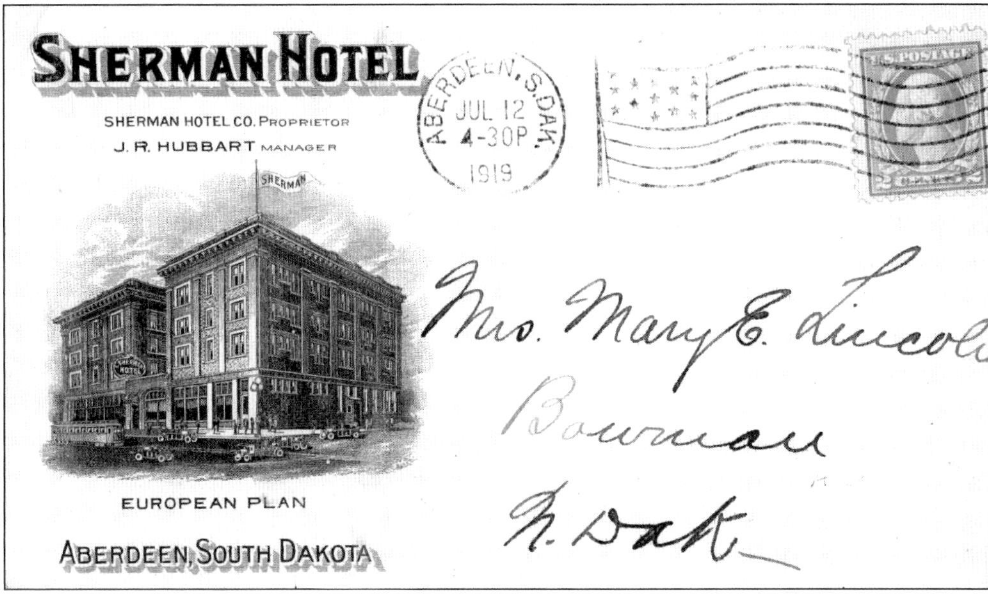

This 1919 full advertising envelope for the Sherman Hotel is from stationary that was provided for the guests to use. The entire back of the envelope was a promotion for the Yellowstone Trail, now known as U.S. Highway 12. The Yellowstone Trail promotion had offices in Aberdeen, but was considered the idea of J.W. Parmley of Ipswich, South Dakota, along with many Aberdonians.

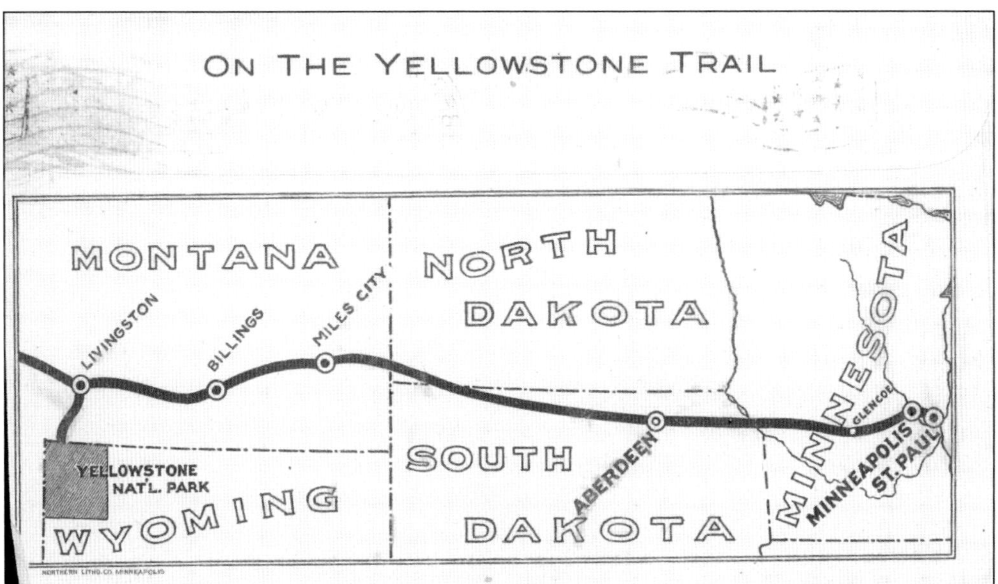

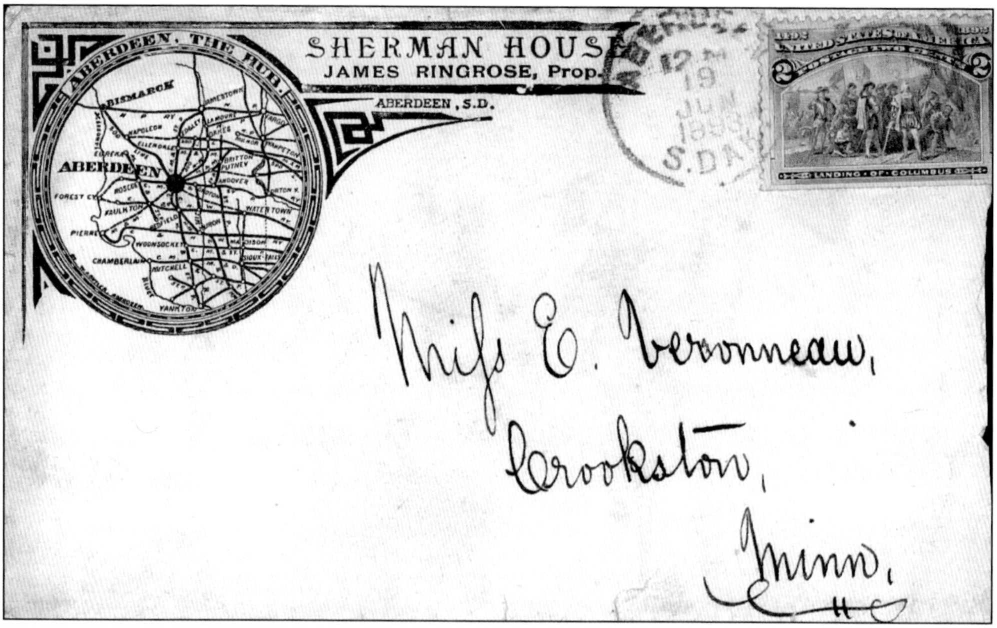

Another Sherman House Hotel envelope, this one from 1893 showing the new "Hub City" logo that was adopted after South Dakota Statehood on November 2, 1889.

This is the First Flight Envelope for the First Air Mail Airplane to carry mail from Aberdeen on July 3, 1934. The sender and receiver of this was a young Bob Perry who was a very dedicated local historian until his death in 1998. His knowledge and friendship will be missed.

Two

OUR BUILDINGS

When the first settlers arrived in the middle of June in 1881 they slept in a wagon on the open prairie. By the end of June, businesses and hotels were set up in tents over a several block area around what is now downtown. By July, wooden buildings were erected with the lumber hauled in. These early buildings were mostly replaced with better buildings in only a few years. By the time the railroad tracks arrived in 1882, we were a thriving community of over 1,000 inhabitants and mostly permanent structures. There was no hesitation in the building of Aberdeen. When the businesses were built and their homes erected, they organized the city government, built churches and schools, then recreational and social gathering places like they left behind when they immigrated to the West. They knew that wintertime meant snow and cold weather. Here is a write-up of some of the earlier and more recognizable buildings.

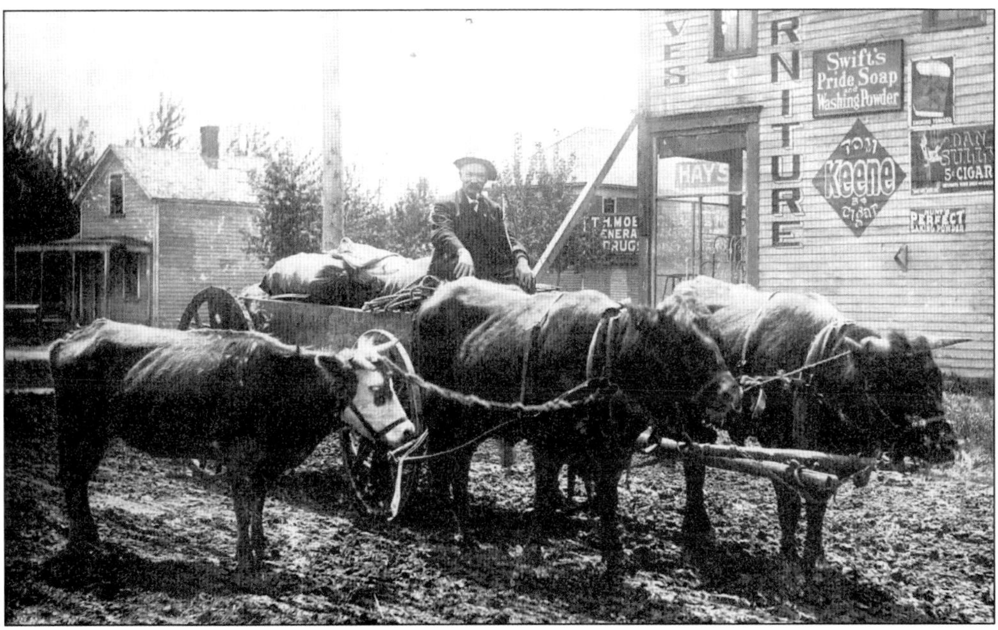

In 1892, C.R. Hay was transporting mules via railroad from Montana to Minnesota to be sold to the U.S. Army. During a layover in Aberdeen to feed and water the mules, Hay found a friendly poker game. His luck was not good; he eventually lost half the mules in the game. He sold the rest of the mules using the money to start a new and used furniture store in Aberdeen. This Hay Furniture building was located on the corner of Seventh Avenue and South Main Street. Hay Furniture remained a family business for the next 110 years, finally closing in 2002.

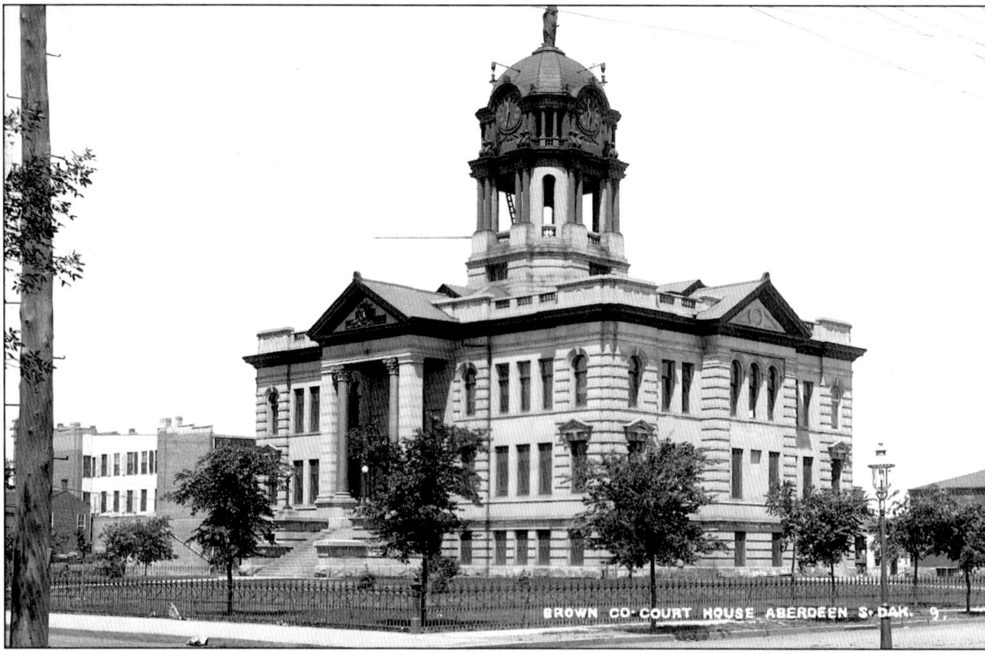

This building in Aberdeen was constructed between 1901 and 1904 after Aberdeen was officially declared the county seat in 1890 following a ten-year struggle for that designation with neighboring Columbia. This is the second courthouse built in Aberdeen, the first being constructed in 1887 at the current Aldrich Park site. That simple frame building served as the courthouse until 1889 when the records were moved back to Columbia after yet another vote on the matter. Aberdeen's second courthouse was built for a total cost of $121,097.10, and is still in service today.

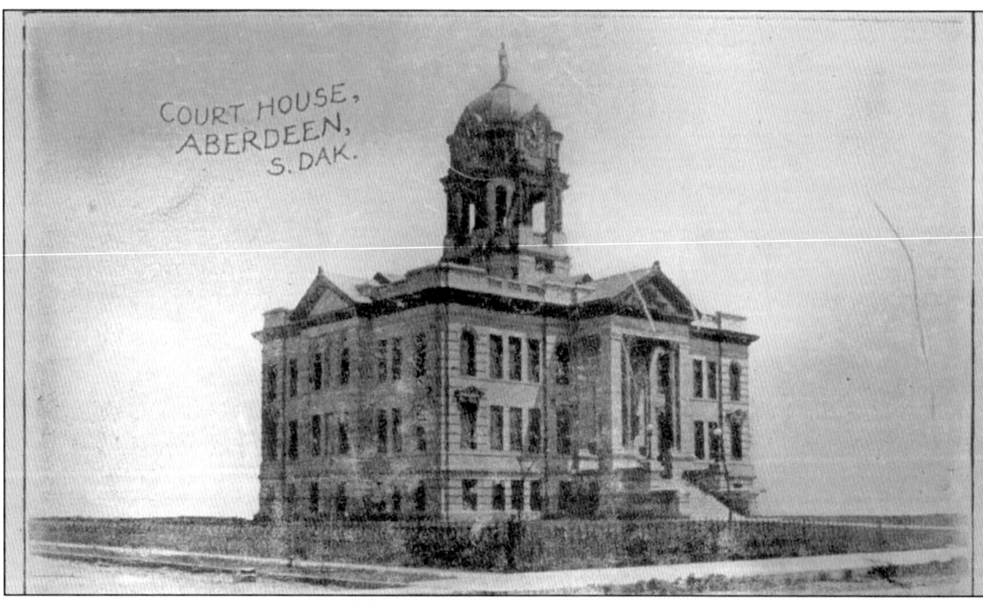

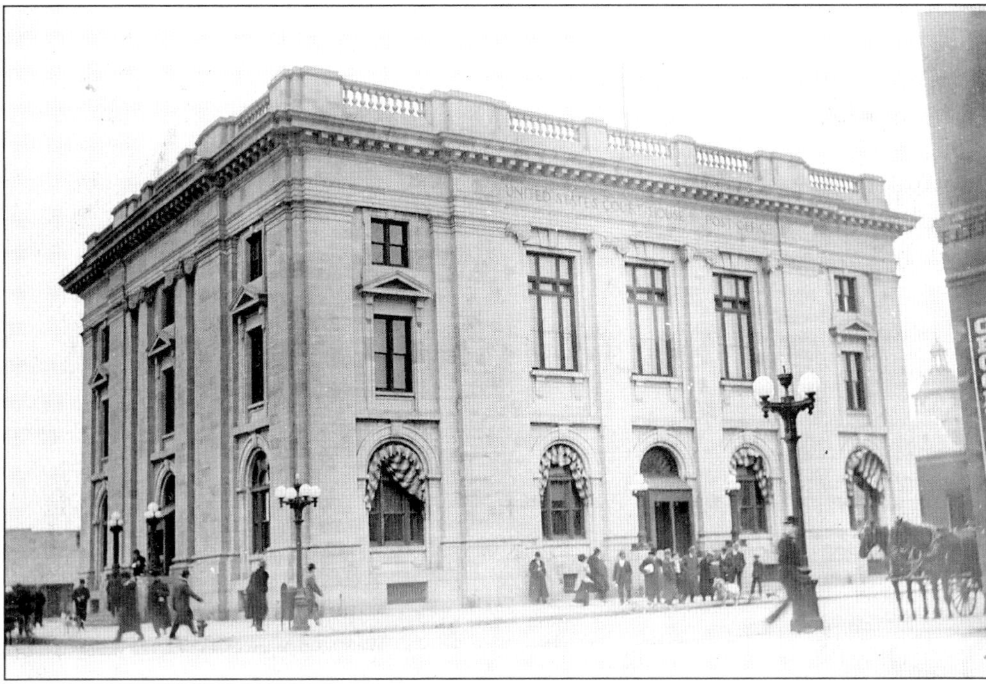

Aberdeen's first U.S. courthouse and post office was completed in 1904 as a result of the efforts of Aberdeen's first U.S. senator, James Kyle, who helped secure funding for the building totaling $175,000. In 1937, the post office and courthouse moved to a new facility, and this structure remained empty for the next seven years. The building was demolished in 1944 and nearly 200 tons of high-grade metal was salvaged and eventually used in the war effort to make battleship hulls.

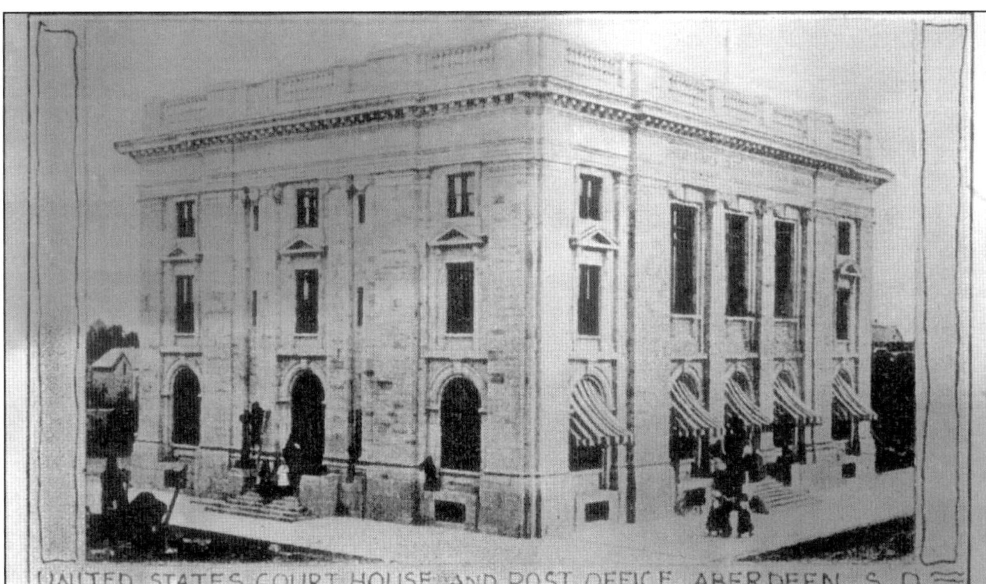

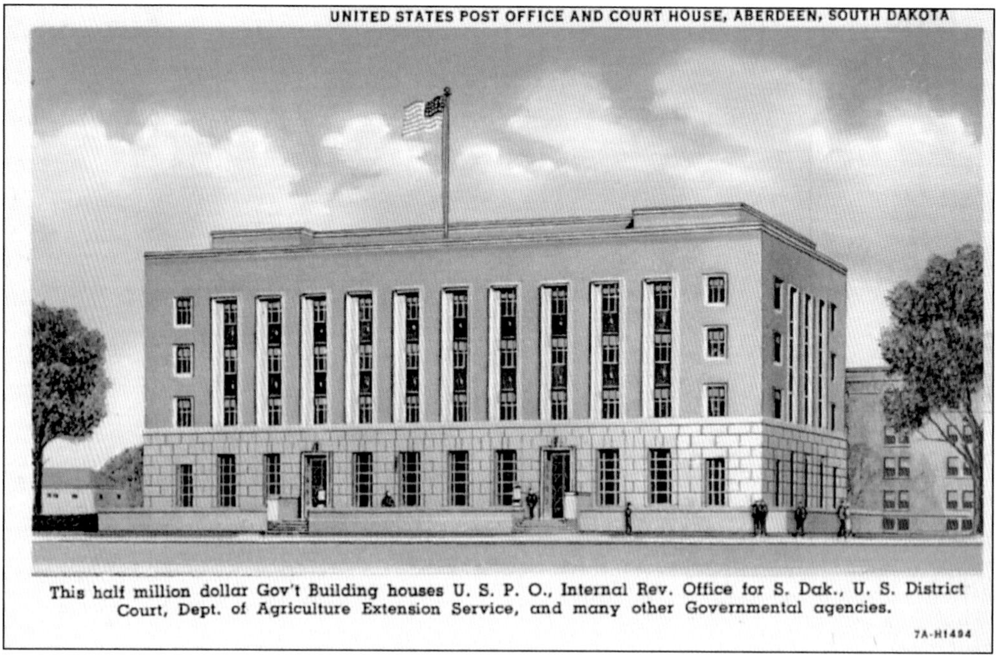

In 1937, the new post office and federal courthouse was completed a block east of the old Federal Building. It is still in use today as the downtown post office and the federal courthouse.

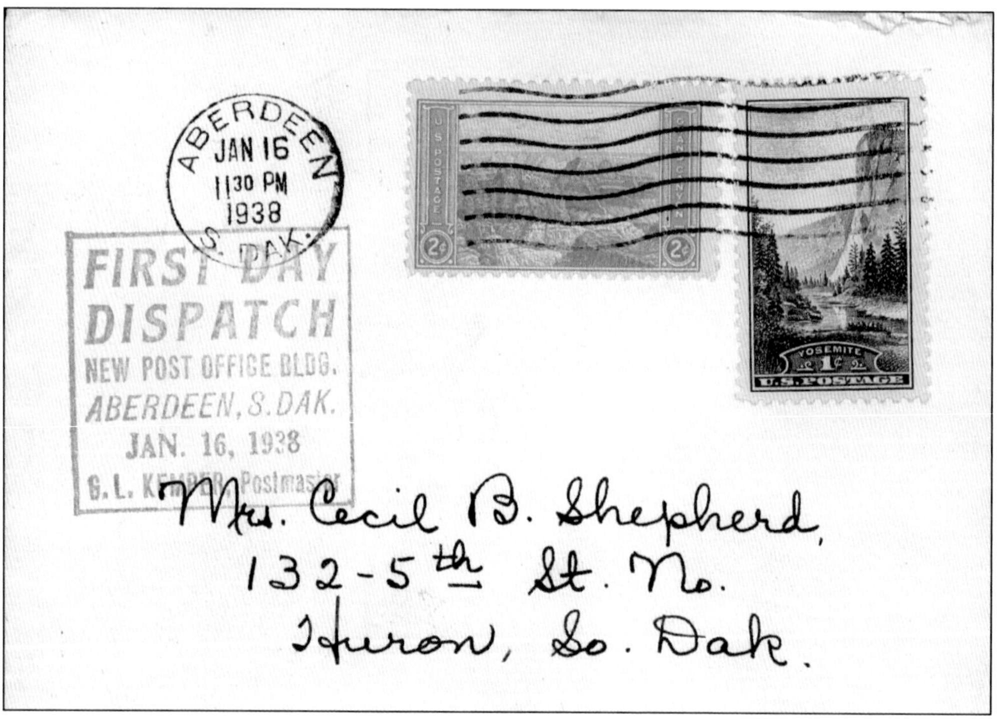

This commemorative envelope was from the "First Mail Dispatch" sent out from the new post office on January 16, 1938. On that day, all outgoing mail was stamped with this logo.

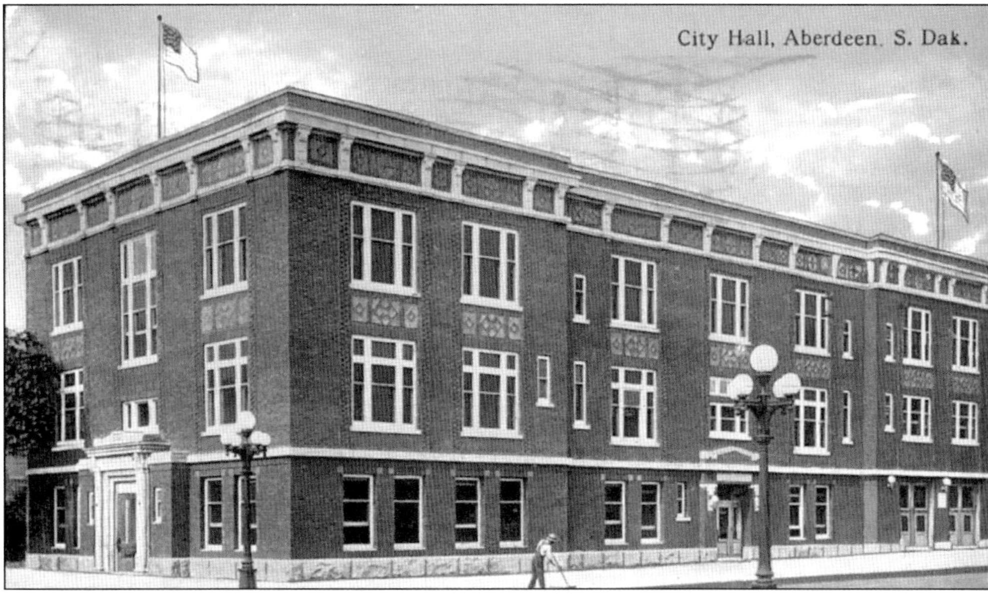

For several years, Aberdeen city officials leased office space in the Brown County Courthouse after its 1904 opening. In 1911, Aberdeen adopted a mayor/commission form of government and replaced its previous justice of the peace system with a municipal court, and the city fathers felt it was time for city government to have its own home. This building, designed by Aberdeen architect George Fossum, opened in 1914 and the press reminded the public: "Nothing has been spent for domes or towers or marble columns. It is the modern ideal of efficiency carried out in brick and stone."

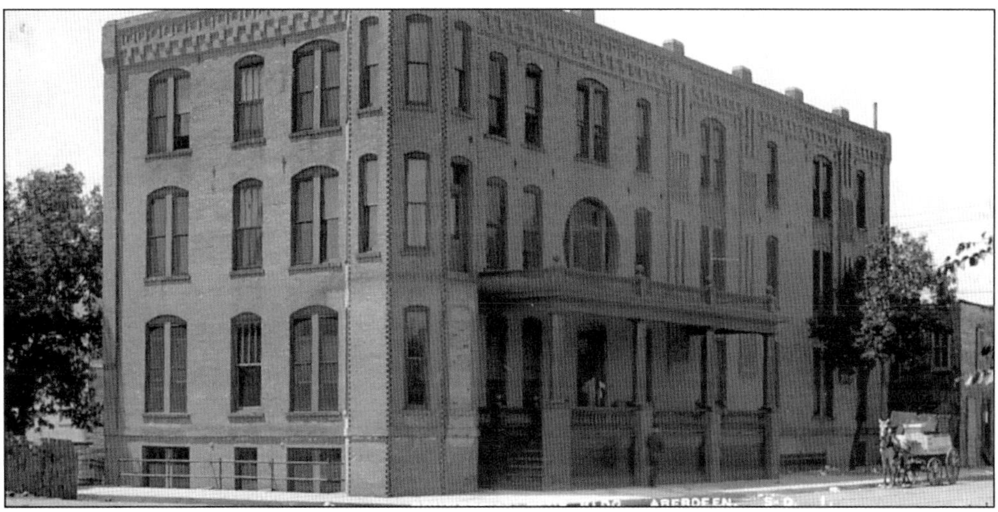

Built in 1887, the Kennard Hotel was Aberdeen's first brick hotel and boasted all the conveniences of the day—steam heat, gaslights, a steam-powered elevator, electric bells, and a fire alarm. The four story 40 foot by 100 foot structure of cream-colored brick stood on the corner of South Lincoln Street and First Avenue. In 1904, the building was sold to the Commercial Club who hosted meetings and social events there. In 1944, the building was sold to the Moose Lodge who used it as their club house for the next 20 years. The building was demolished in 1965 and Bill Clark then built his Clark Title Co. Building on the spot.

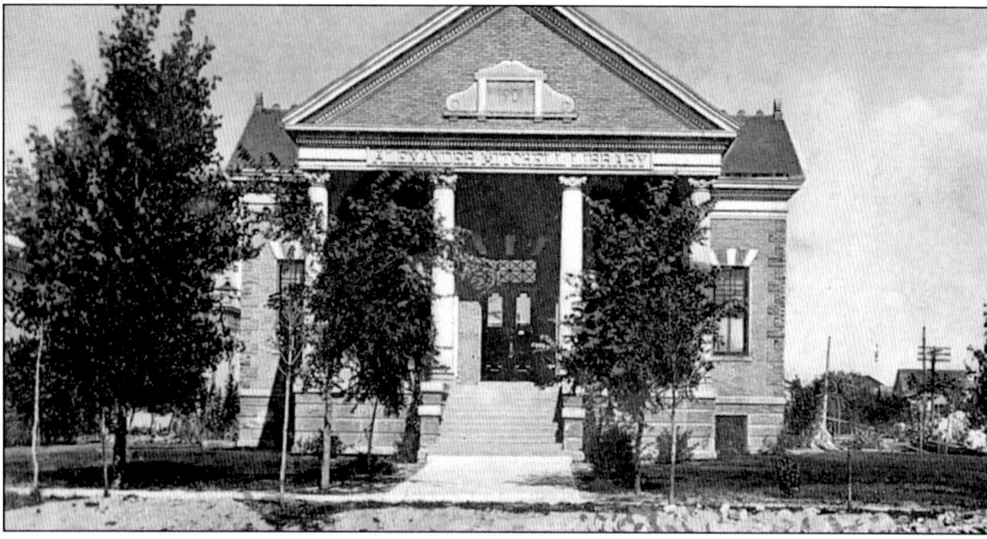

Andrew Carnegie donated $15,000 to the city of Aberdeen to construct a library. This building was built in 1901 and is the only Carnegie Library in the country that does not bear the Carnegie name. One of the conditions of Carnegie's generous donation to Aberdeen was that the library be named after his friend Alexander Mitchell, president of the Chicago, Milwaukee & St. Paul Railroad. This building served Aberdeen until it was condemned in 1950 because the weight of over 38,000 books was causing the floor to collapse. The structure no longer stands.

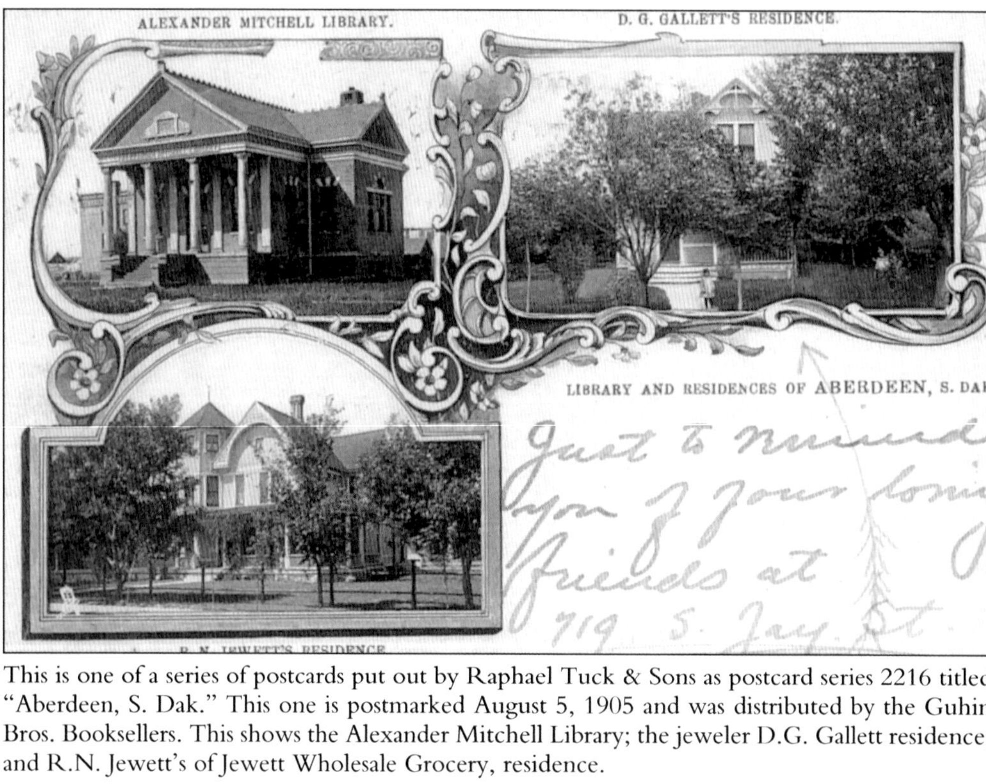

This is one of a series of postcards put out by Raphael Tuck & Sons as postcard series 2216 titled "Aberdeen, S. Dak." This one is postmarked August 5, 1905 and was distributed by the Guhin Bros. Booksellers. This shows the Alexander Mitchell Library; the jeweler D.G. Gallett residence; and R.N. Jewett's of Jewett Wholesale Grocery, residence.

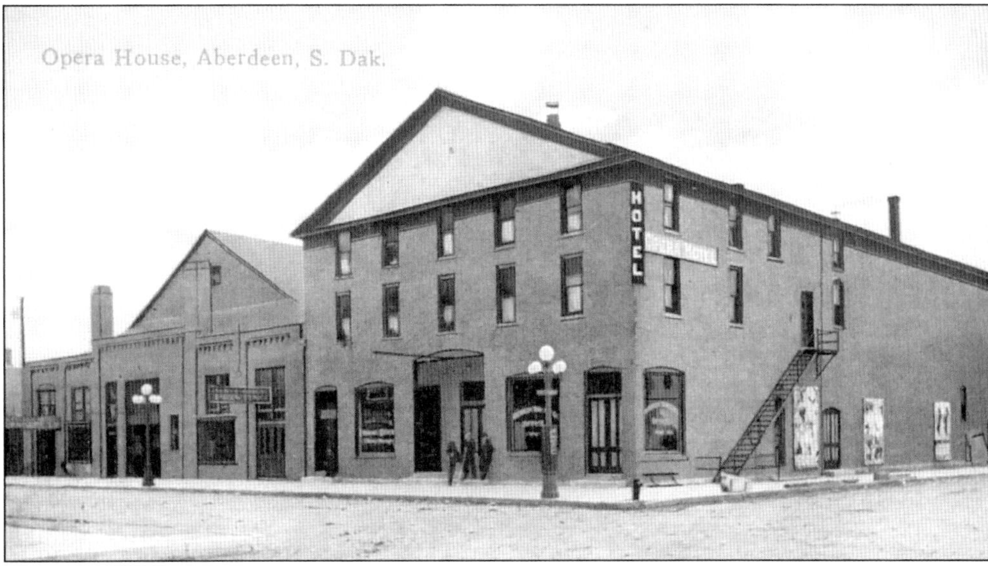

In 1902, the Gottschalk Opera House opened and was declared to be one of the best playhouses west of the Mississippi River with seating for nearly 1,000. The acoustic properties were perfect and the stage was larger than many twin city theaters. It allowed the use of very large scenery props used in the most ambitious plays. The audience for the theater's opening night performance was claimed by the local newspaper to be "the most elegant that has ever assembled in the state of South Dakota."

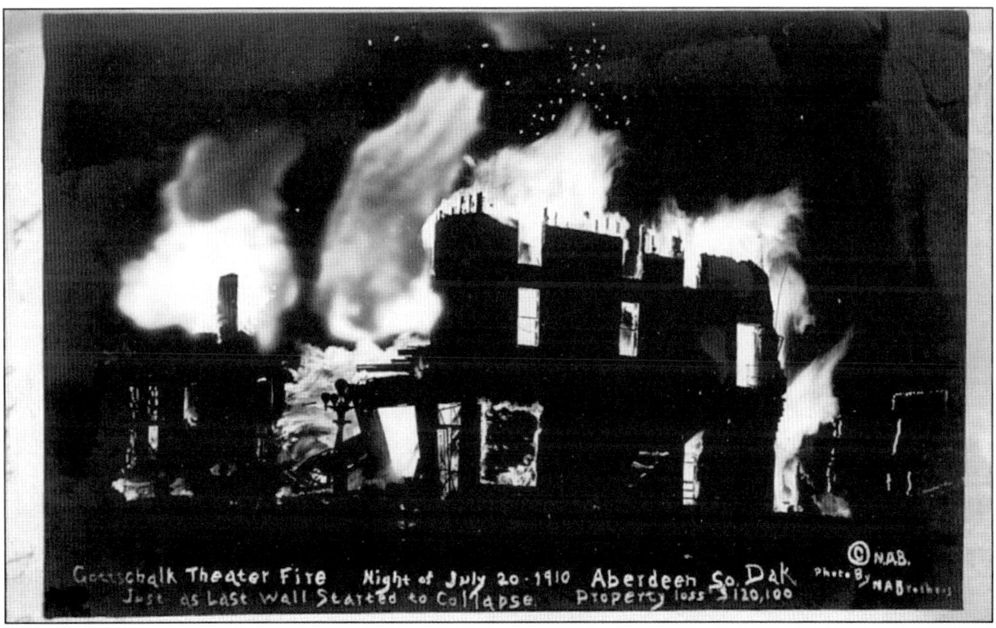

On July 20, 1910, Aberdeen's fine opera house and several adjoining businesses were destroyed by fire with losses totaling $120,000. The fire started in the electrical system, spreading quickly throughout the structure, which housed several other businesses on the upper floors. The building burned to the ground in less than two hours. After this fire, the Aberdeen Fire Department purchased its first pumper truck.

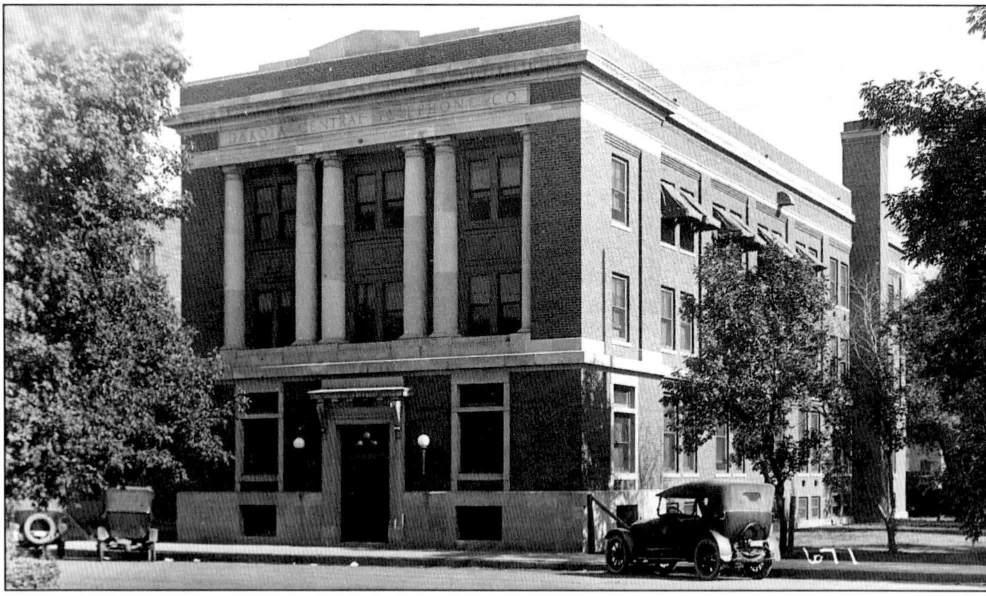

This early real photo postcard of the new Dakota Central Telephone Building was taken at a time when they had been renting at several locations. Because of the owner, J.L.W. Zietlow, Aberdeen had telephones before most places on the prairie. His designs prevailed over the Bell phones because his were based on a different and better principal. He gave his invention to the world instead of becoming rich.

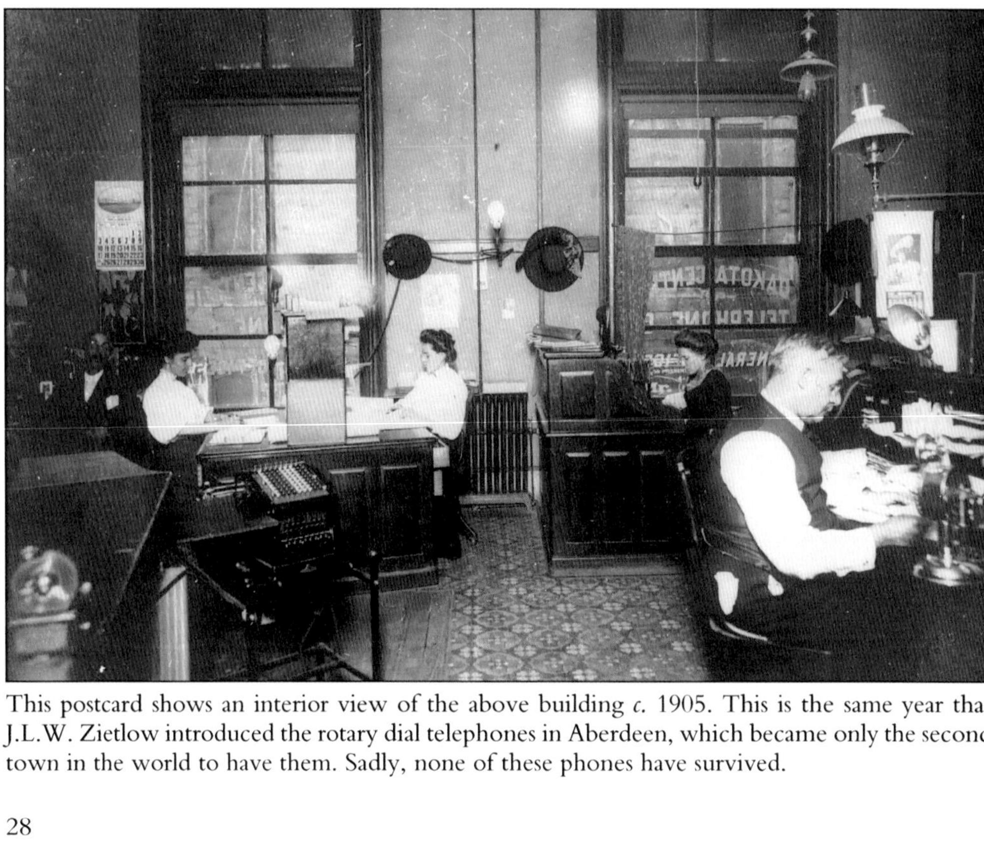

This postcard shows an interior view of the above building *c.* 1905. This is the same year that J.L.W. Zietlow introduced the rotary dial telephones in Aberdeen, which became only the second town in the world to have them. Sadly, none of these phones have survived.

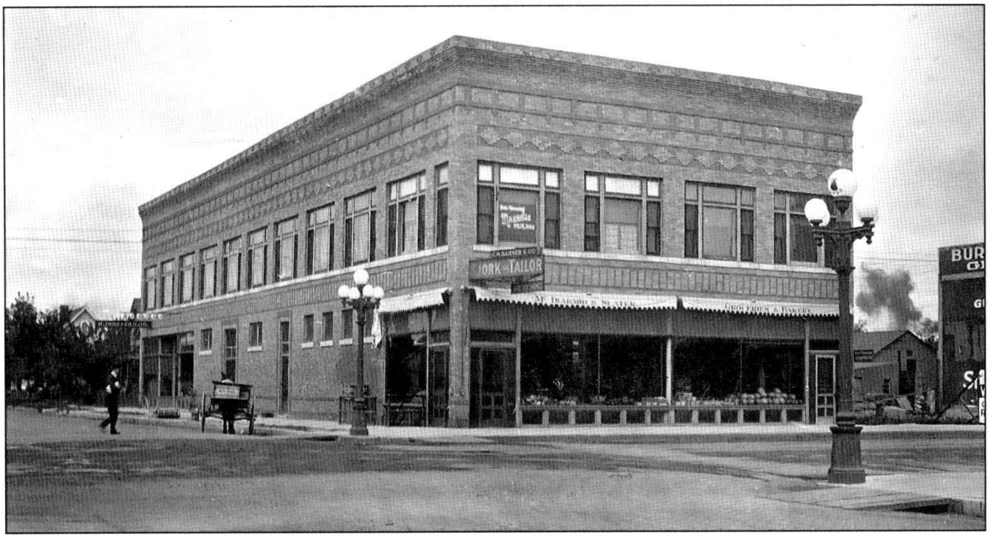

James McDiarmid and George Slater built this building to house their grocery business. The cashier worked in a carved polished wood cage with a glass grill in the center of the store. The store also boasted its own bakery in the basement so shoppers could buy fresh bread for five cents a loaf and have it sliced while they shopped for other needs. This store also introduced the "deli" concept to shoppers by making prepared food available to the employees in the neighboring businesses. They used "merchant tokens" from five cents to $1 for making change. These tokens had their business name on them and can still be found at coin shows and antique stores.

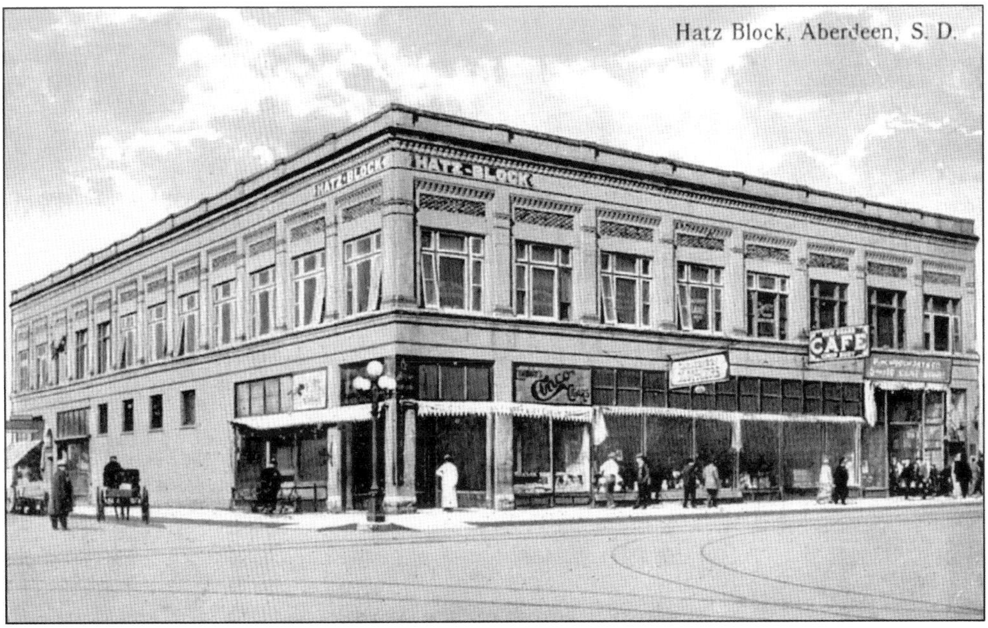

The Hatz Block opened in 1906 and was named for Casper Hatz, the building's developer. The Golden Rule Department Store moved into the building from its Ward Hotel location to become the building's first tenant. At the time, the Golden Rule was the largest department store in the state, but by 1911 it was out of business. Over the years, Gamble's, Woolworth's, and Montgomery Ward stores called the Hatz Block home. The building was torn down in 2002.

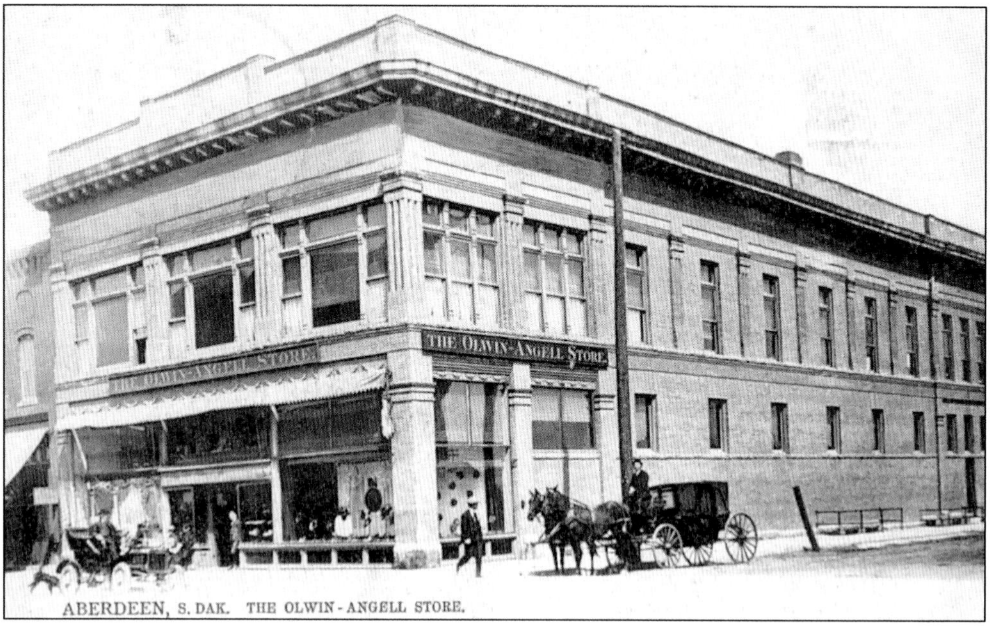

A.H. Olwin and Robert Angell built this building in 1903 for their dry goods business, which had outgrown its original building across the street. This new structure, billed as two floors light as day, was equipped with the city's first pneumatic tube system which delivered cash from sales in all department to the accounting office on the second floor. Soon after, the tube would return with change and/or a receipt for the sale. A third floor was added in 1914.

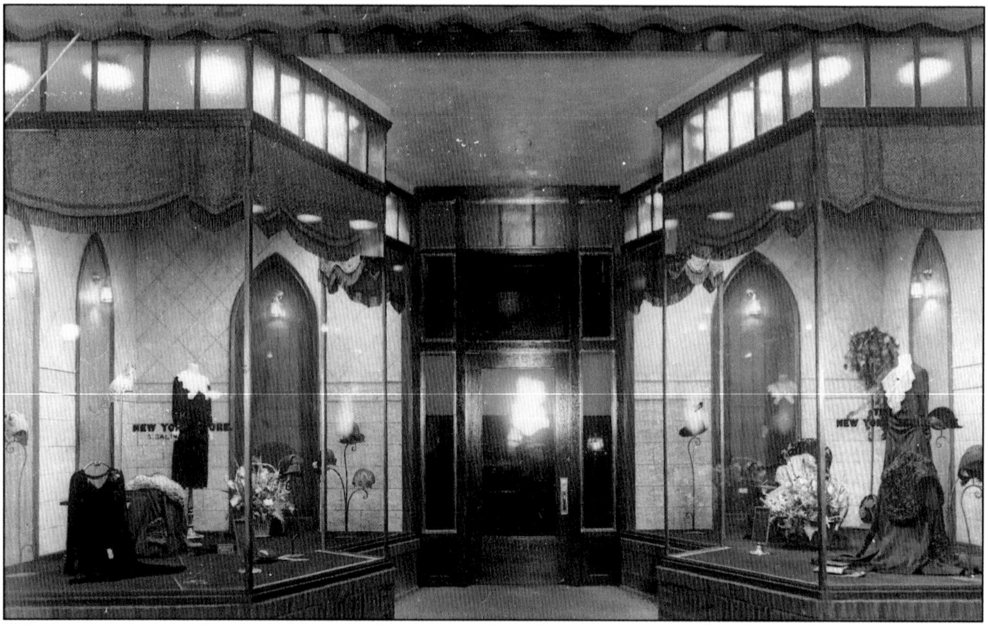

This real photo shows the New York Store about 1926. Its recessed entrance was not uncommon for Main Street businesses of that era. The store, located in the Sherman Hotel, occupying space once used as the hotel's lobby, featured women's apparel and always the latest in millinery (hat) styles.

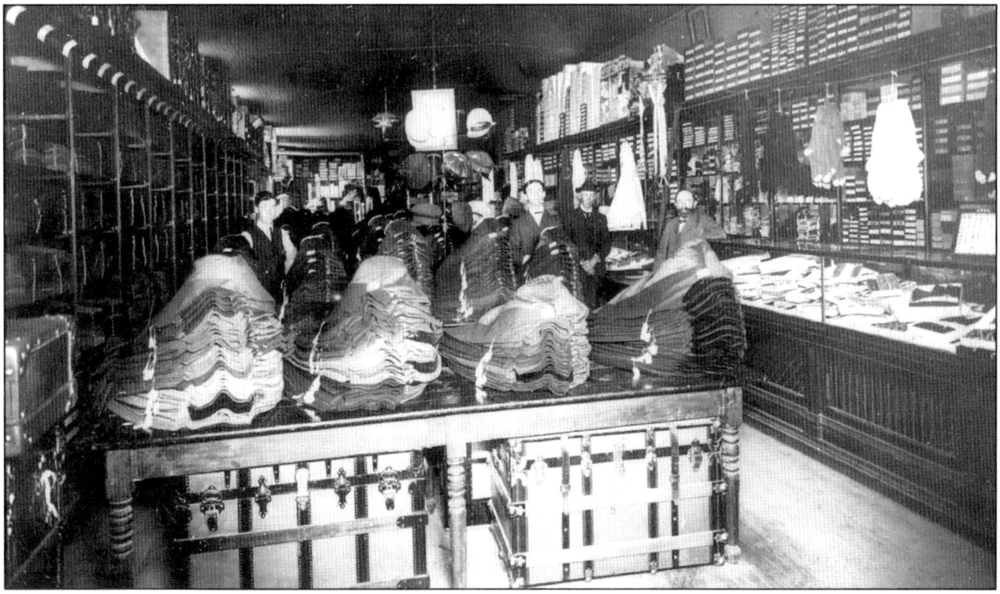

The Strauss Clothing House was opened in 1887 by David Strauss, who moved to Aberdeen from Iowa. First called the Golden Eagle, the store opened in the Sherman Hotel addition. After renaming it Strauss Clothing in 1916, David Strauss put up a two-story building on Main Street, south of the Ward Hotel that housed his business until it closed in 1934, 47 years after it was founded.

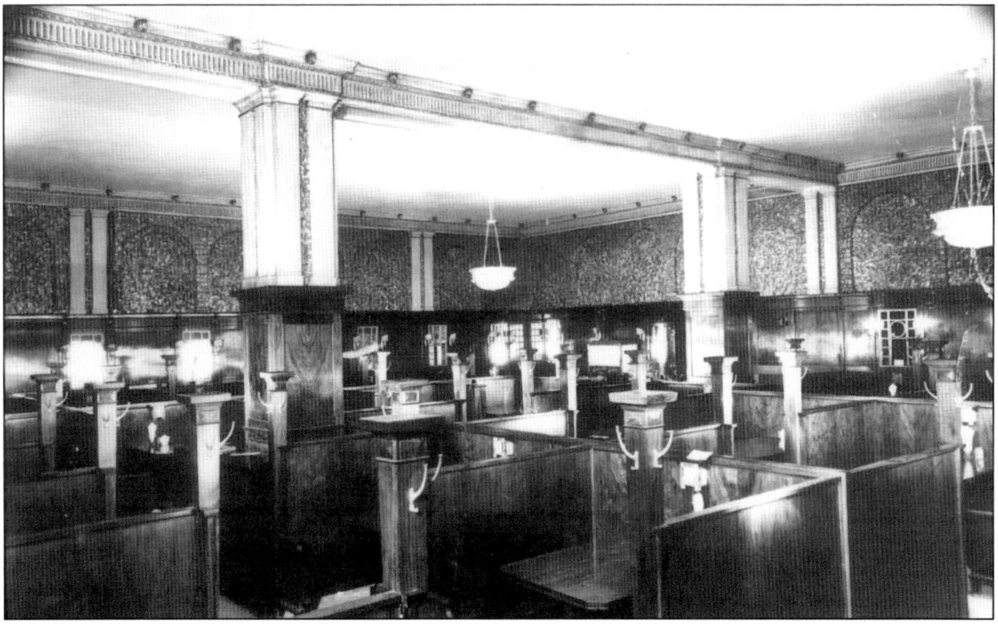

John Combs opened his Chocolate Shop in 1905 and in 1926 built a building to house his new restaurant. This restaurant was very large and had booths enough to seat 225 customers. Electric push buttons at each booth were used to call the waitress for service. Combs' became a popular spot for youth because it was open late and had a jukebox. Combs' served more hamburgers and shoestrings than anything else on the menu. The restaurant closed in 1954.

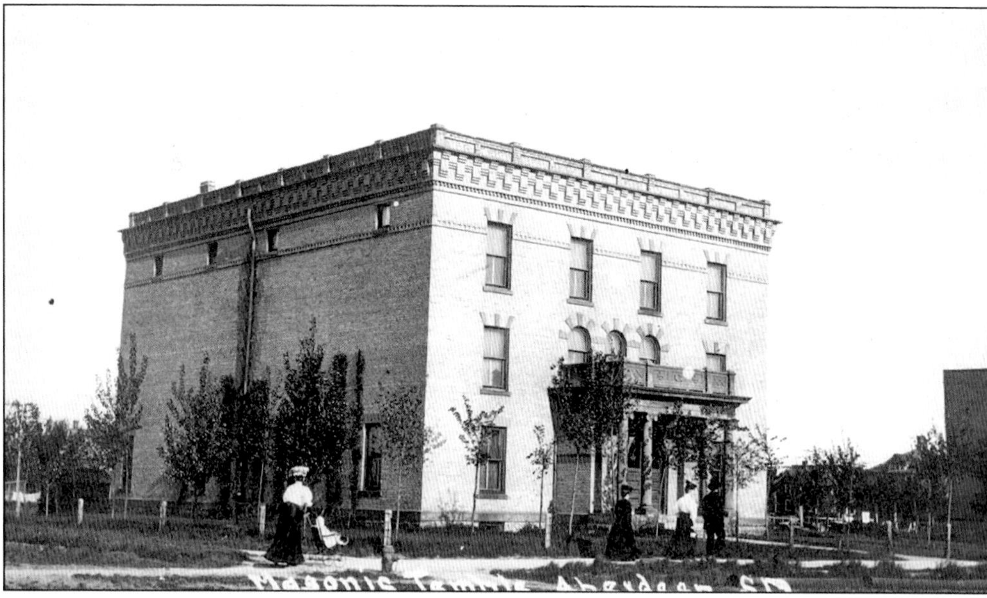

This is the first building west of the Mississippi River to be built entirely as a Masonic Temple. This is how it originally looked in 1897 before an addition to the rear and a front sun porch was added. It is still in use entirely as a Masonic Temple.

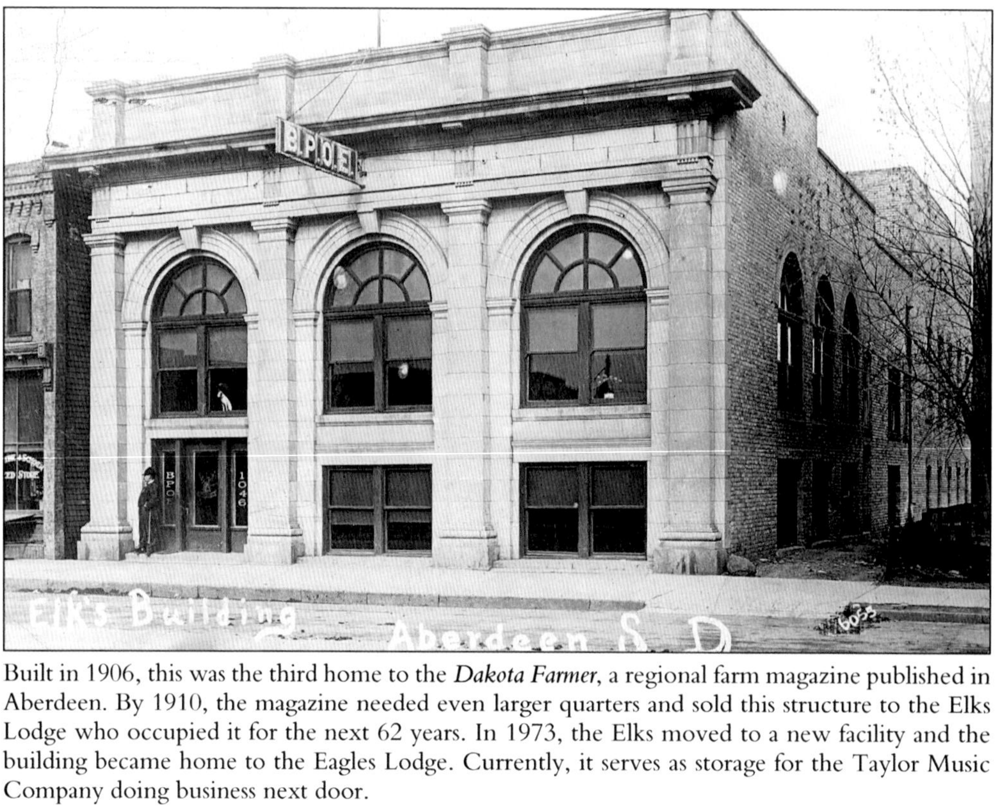

Built in 1906, this was the third home to the *Dakota Farmer*, a regional farm magazine published in Aberdeen. By 1910, the magazine needed even larger quarters and sold this structure to the Elks Lodge who occupied it for the next 62 years. In 1973, the Elks moved to a new facility and the building became home to the Eagles Lodge. Currently, it serves as storage for the Taylor Music Company doing business next door.

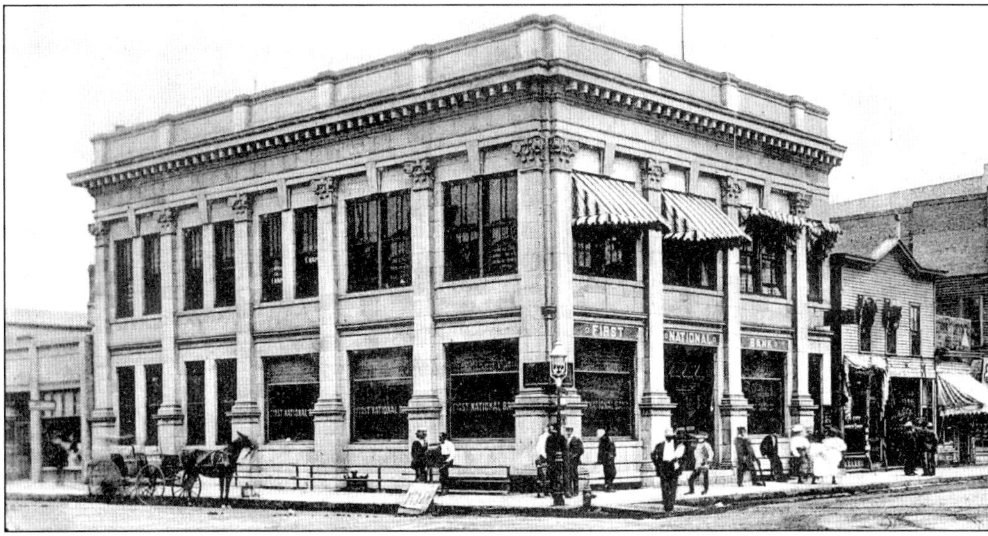

In 1883, Samuel H. Jumper founded the Farmers and Merchants Bank in Aberdeen. Within a few months the bank became the city's first federally authorized financial institution and Jumper changed its name to First National Bank. In 1907, the bank moved into this grand structure, built in 1906. Rental space was available on the second floor and in the basement. One of the tenants was The National Barber Shop, which employed six barbers and offered not only shoeshines, but also Turkish Baths. When the bank moved to new headquarters in 1959, Stewart's School of Hairstyling moved in. Later Tony's Gym occupied the space which today stands vacant.

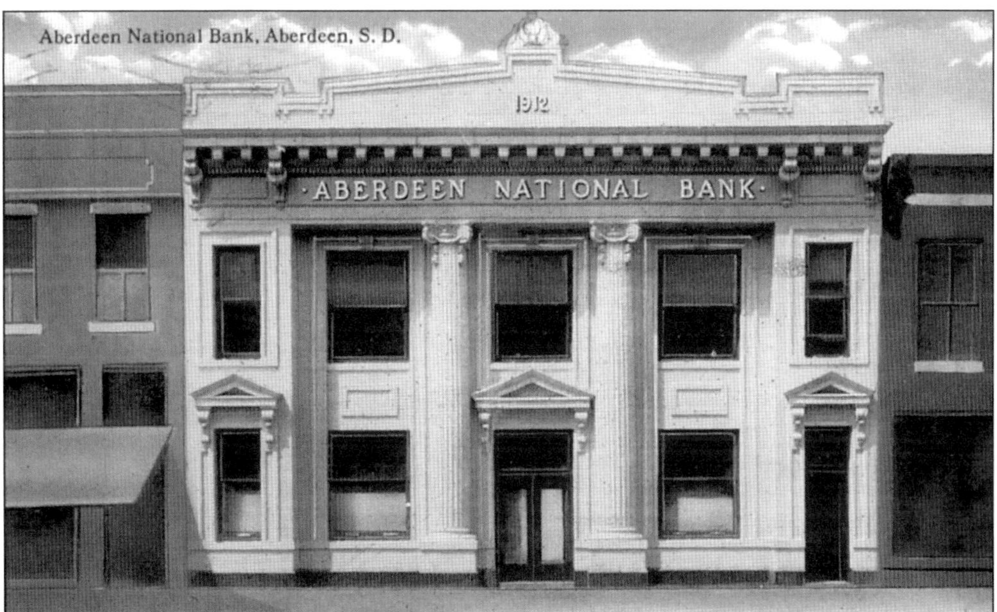

In 1912, the Aberdeen National Bank constructed this 50 by 100 foot building that was billed as a "palace of finance" by the local press. The $75,000 price tag included Knoxville marble floors, Pavanazo marble wainscoting, and Alpine marble counters. The five tellers' cages were surrounded with bronze grillwork. The front of the bank featured two terra cotta pillars 25-feet high and 4 feet in diameter.

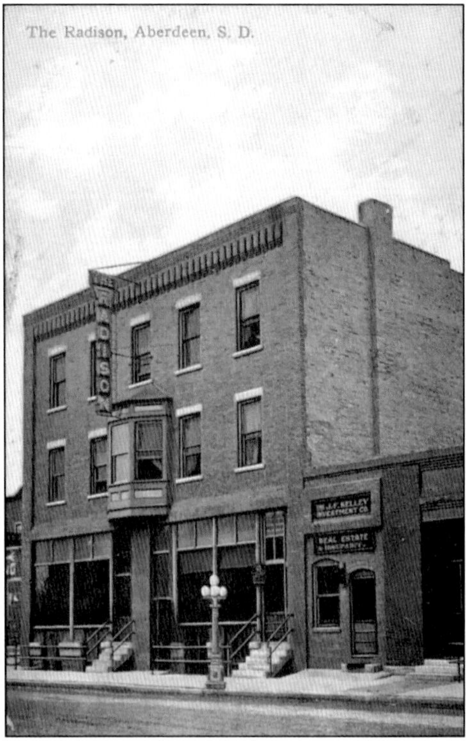

Ben Ward built this hotel on Lincoln Street after he found his original Main Street location was inadequate. This 130-room brick structure joined the original hotel with a passageway above the alley, a novel idea in the early 1900s. The remnants of an underground tunnel between the two hotels was discovered when new owners were making repairs on the Lincoln Street hotel in the late 1920s.

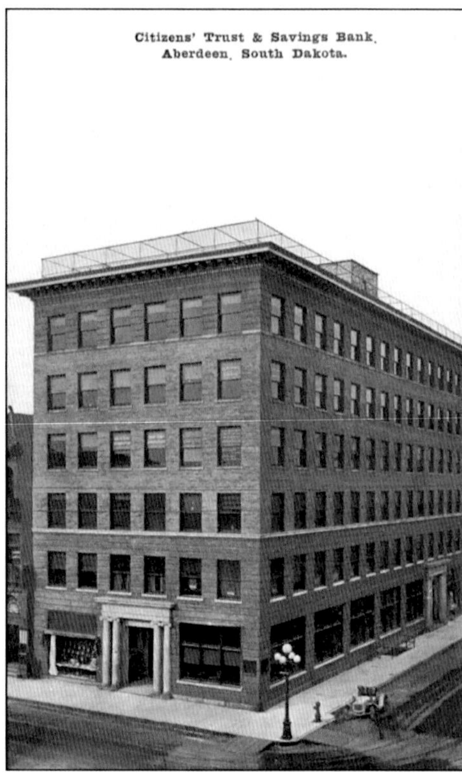

In 1909, a group of Aberdeen businessmen sold $100,000 worth of bonds to finance construction of the Citizens Building, which would be the finest office building in South Dakota at the time. The six-story building was also the tallest in the state, as well as one of three in Aberdeen to be designated as "fireproof." Two elevators in wrought-iron cages dominated the lobby. A glass mail chute carried mail from the upper floors to a receptacle in the lobby. This feature fascinated young and old alike as they watched letters drift slowly downward from above.

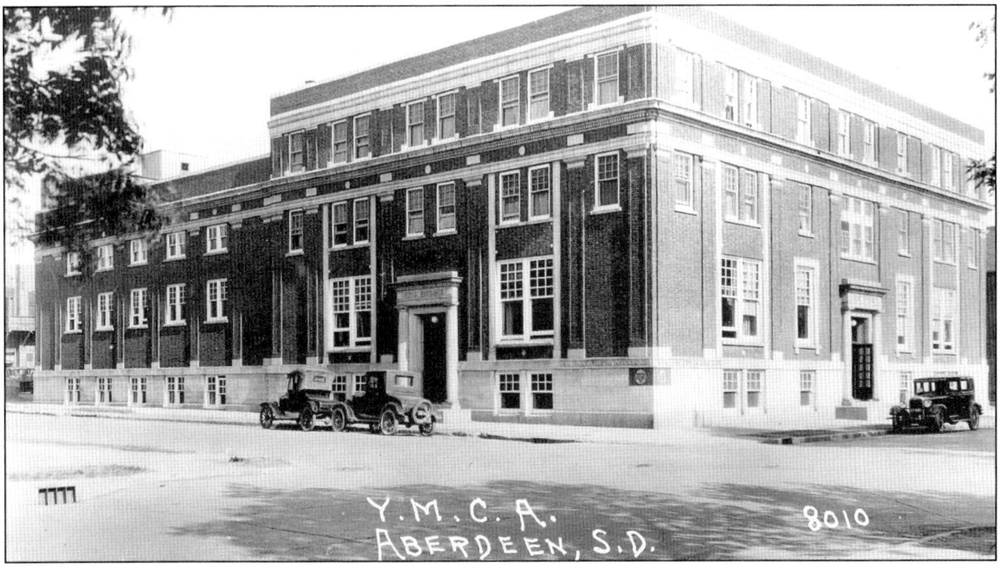

On April 12, 1920, a building fund campaign was started for this building after Mrs. A.E. Boyd donated the corner of Fifth Avenue and South Lincoln Street to the Y.M.C.A. in 1915 with the provision that a facility be erected on the site within five years. The corner stone was laid September 25, 1921, but work was halted in January of 1922 after the funds were depleted. The building was closed for three years until a second campaign opened in 1925. Twelve days later the required $75,000 was in hand and the work proceeded. The completed building was dedicated on October 19, 1926.

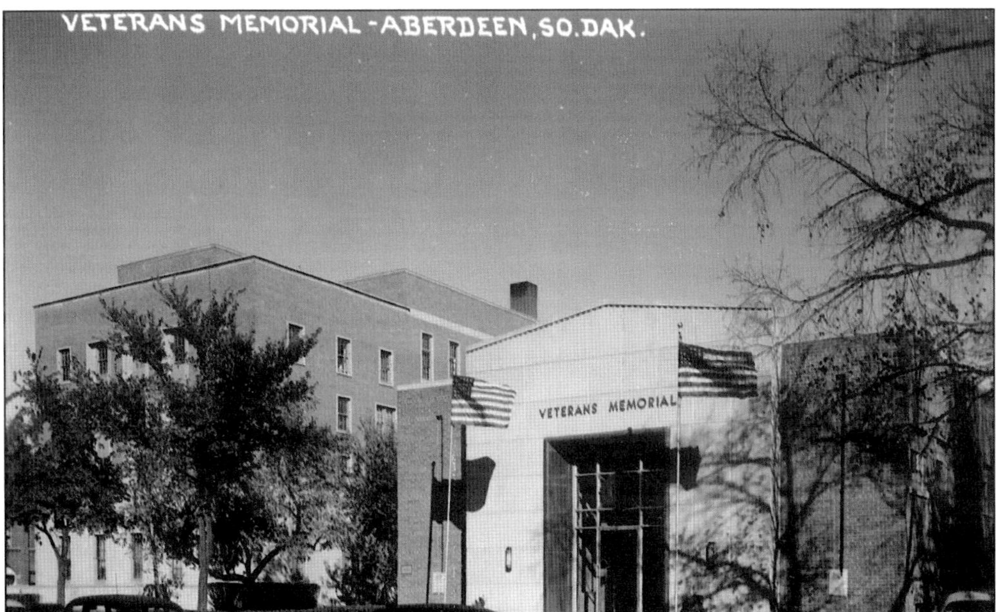

The American Legion Sidney L. Smith Post Number 24 was organized in 1919 by World War I veterans and was named for the first Aberdonian to die in France. The group purchased the Lincoln Street lot left vacant after the moving of the Lincoln Hospital in 1940 and built this building. Today, this building serves as headquarters for the Native American Tea Company.

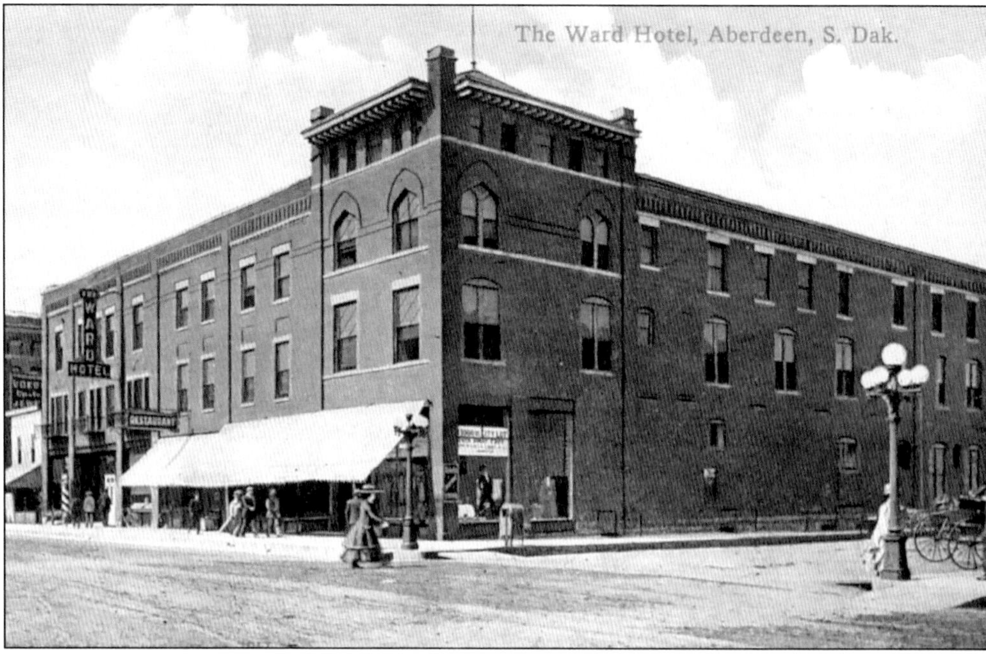

Alonzo LaRue Ward came to Aberdeen in 1883 and started a small lunch counter on Main Street. Little by little he purchased neighboring properties to add a small hotel to his operation. Eventually he had 125 feet of Main Street frontage and had added a third floor to his property. On the day before Thanksgiving 1926, this hotel was destroyed by fire. Firemen battled for over nine hours, but ultimately only the hotel's walls were left standing on three sides of the building.

PLEASE

Be careful not to soil room carpets when oiling your gun or greasing your boots.

Dogs are not allowed in the Coffee Shop or Grill Room.

ALONZO WARD HOTEL

This card was attached to the inside of the doors of all of the rooms in the old Ward Hotel in the 1890s to about 1910.

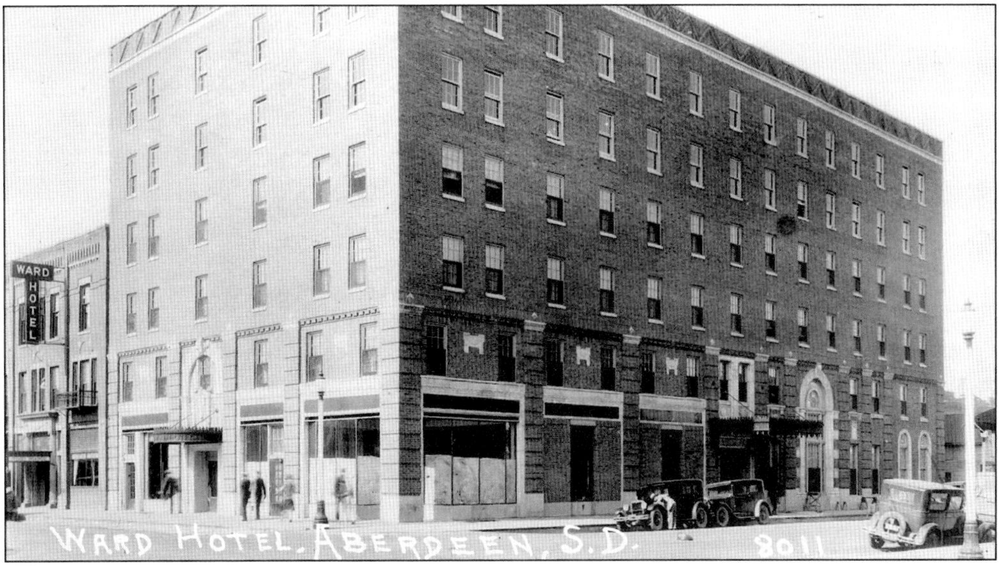

Alonzo Ward rebuilt his burned-out hotel on the same site in 1928. Mayor John Wade ceremoniously registered as the first guest on May 15, 1928. The new, six-story hotel would be equipped with 140 guest rooms and a large staff consisting of four clerks, one bookkeeper, one operator, two elevator operators, four bell boys, one engineer, one porter, one night fireman, one chef, four cooks, a storeroom steward, a yard man, two dishwashers, thirteen waitresses, and one cashier. Alonzo Ward passed away unexpectedly in 1929, leaving management of the new facility up to his children.

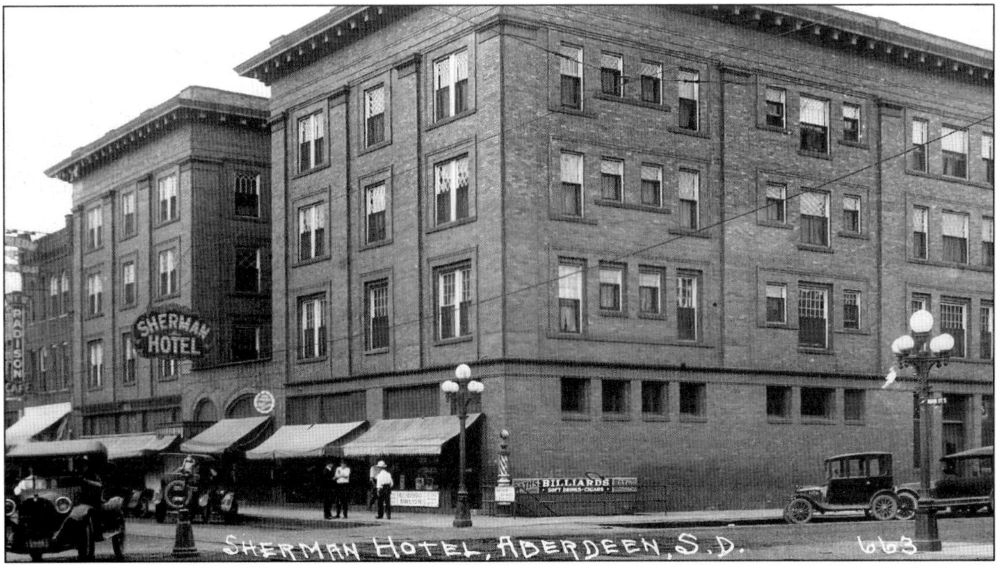

This new four-story hotel with 120 guest rooms and fifty baths, mostly placed between two guest rooms, was built in 1907 to replace the original Sherman Hotel that was destroyed by fire the previous year. When the building was finished in 1908, a grand opening ball and reception were held with approximately 1,000 people attending. This hotel burned to the ground on June 26, 1926. Newspaper reports of the fire estimated that "practically every resident of Aberdeen not sick in bed or too aged to appear was on Main Street and the adjoining avenues watching the fire."

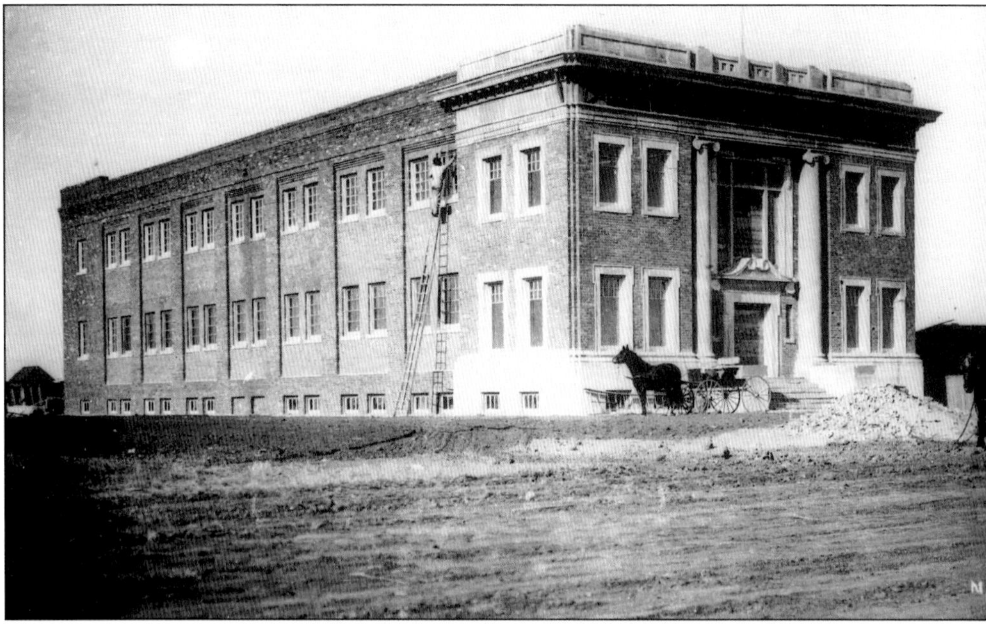

The *Dakota Farmer* was established in 1881 in Huron, Dakota Territory, and was moved to Aberdeen in 1887. Growth of the magazine necessitated moving the operation several times until this final home was built in 1911 on the 1200 block of South Main Street. The magazine was published in this Aberdeen building until the 1980s. Hollis & Jean Hurlbert converted the building into upscale apartments in the 1990s.

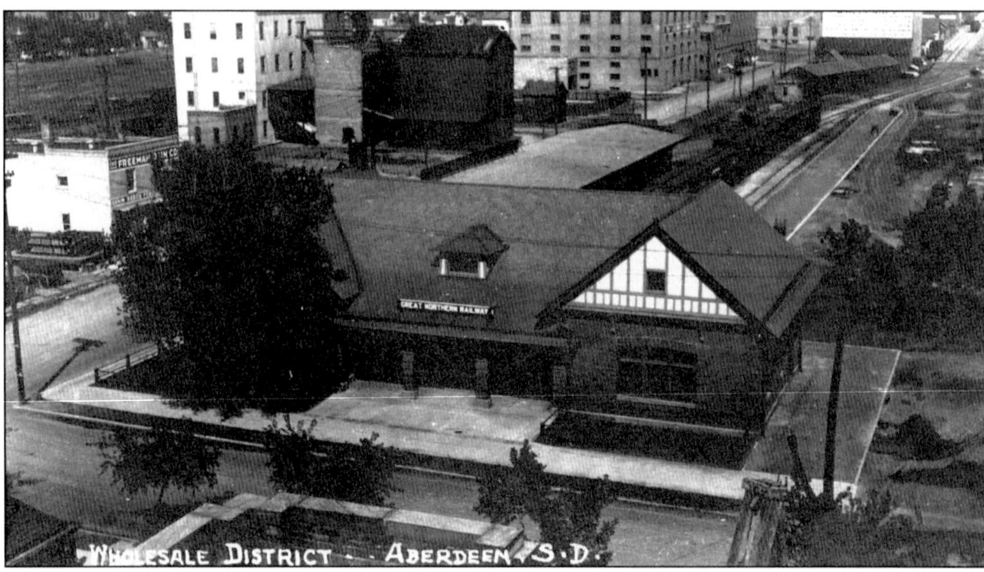

Aberdeen was the preeminent wholesale location in the Dakotas with its four railroads and nine lines. Many of Aberdeen's early businesses eventually erected wholesale houses near the railroad depots. Jewett Brothers Wholesale Grocers established the first permanent wholesale house in 1886. By 1907, Jackson Hardware, Aberdeen Wholesale Grocery, Gamble-Robinson Fruit Co., McArthur Piano Co., and Val Blatz Brewing Co. had erected large buildings, with a total value of upwards of $200,000, east of the Milwaukee Depot in this wholesale district.

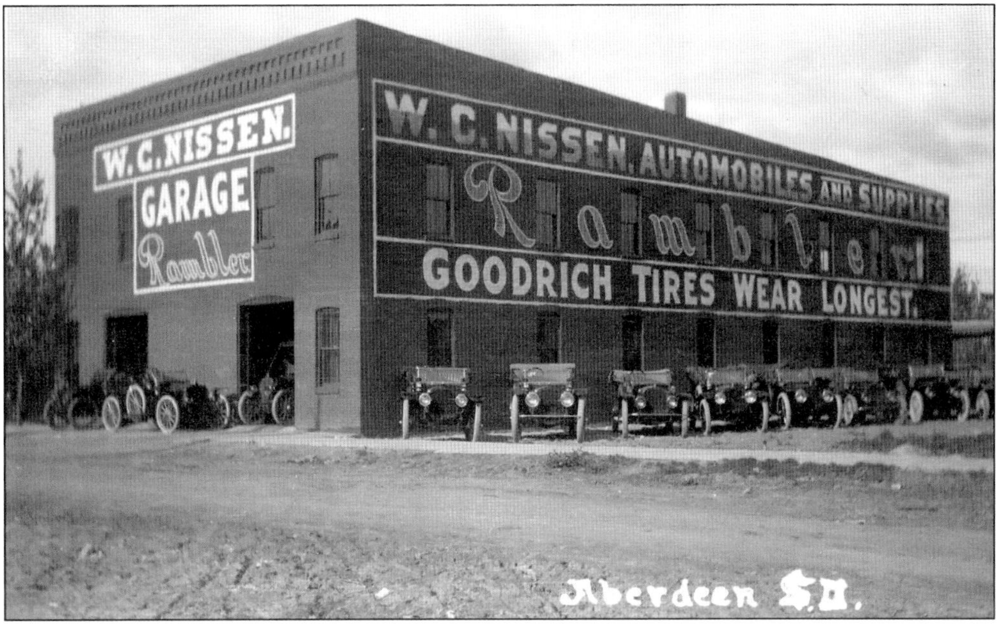

William C. Nissen opened this garage in 1909 at 113 Third Avenue S.W. where he sold Jackson, Rambler, Fuller, and the "Invincible Schact" brands of the newfangled automobiles. He also handled engines and threshers, perhaps as a hedge against the fragility of the infant auto business.

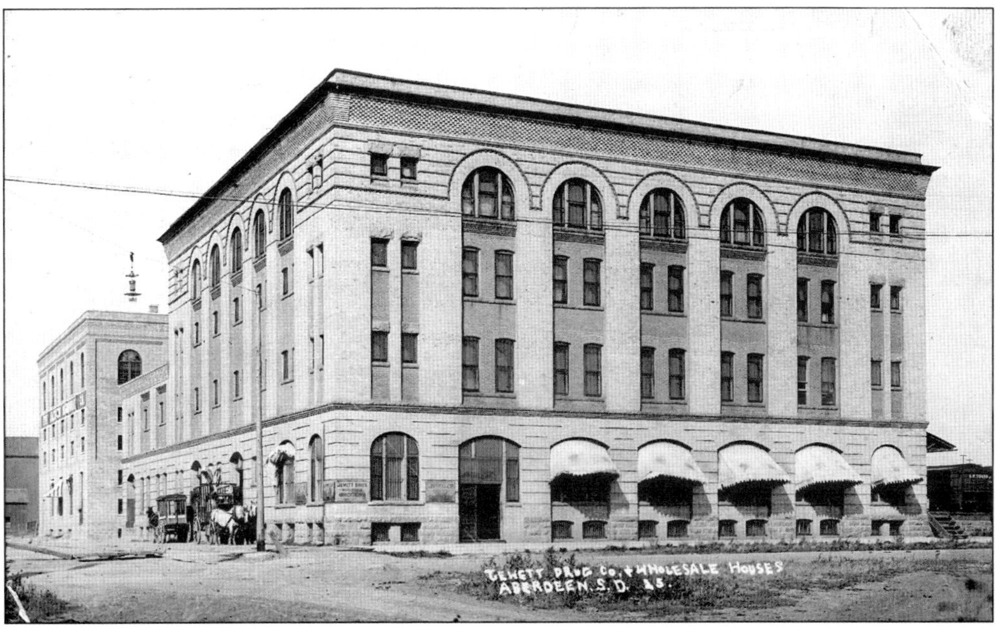

Brothers Harvey, Charles, and Rollin Jewett built this building in Aberdeen's wholesale district in 1909 to accommodate their ever-growing grocery and drug wholesale business. The Jewetts had come from Ohio in 1883 to establish their wholesale grocery business, the first business of this kind in Dakota Territory. In the early 1900s, the Jewett's established a wholesale drug division. In the 1950s, Aberdeen was the smallest U.S. city to have a wholesale drug company carrying a full line of drugs.

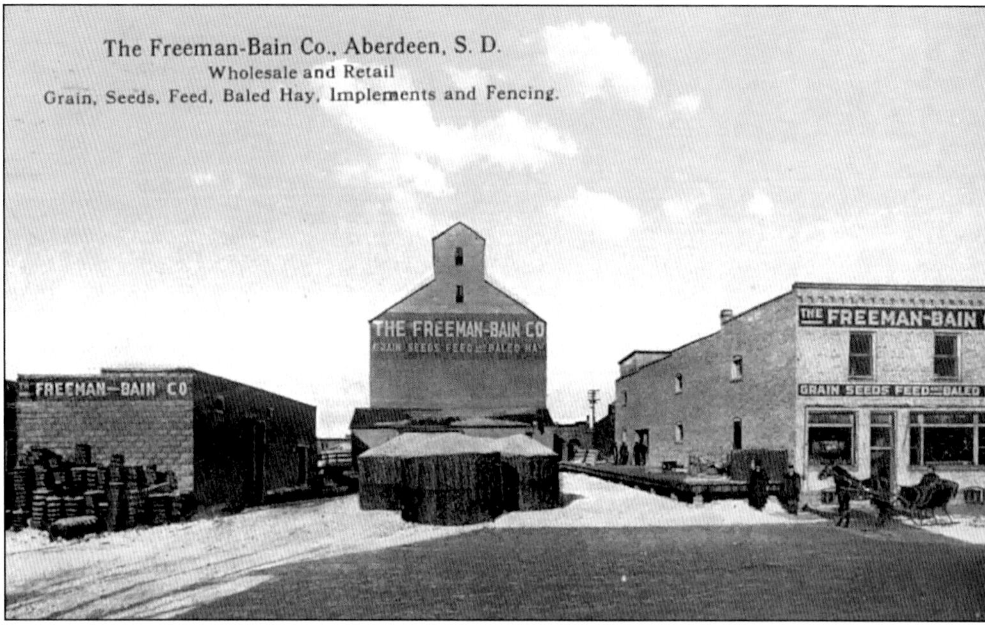

The Freeman Brothers bought this grain business from the Bagley Company in 1906. In 1909, the buildings in this photo replaced those that were destroyed by fire. In 1940, the Sheldon Reese Company that already had elevators in 27 South Dakota towns purchased this operation. This elevator was demolished in the late 1940s when Sheldon Reese sold the grain business. The real photo postcard below shows the interior.

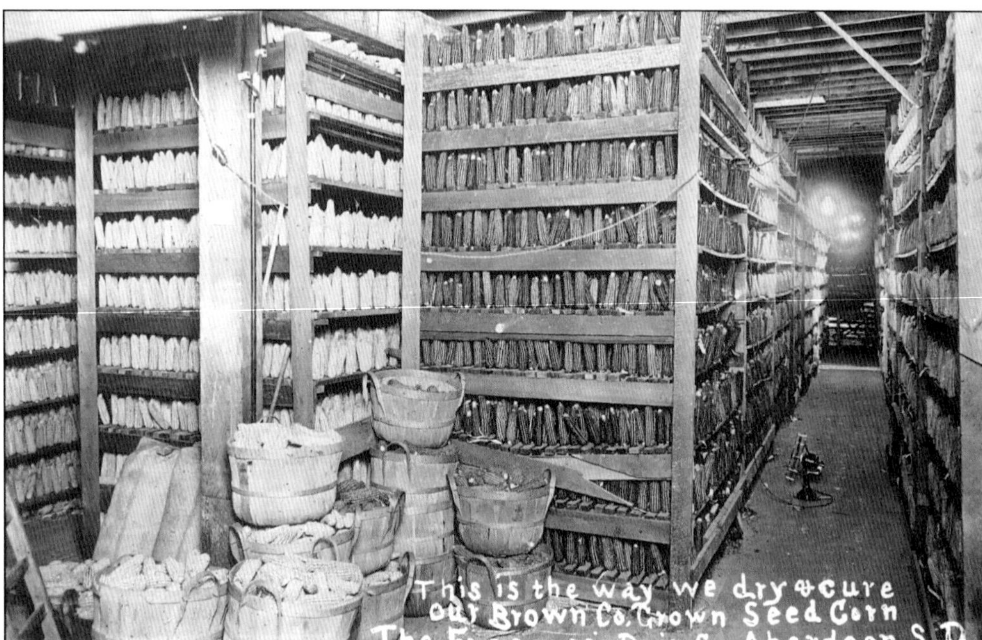

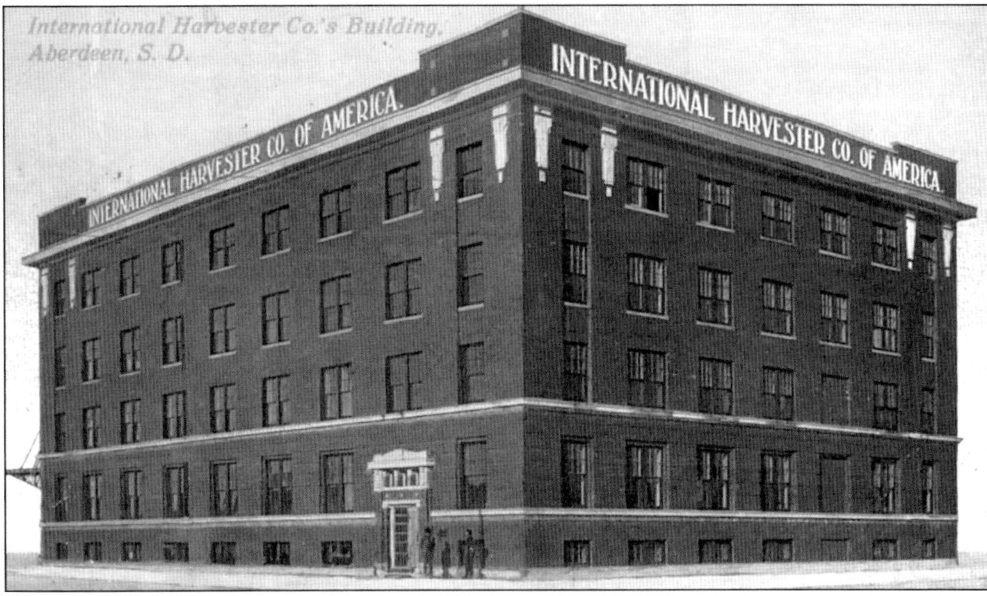

This massive five-story building was constructed in 1911 for Aberdeen's International Harvester Company, who called it home for the next 50 years. IHC fell victim to changing times and advanced technology and closed this operation in 1961. It was then sold to Hub City Iron Co. and extensively remodeled to suit their business needs. On Friday, November 11, 1972, a fire that apparently started in a paint room in the southwest corner of the building destroyed the structure. Because of a strong northeast wind, charred embers from the fire could be found blocks away on Saturday morning.

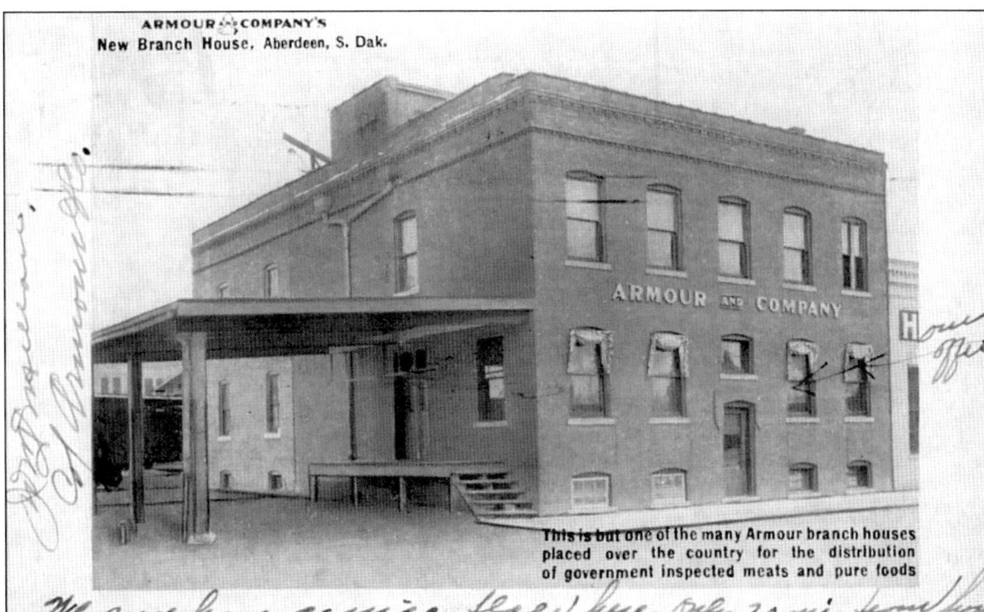

This postcard is dated 1912 and features the Armour & Co. Branch House at 115 SE Railroad Avenue. Formerly used by Armour until 1964 when it became Mathes Electric Co., it is now occupied by Custom Sheet Metal and owned by Gordy Nelson.

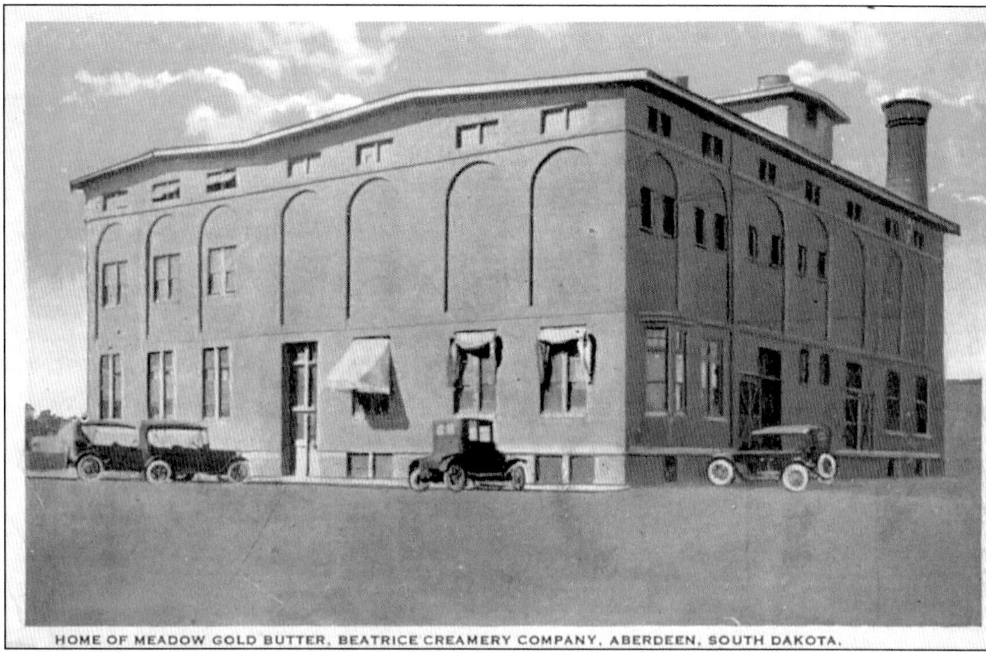

No information could be found about Beatrice Creamery, the Home of Meadow Gold Butter, in any of the old city directories, history books, or from anyone at the Dacotah Prairie Museum.

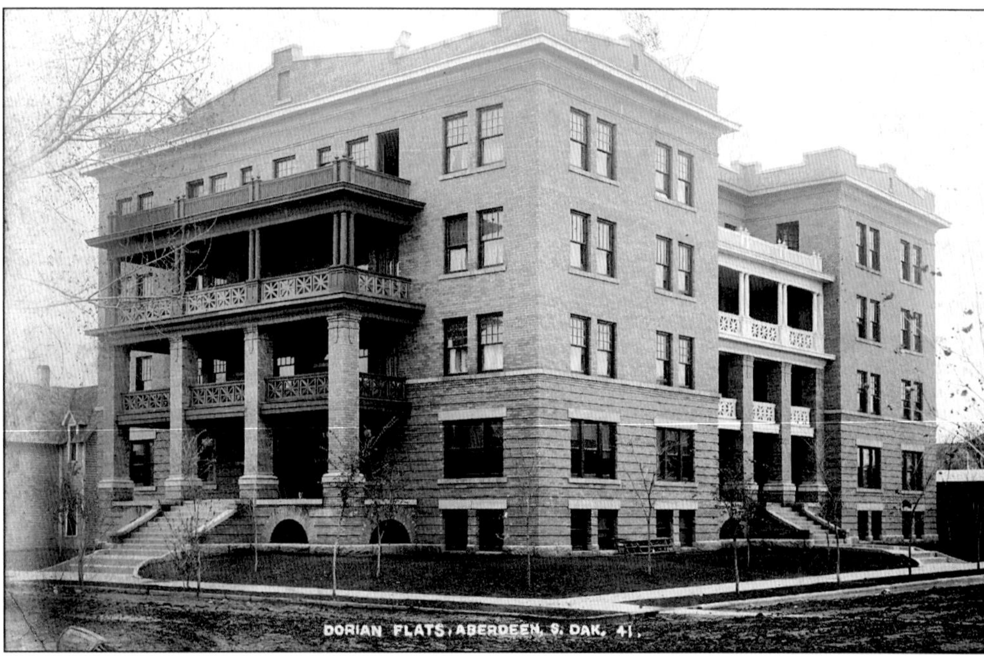

George B. Narregang built the Dorian Apartment complex in 1909 on the corner of southeast Seventh Avenue and South Lincoln Street. Until that time, multiple family dwellings were very scarce in Aberdeen. One six-family apartment house was built in 1888, but all six apartments shared one kitchen!

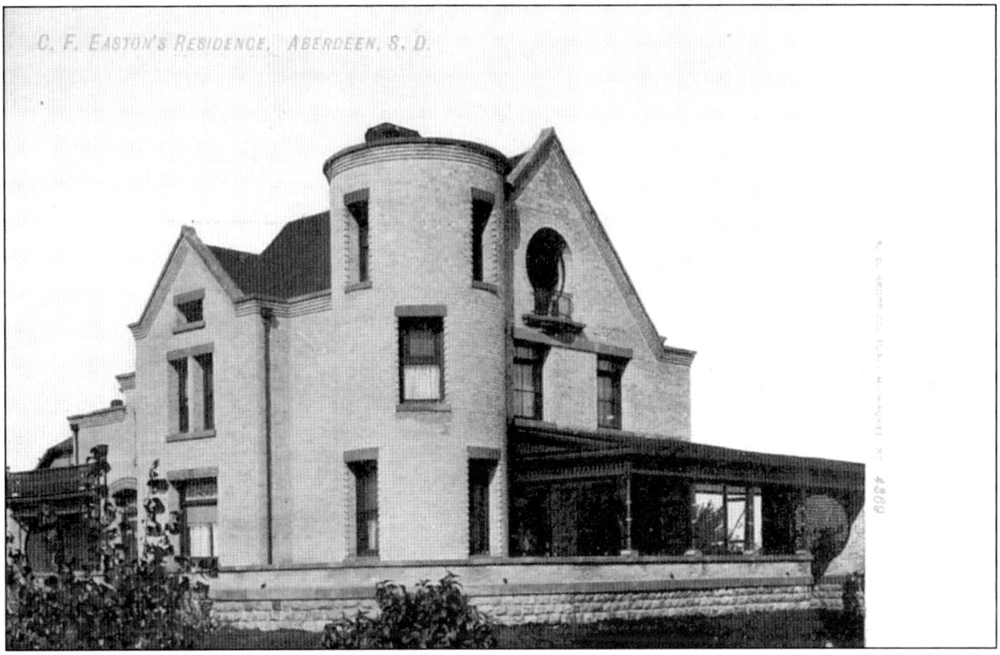

The C.F. Easton residence was a unique home that was built in 1890 and was long owned by the Easton family. Its distinctive features include a three-story tower, a balustrade with a keyhole opening on the third floor, and baled roofs with parapet eaves. It was originally a frame building but was bricked over in 1904.

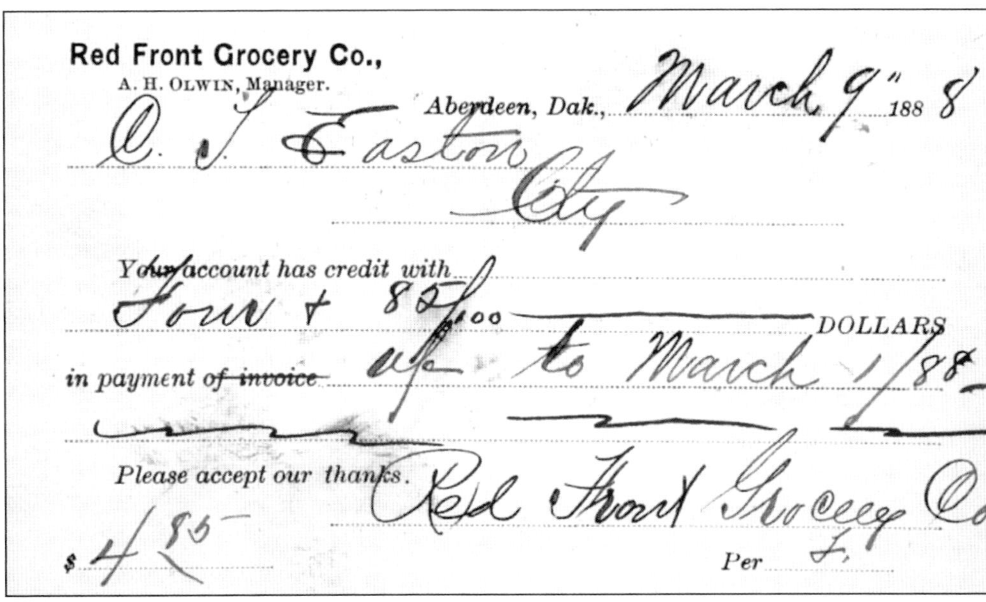

Red Front Grocery Co.,
A. H. Olwin, Manager.

Aberdeen, Dak., March 9" 1888

C. F. Easton
City

Your account has credit with
Four + 85/100 DOLLARS
in payment of ~~invoice~~ up to March 1/88

Please accept our thanks. Red Front Grocery Co

$ 4 85/

Per L.

This is a bill to the owner of the above Easton home in 1888 from the Red Front Grocery Company, which was located on the northwest corner of Main Street and Third Avenue. A.H. Olwin and W.P. Butler then owned it. About 20 years later, Mr. Olwin started the Olwin Angel Store, a fine department store that remained in town for over 70 years.

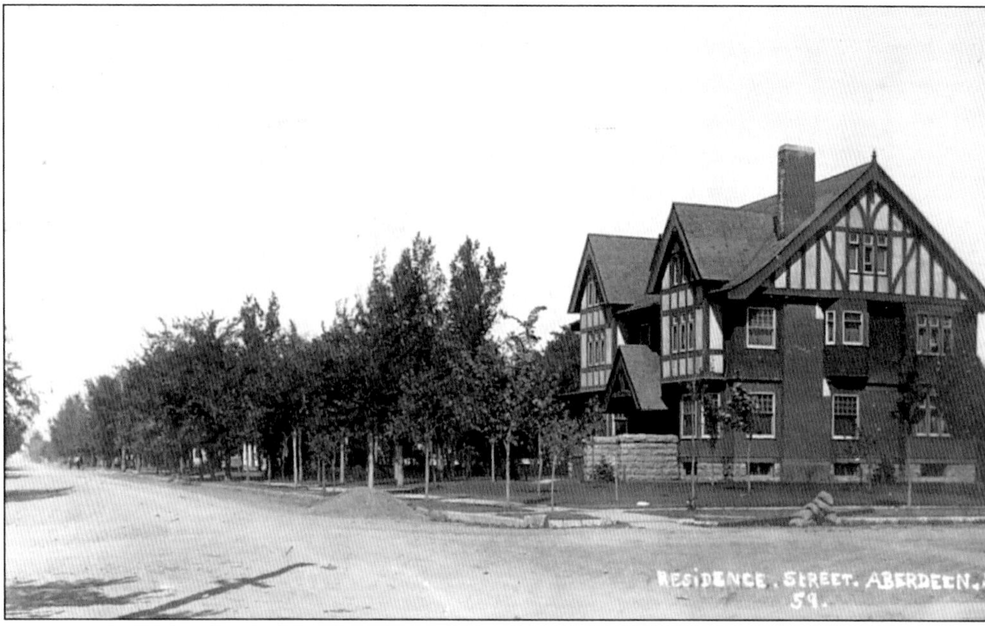

Pictured here is the home of A.F. Milligan, a local insurance man. This home, built *c.* 1906, stood on the northeast corner of South Kline Street and Sixth Avenue. This house was moved in the early 1960s when the Milligan family donated the land to the city of Aberdeen as a site for the new Alexander Mitchell Library. The elder Milligan served as president of the library board for 20 years prior to his death in 1939.

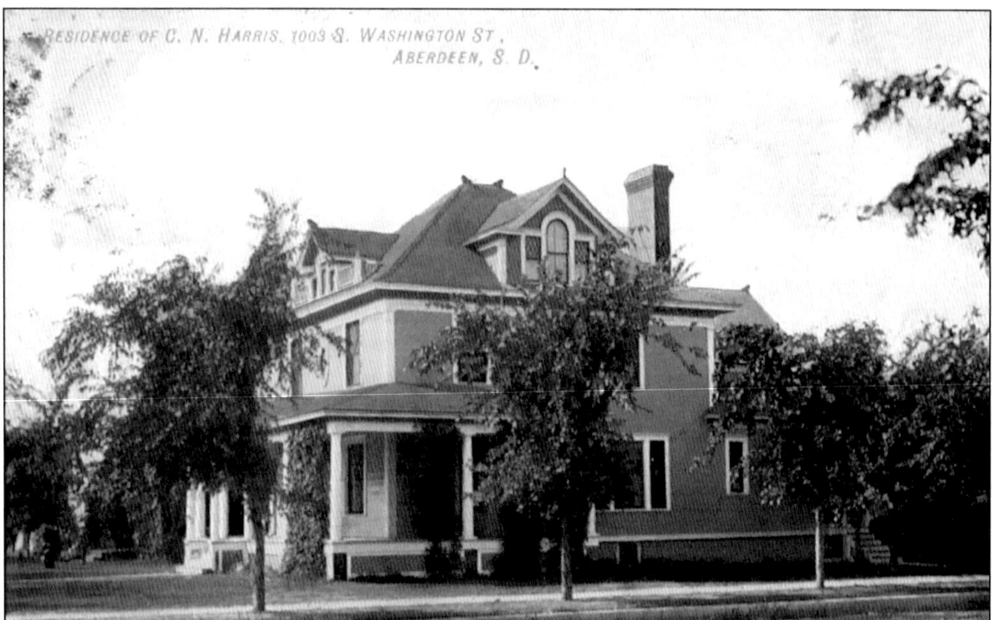

C.N. Harris was an attorney and judge. This home was built in the early part of the 20th century on Ninth Avenue southeast and Washington Street, where it still stands today serving as an apartment house.

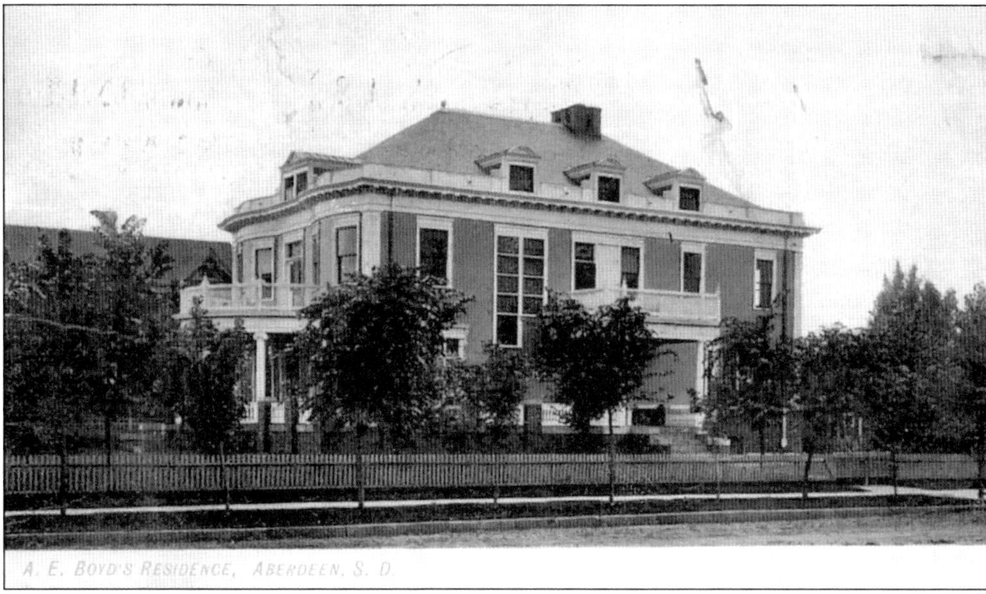

Arthur E. Boyd and his wife Della built this home in 1906. The massive home featured solid oak woodwork, leaded and stained glass windows, pocket doors, and a dumbwaiter to serve meals from the basement kitchen to the first floor dining room. The third floor housed the servants. A coal-fired boiler heated the entire structure. The home eventually became the Gates Funeral Home but was torn down in 1995.

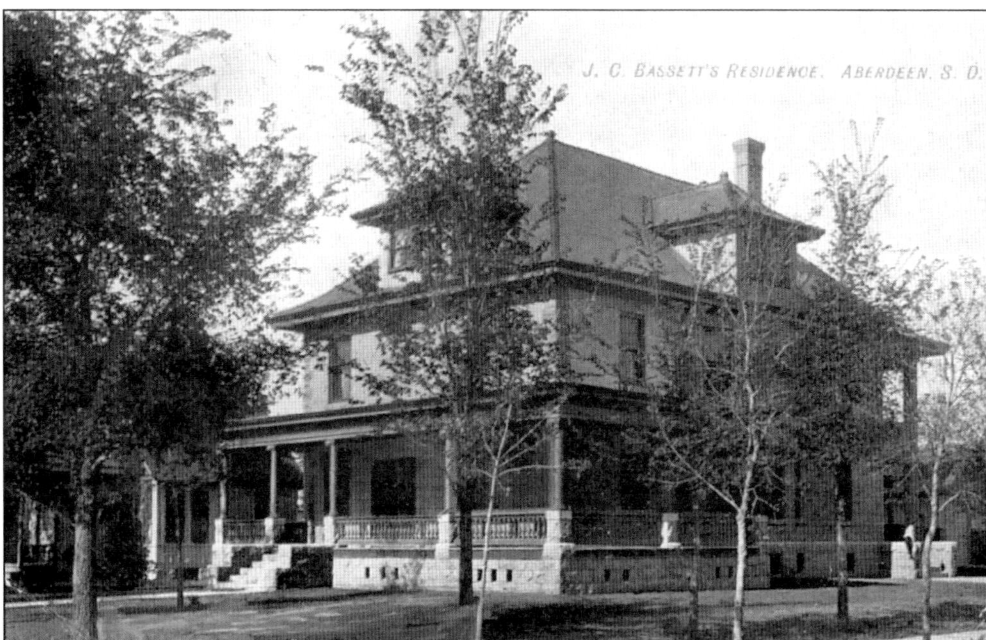

John C. Bassett and his wife Harriet moved from Langford to Aberdeen in 1900. As a successful banker, Bassett served as president of the Aberdeen National Bank, the Ninth District Federal Reserve Bank, and the First Bank Stock Corporation.

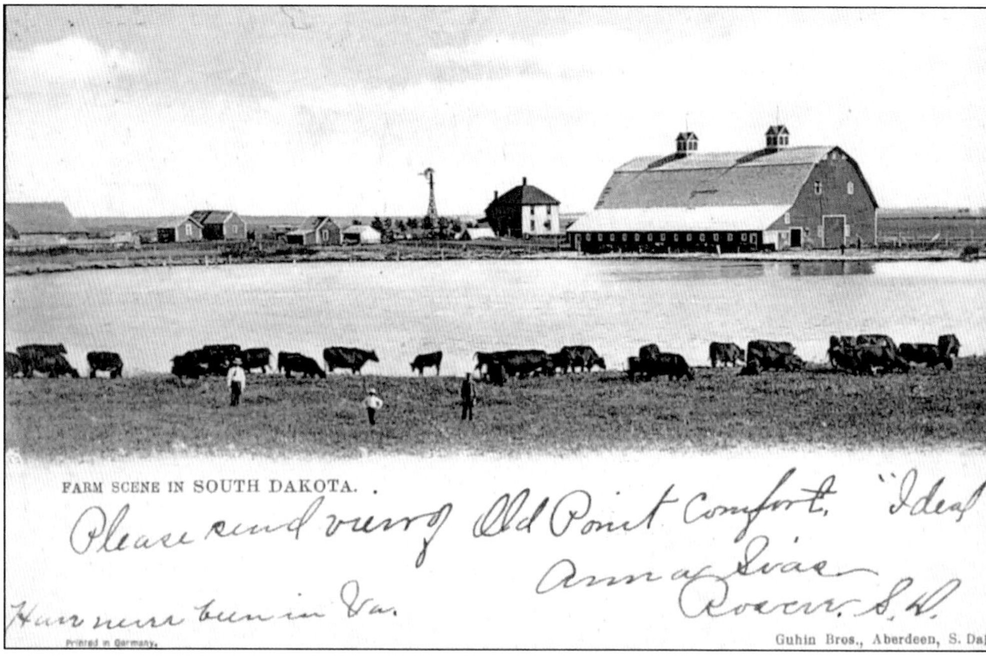

This is one of the 1905 Raphael Tuck & Sons postcard series 2216 titled "Aberdeen, S. Dak." It was distributed by the Guhin Bros. Booksellers.

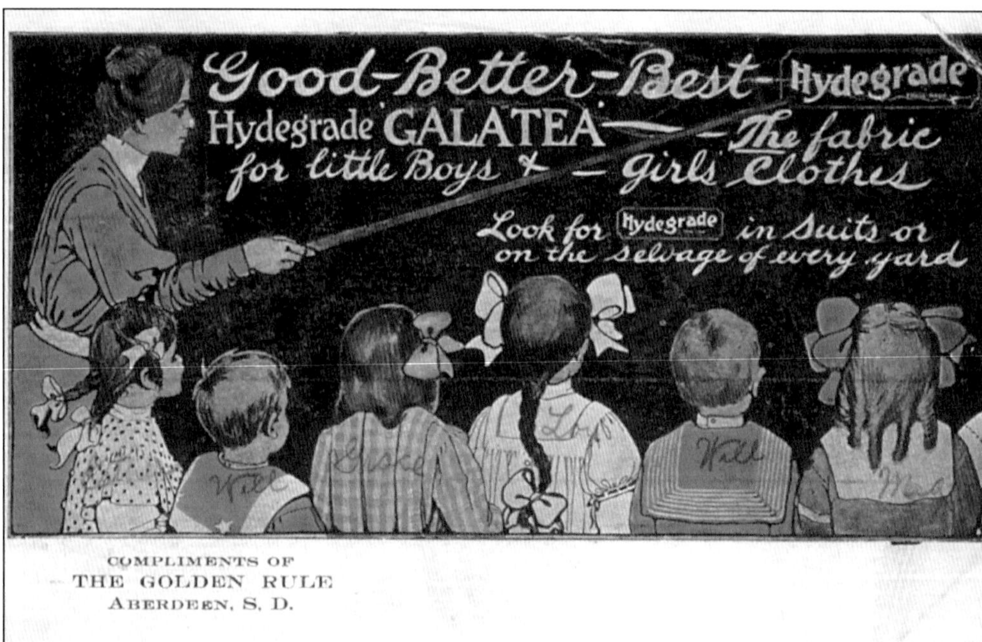

This is a pre-1907, undivided-back postcard from the Golden Rule Store at 202 South Main Street. It was an advertisement for one of their product lines, Hydegrade.

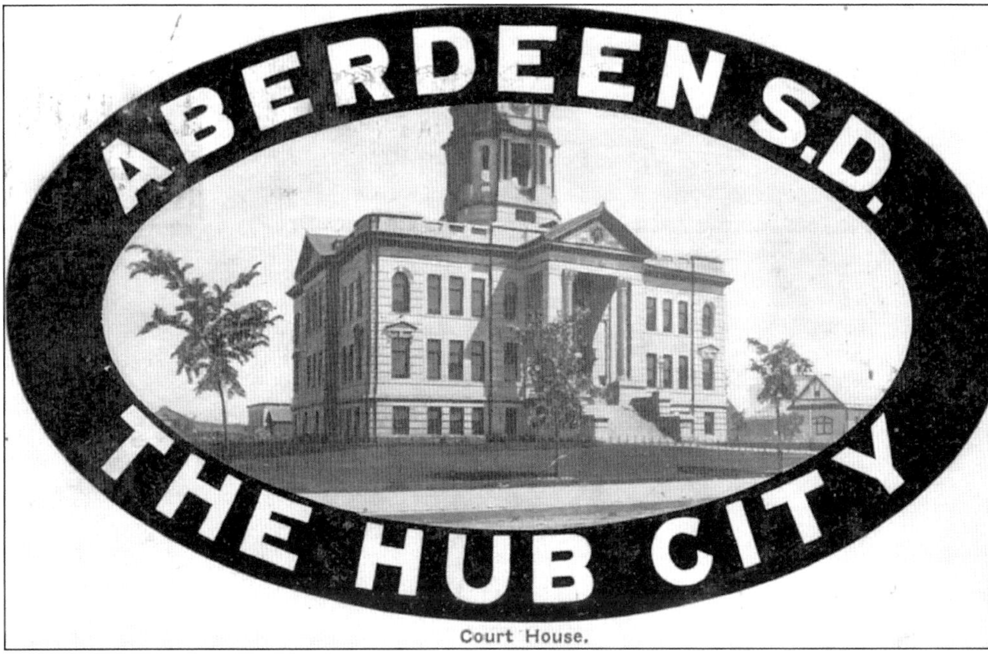

These next eight postcards comprise the complete set of "Aberdeen, South Dakota, The Hub City" oval postcards. Each is described in more detail in other sections of the book. Above is the 1904 Brown County Courthouse; below is the high school that was used until the new high school was built in 1910.

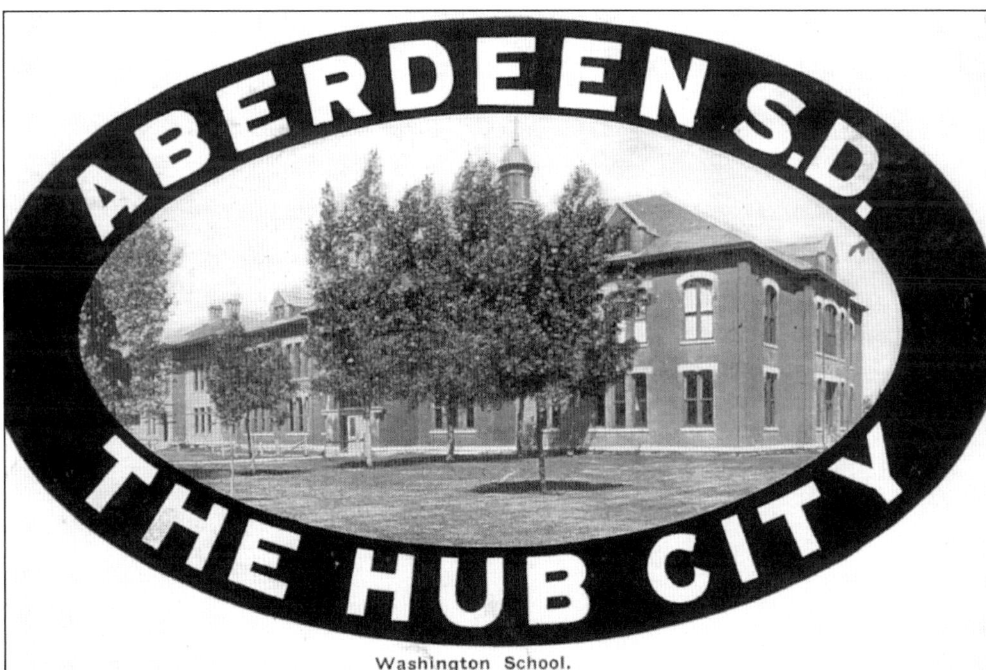

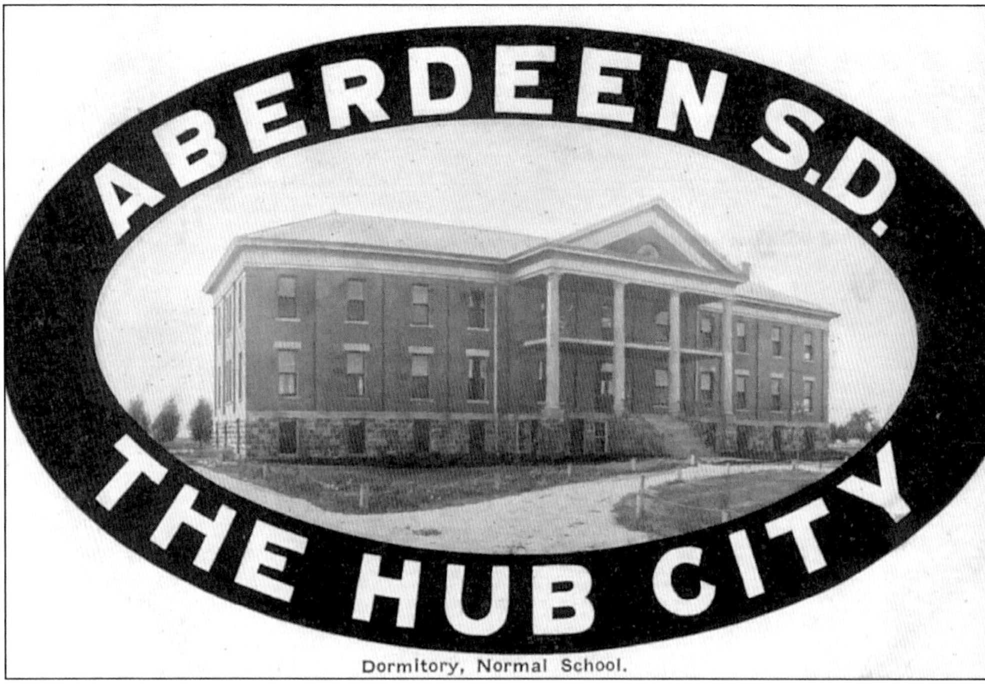

The Hub City "ovals" came in two varieties, either in black and white or colored. Above is the first dormitory built at Northern in 1902 and below is the original Chicago, Milwaukee & St. Paul Railroad depot.

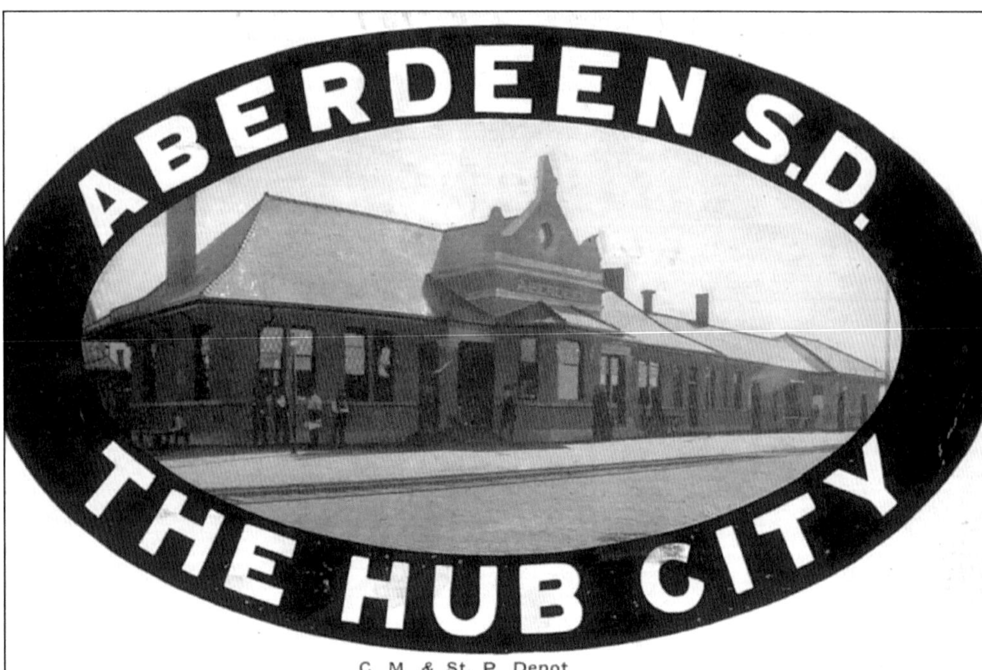

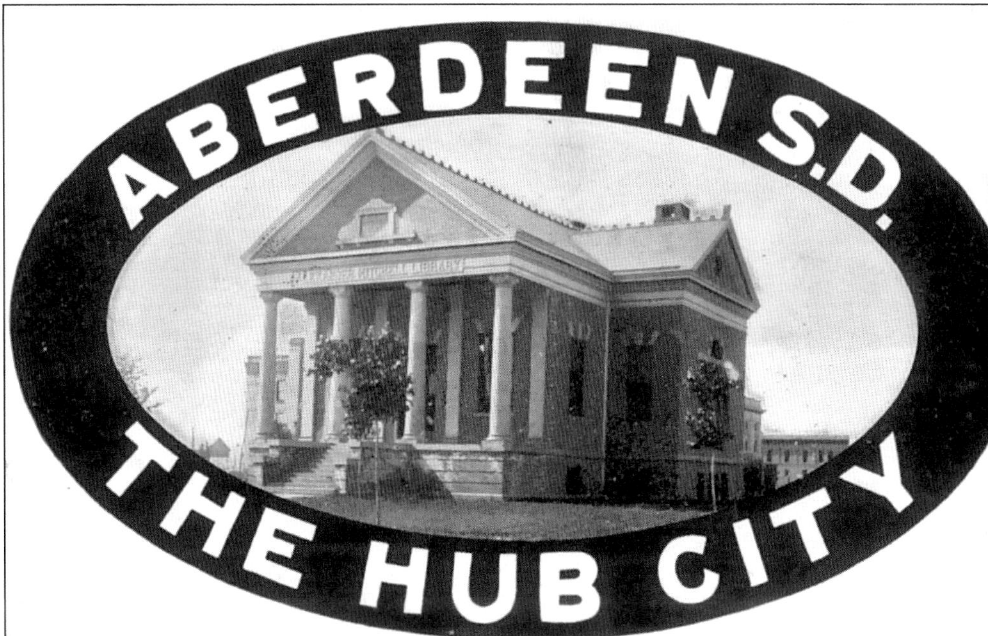

Aberdeen Public Library.

We are aware that two other South Dakota towns had similar oval style postcards. They were Watertown and Huron. Above is the Alexander Mitchell Library that was just south of the United Methodist Church and has been a parking lot since the late 1950s. Below is the Main Building or Central Building at Northern that burned down in 1960.

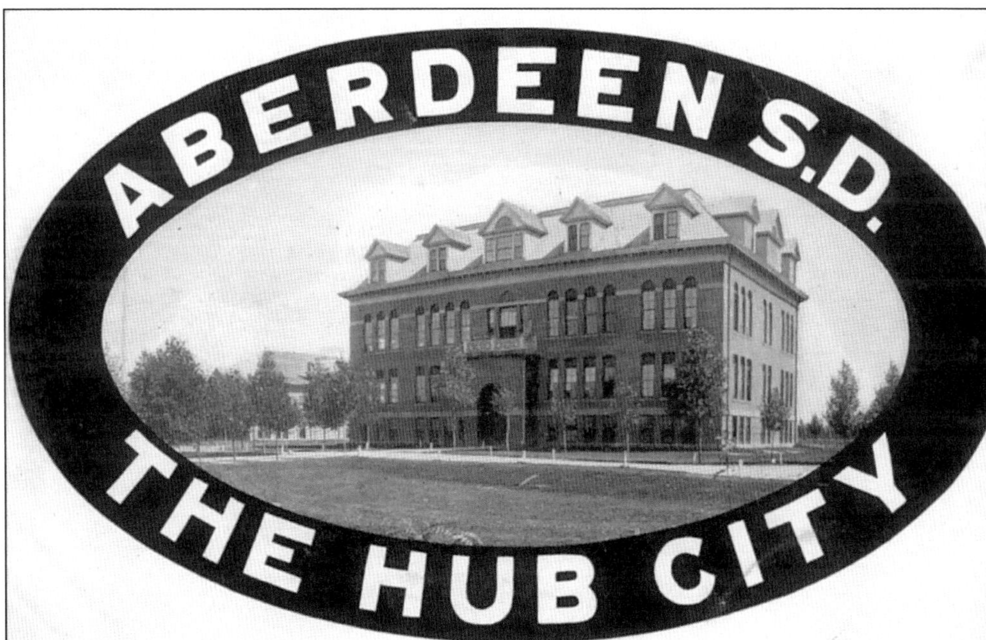

Main Building, Normal School.

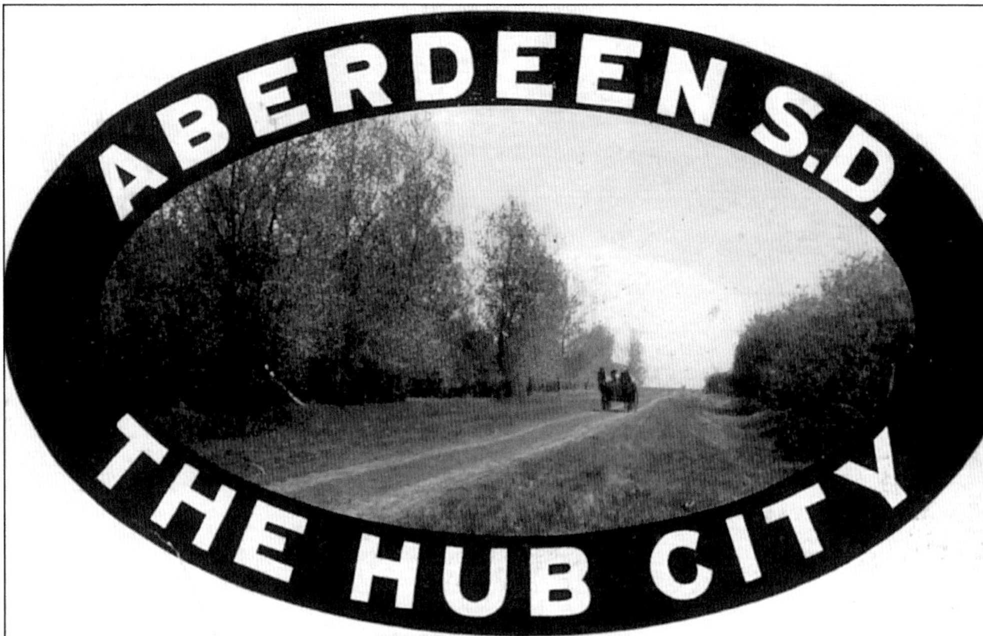

A Drive to Melgardes.

These oval postcards were sold starting in late 1907 or early 1908. Melgaard is misspelled in the above postcard. At this time, Melgaard was still several blocks outside of town. Below is a Main Street view looking south from Railroad Avenue.

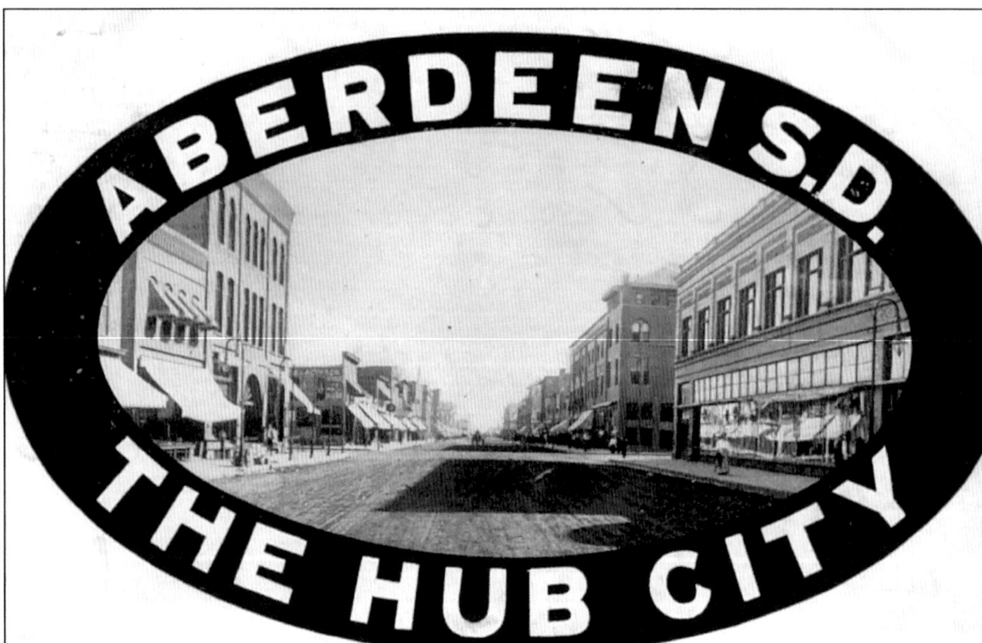

View South on Main Street.

Three

Churches and Hospitals

Since the founding of Aberdeen, when it was located in Dakota Territory, the presence of religion through its worship services, the clergy, the missionaries (of which some were here before the county was platted), and finally the actual church buildings have been important. Before the churches were built, worship services were held wherever they could find room. The Presentation Sisters were early arrivals and they were very instrumental in starting the schools, the medical clinics, and finally the first hospital. After 116 years, the Presentation Sisters are still committed to Aberdeen, the schools, and to medicine.

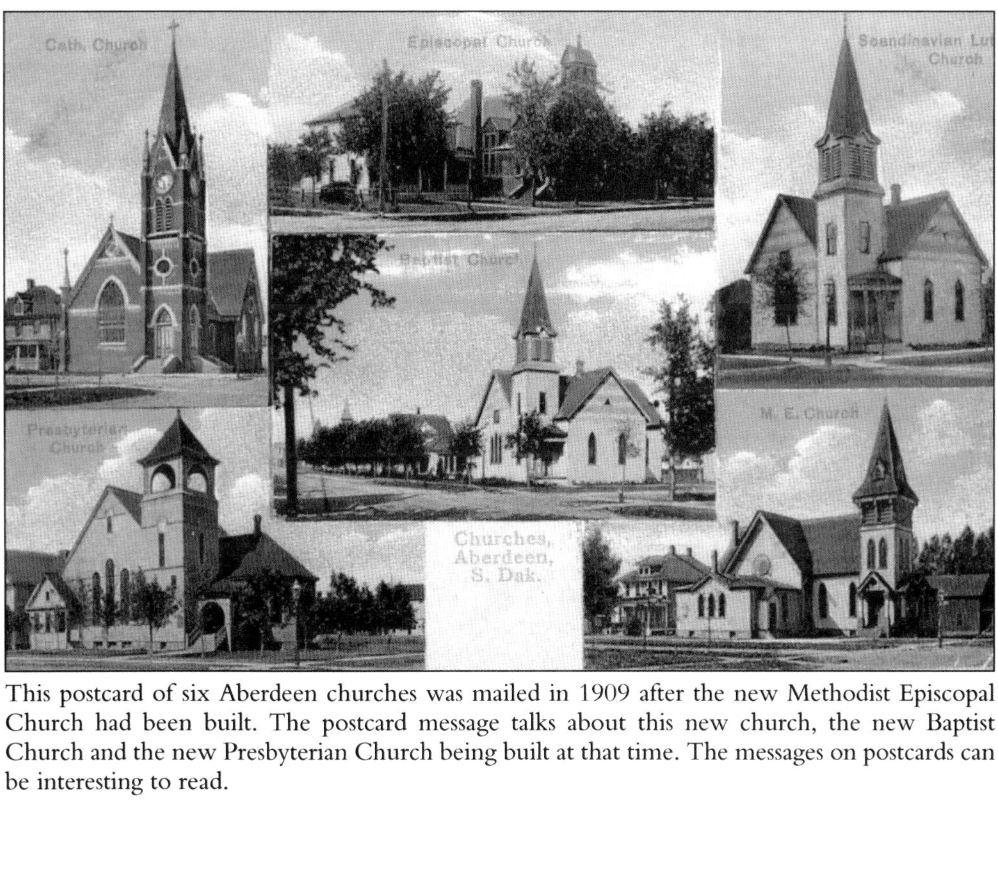

This postcard of six Aberdeen churches was mailed in 1909 after the new Methodist Episcopal Church had been built. The postcard message talks about this new church, the new Baptist Church and the new Presbyterian Church being built at that time. The messages on postcards can be interesting to read.

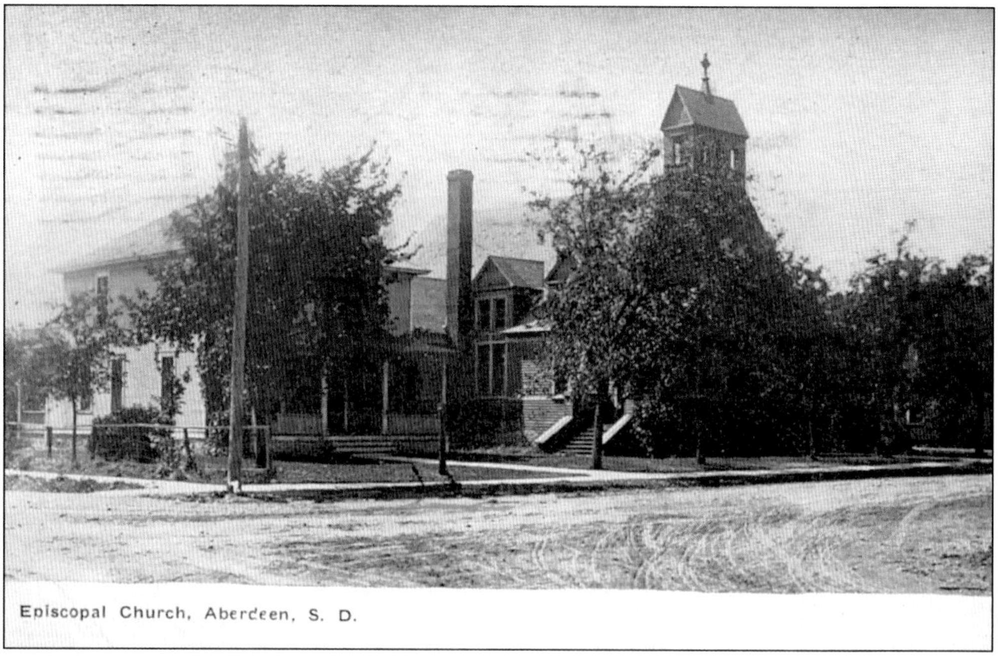

In 1909, St. Mark's Episcopal Church was located at 20 Sixth Avenue SE. The Rev. J.W. Hyslop was rector and he lived at the house next door at 24 Sixth Avenue SE. This location is now home to Aberdeen TV & Appliance, before that it was the Red Owl Grocery Store.

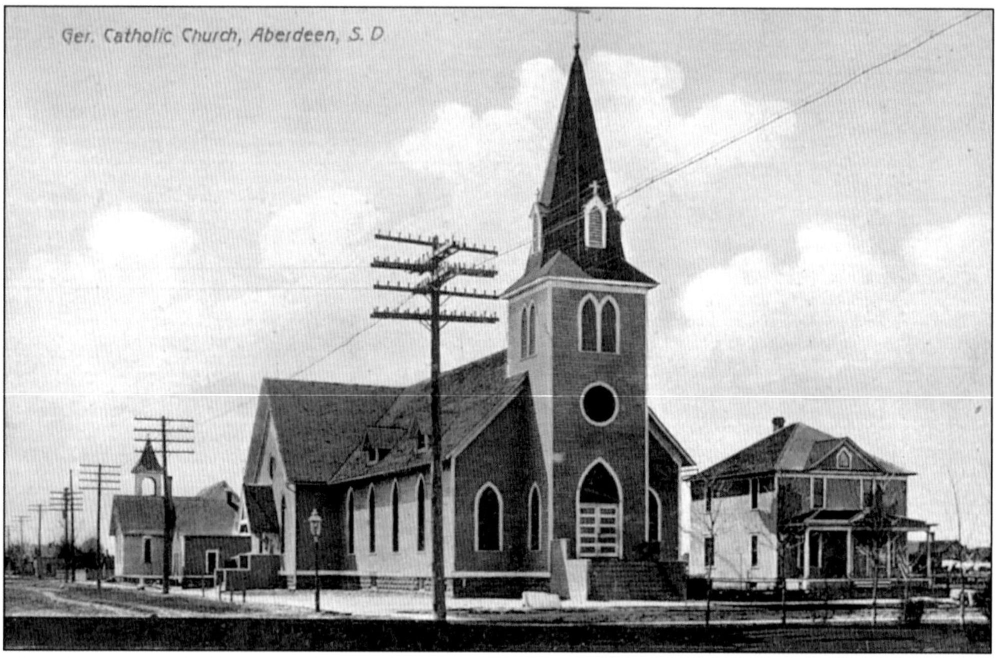

The German Catholic Church was located at 201 North Arch Street and is more properly known as St. Mary's Catholic Church. The German name was changed because of World War I influences. In 1909, the Rev. Father Dahlmans was the priest.

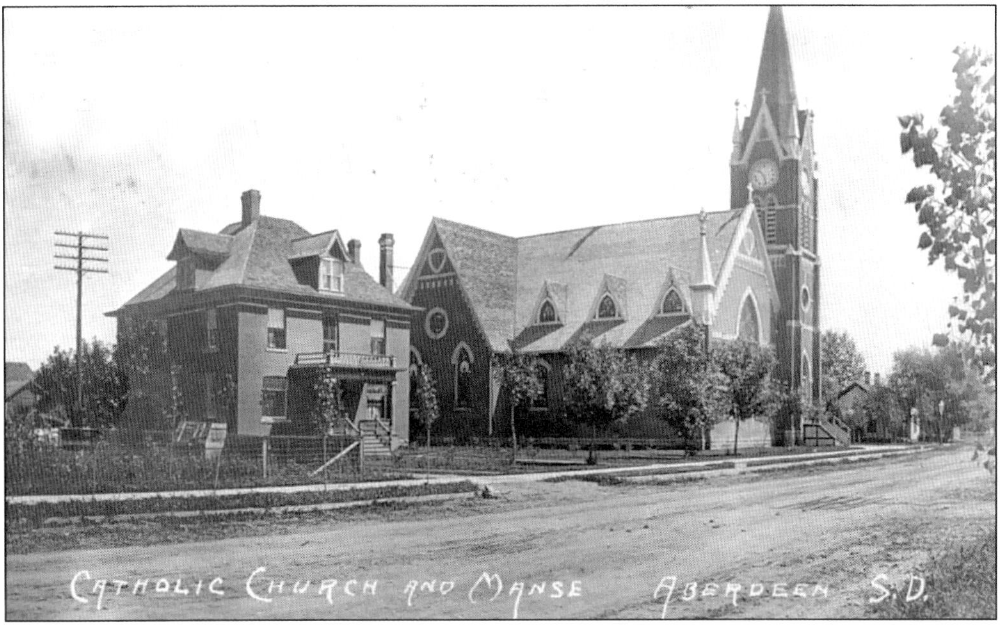

This 1909 postcard of the Sacred Heart of Jesus Christ Catholic Church at 423 Third Avenue SE also shows the manse or rectory on the left. This church was built in 1899, and the manse in 1900. The current neo-gothic cathedral was built in 1933 and the current rectory in 1950. In 1909, the Rev. Father Dermody was the priest.

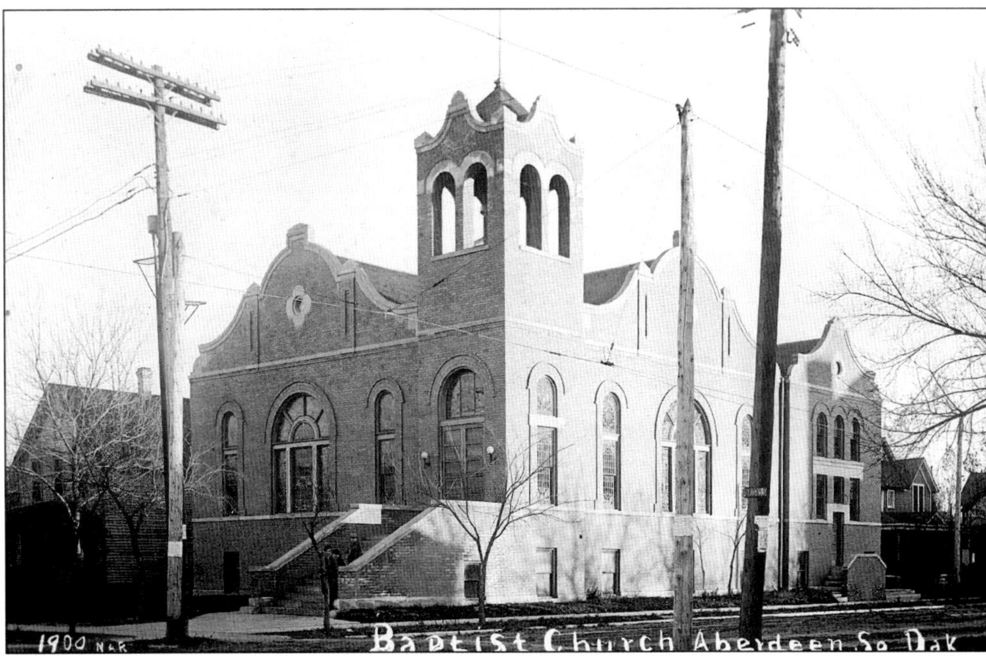

This *c.* 1910 real photo postcard shows the new Baptist Church at 102 Sixth Avenue SE. The Rev. E.J. Parsons was the pastor. The church's new building is on Melgaard Road and this is now a parking lot for the South Dakota Wheat Growers.

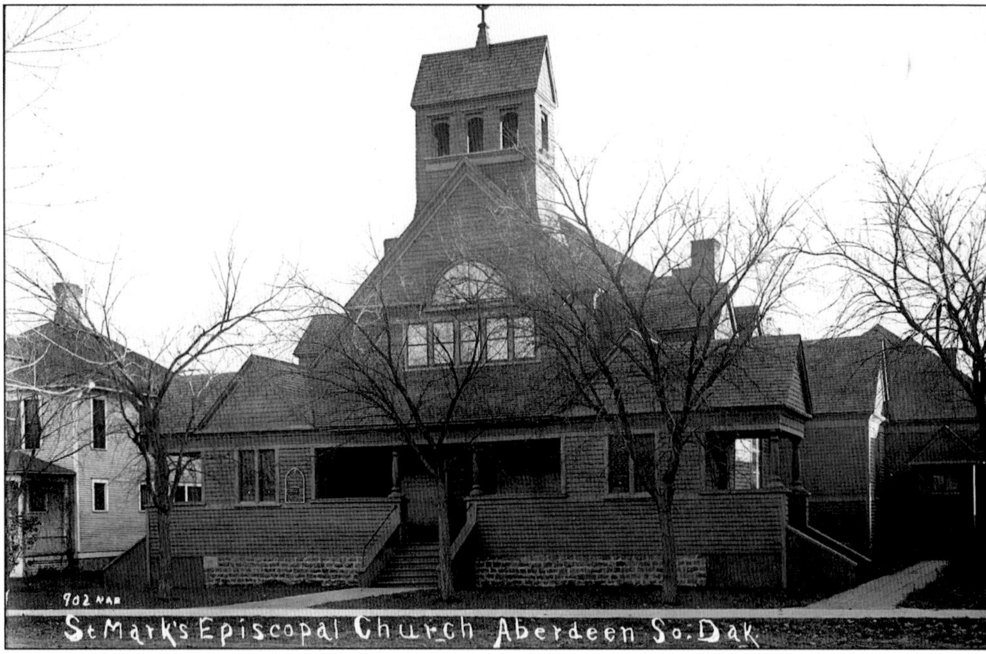

This *c.* 1910 real photo postcard shows a front view of St. Mark's Episcopal Church at 20 Sixth Avenue SE.

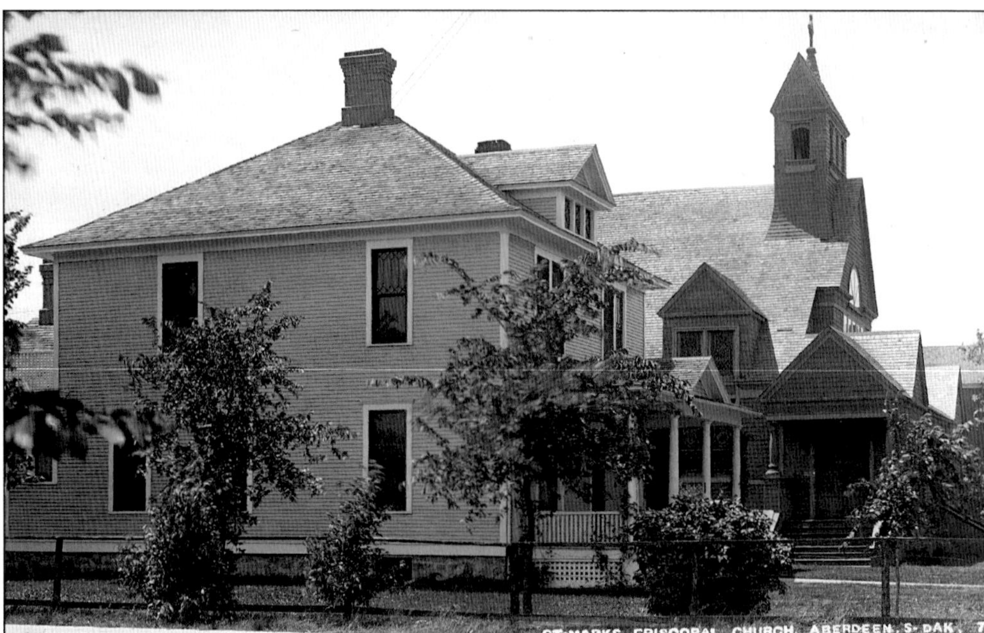

This *c.* 1910 view was taken from the east and features the Rev. J.W. Hyslops parsonage next to his church.

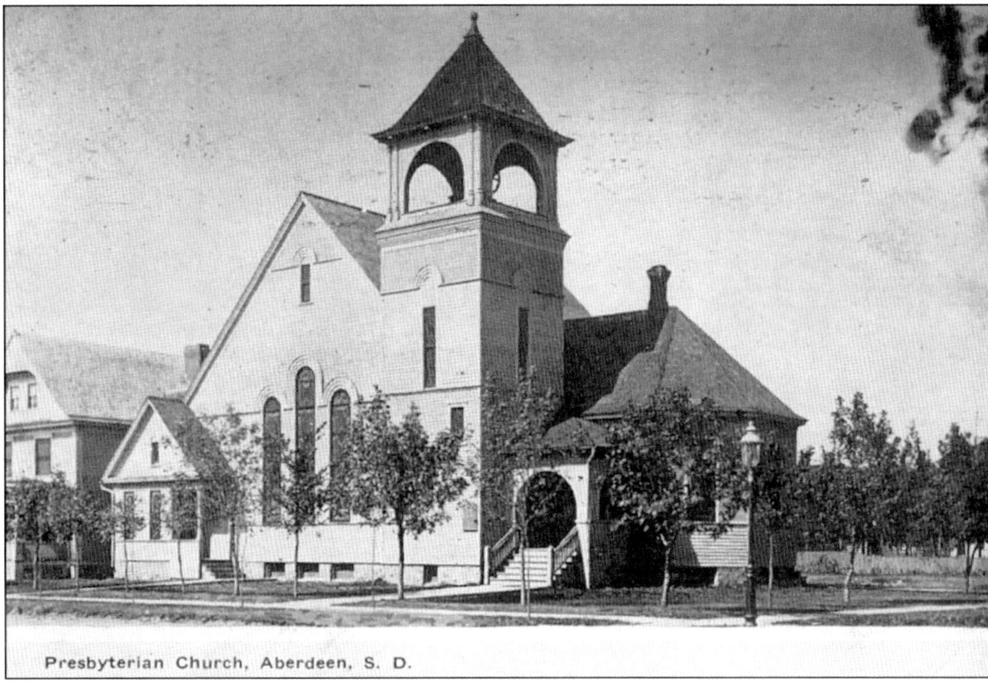

This is a *c.* 1908 postcard of the original Presbyterian Church located at the corner of Fourth Avenue and South Kline Street. An earlier city directory erroneously had this church listed on the north side of town. The Rev. Chas H. Bruce was the pastor in 1908. A new church was built in 1927 and is still in use.

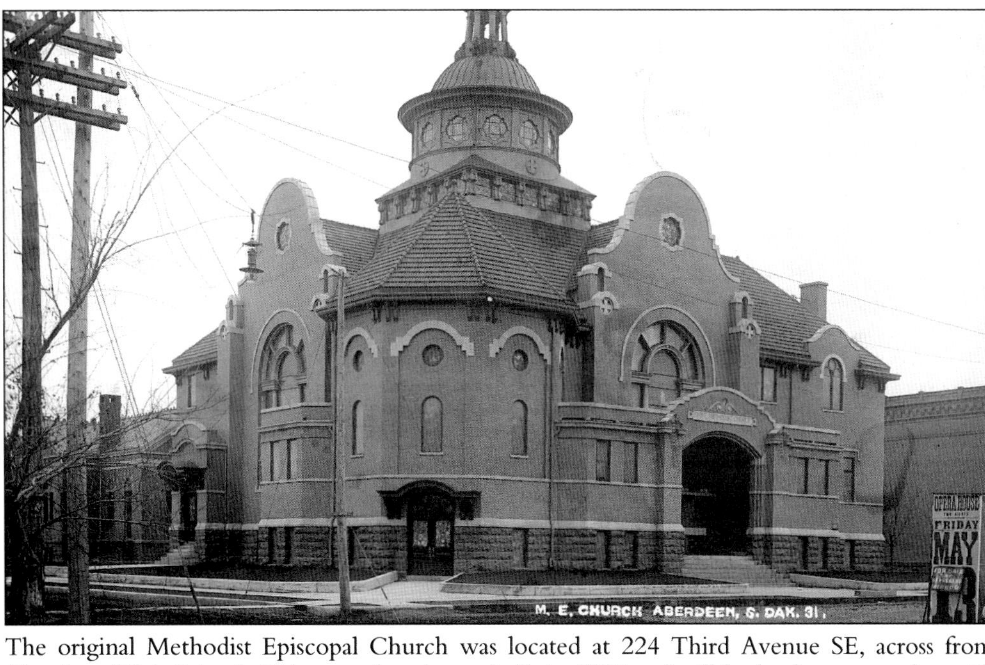

The original Methodist Episcopal Church was located at 224 Third Avenue SE, across from Aberdeen High School. This new church was built in 1908 and still looks the same today with several additions added. The Rev. J.W. Taylor was the pastor in 1908.

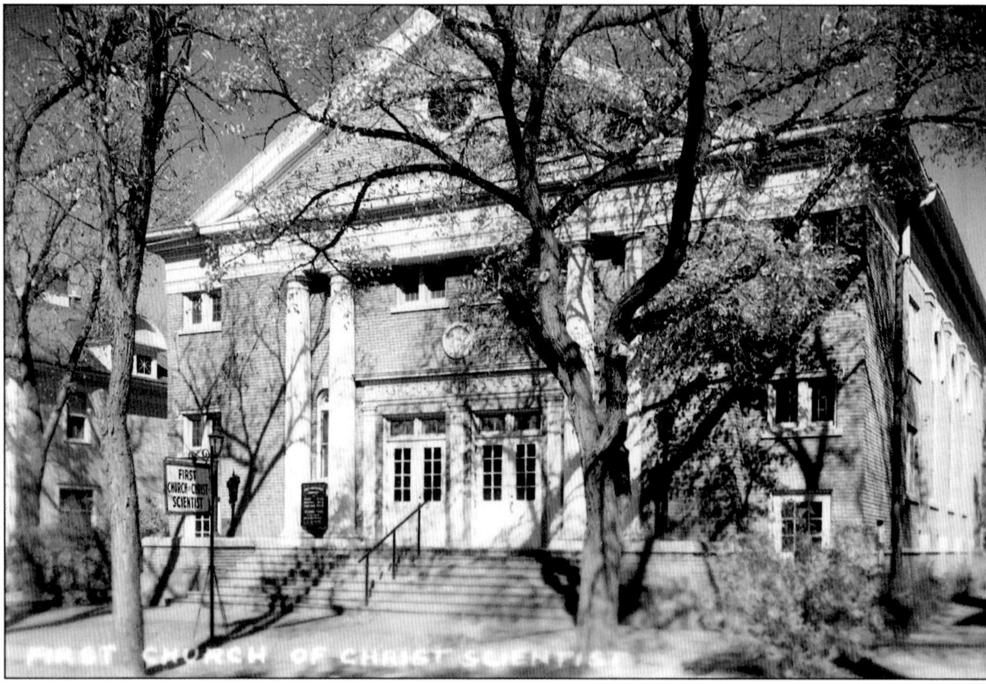

The First Church of Christ Scientist used to meet in the Elks Hall at 315 South Main before building its own church in 1928 at 305 Sixth Avenue SE. The Scientists no longer have a church in Aberdeen and this building's interior has been remodeled for law offices while maintaining the original exterior.

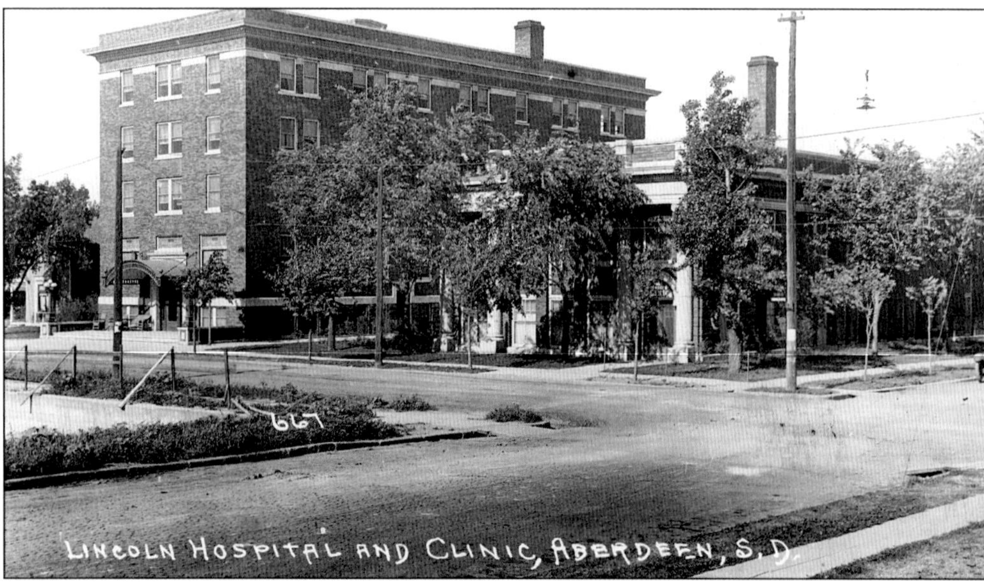

The Lincoln Hospital and Clinic opened in 1920 at 421 South Lincoln and was built by Dr. R.L. Murdy. The hospital was moved by horses in 1940 to where it sits today by St. Luke's Hospital. The clinic was used by several generations of Dr. Murdy's until the death of Dr. Carson Murdy. It is now an apartment complex owned by the young Carson Murdy.

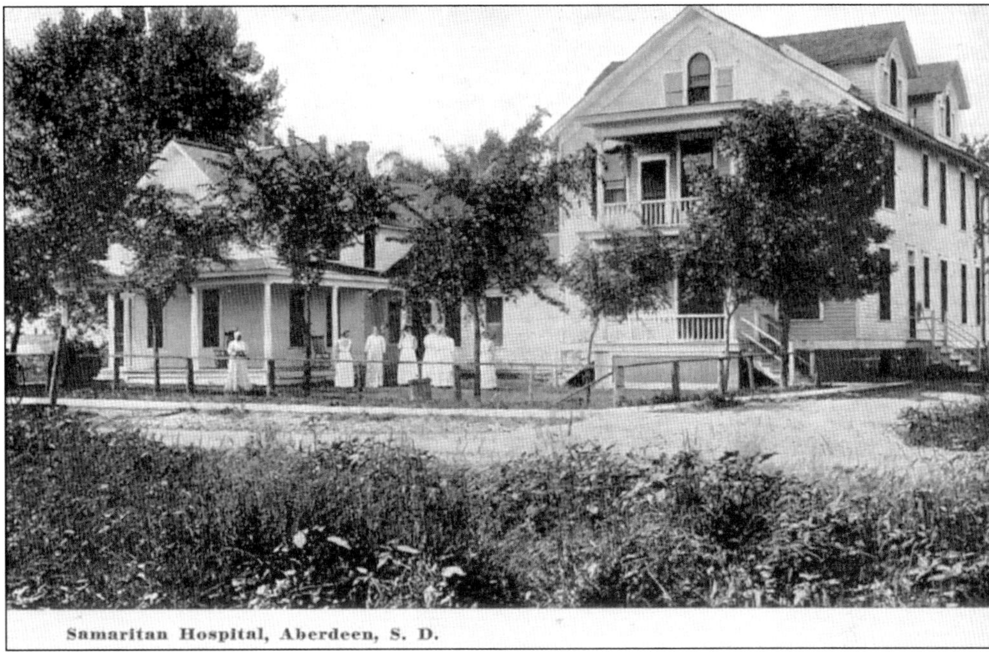

Here are two views of the Samaritan Hospital, which was also known as the German Baptist Hospital until the political correctness caused by World War I. It was located at 205 Eighth Avenue NE. Eighth Avenue used to be known as Spruce Avenue. In 1909, B.H. Rice was the superintendent. In the above picture, the nursing staff is standing in front of the hospital.

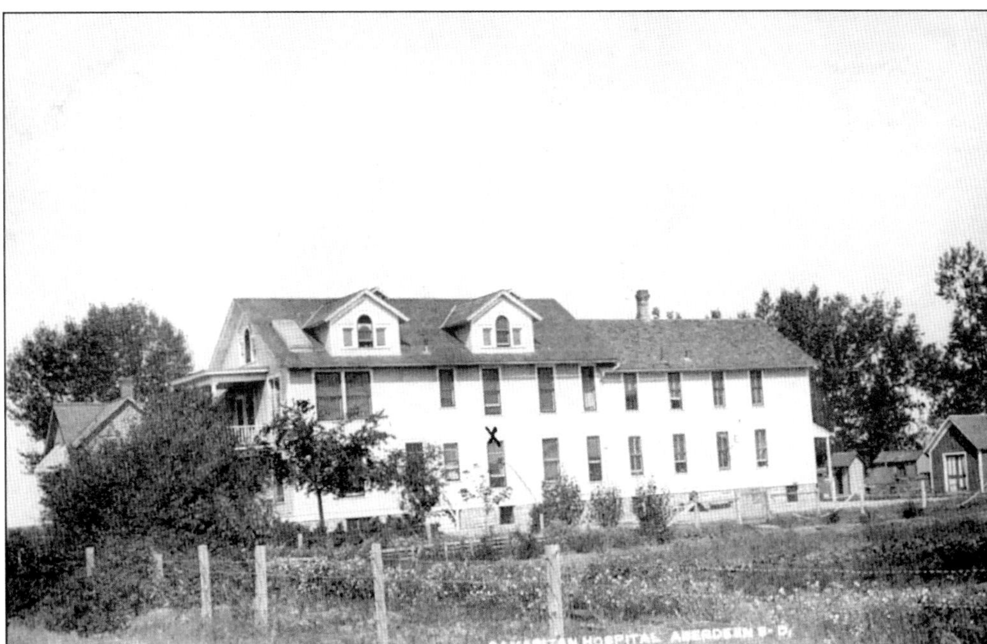

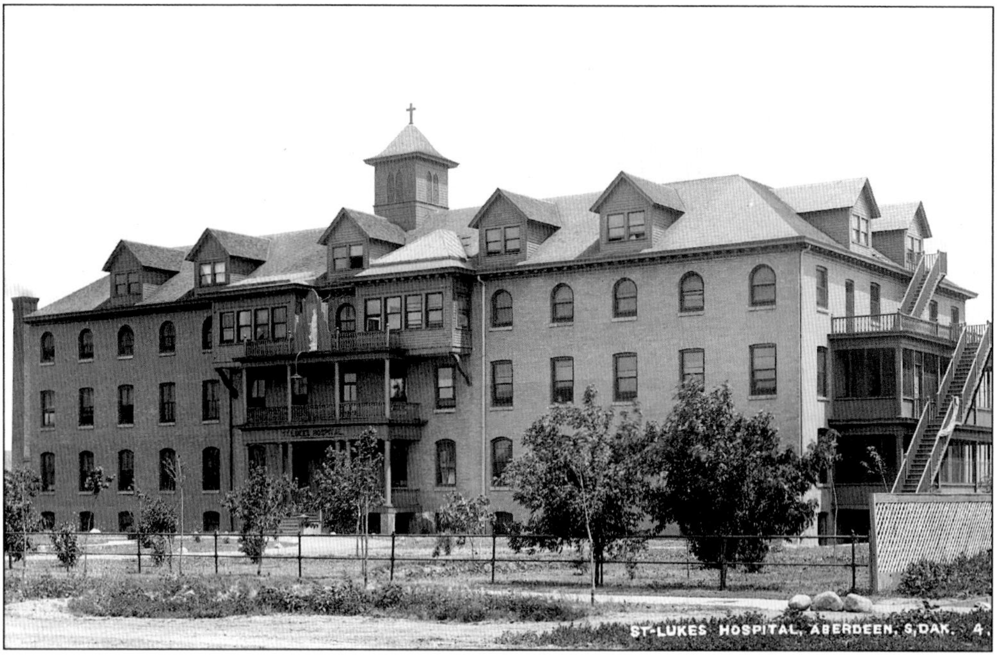

Mother Joseph Butler first organized St. Luke's Hospital in 1902 and the hospital is just celebrating its 100th anniversary. Originally located on the northeast corner of Fourth Avenue and South State Street, it now covers the whole block and then some.

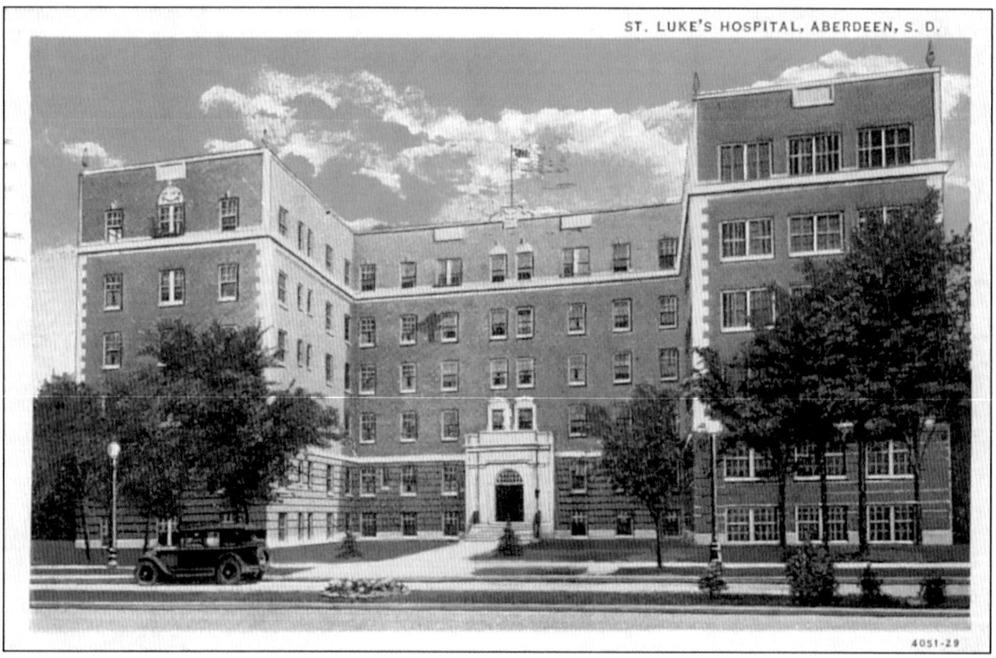

This is the new six-story St. Luke's Hospital built on the same site and just a little north of the original hospital. This structure still stands with many modifications and additions. It was in this hospital that Dr. James Berbos delivered the Fischer Quintuplets on September 14, 1963.

Four

Main Street and Views

For the first 110 years, Main Street in Aberdeen was the central business district for the town. In recent years, businesses have become more spread out, especially along Sixth Avenue, the mini-malls, and Lakewood Mall. Downtown still has banking, finance, law, and business offices, as well as all forms of government, and a nice selection of stores. Burt Frank's, the main clothing store, still occupies a prominent place on Main Street and is now being continued by his son Steve. Businesses on Main Street have come and gone, but each building still holds many memories. At one time there were at least seven businesses on Main Street that rolled cigars, or in other words, they were made in Aberdeen. Do you remember all the restaurants and all that food they served before all this fast food came along?

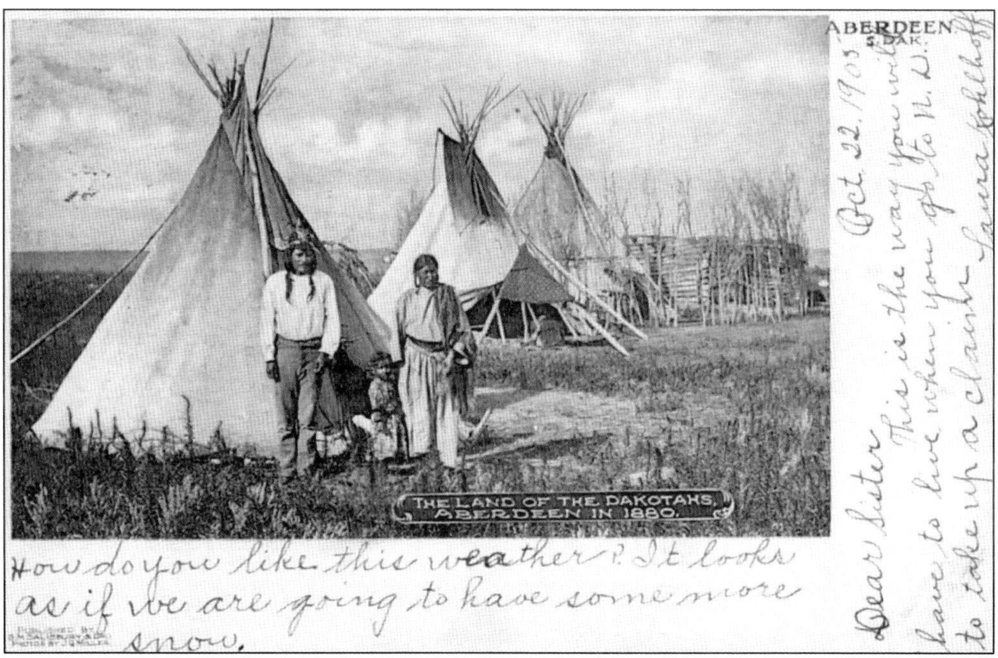

When the first settlers arrived in Brown County, Dakota Territory, there was a small band of Indians roaming in the area lead by Drifting Goose, a leader of the Hunkpati band of the Sioux, who was chief from the 1850s until his death in 1909. Naturally he resisted settlements, but without resorting to bloodshed, and came to be regarded as a friend of the whites and pretty much went wherever he wanted to go.

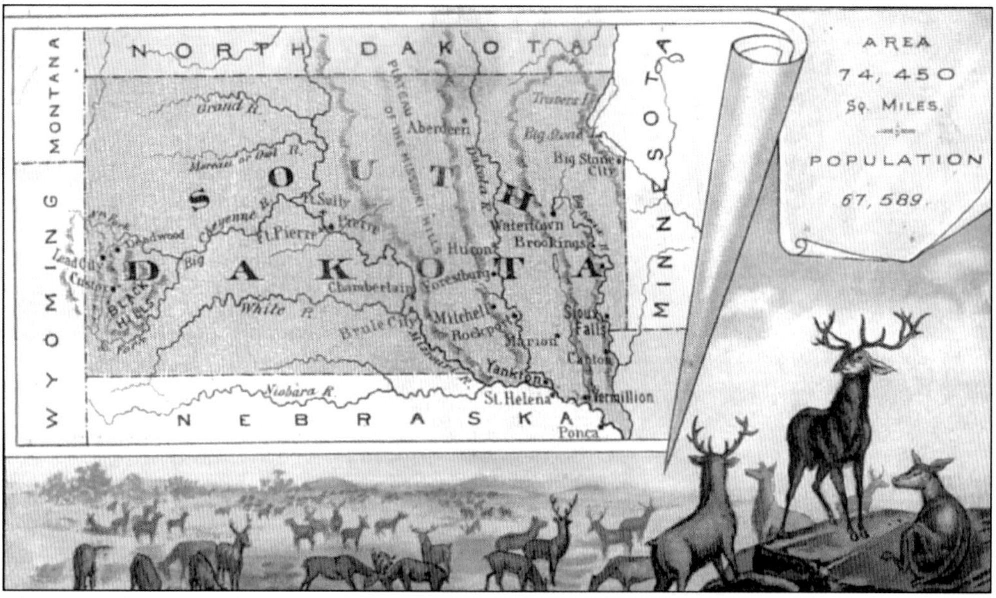

This map of South Dakota is from the State Series Collector cards from Arbuckle Bros. Coffee Co. of New York.

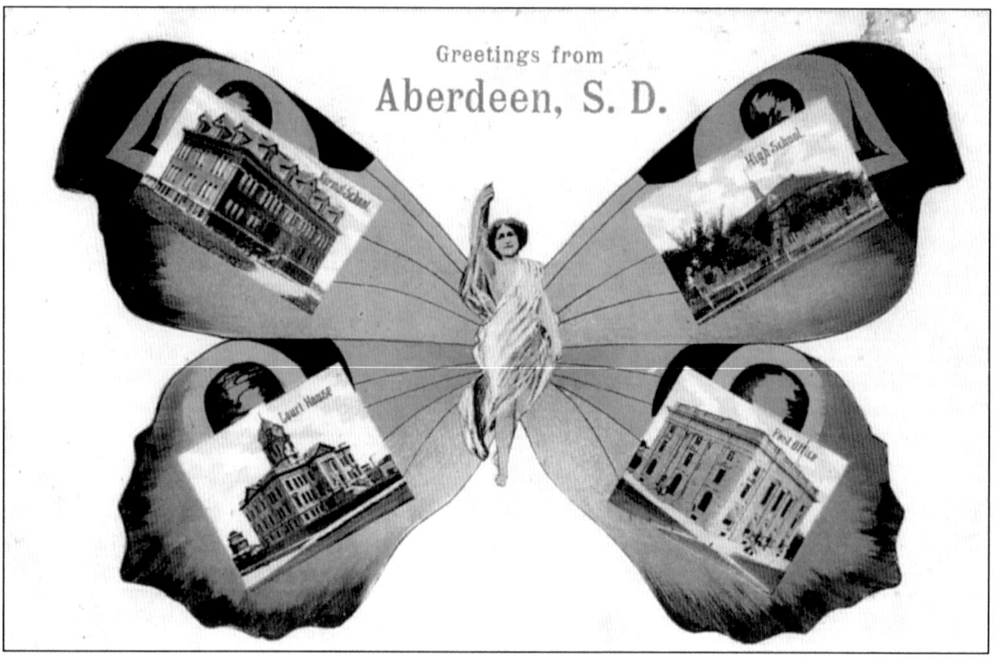

This is a colorful example of a multi-view postcard featuring Aberdeen's education and government buildings. Multi-views were used to highlight several images of a community.

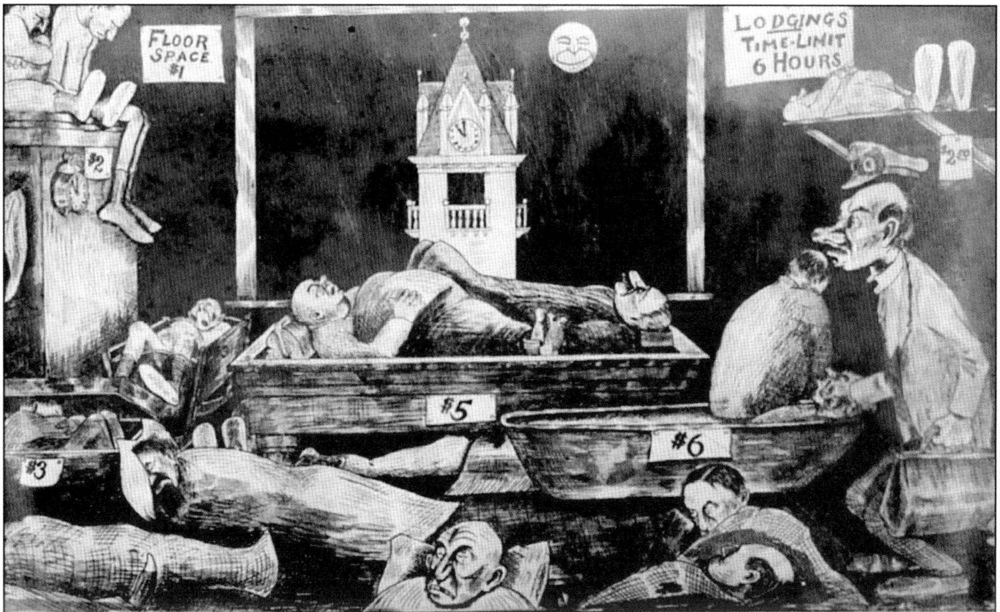

Land Opening, Aberdeen, S. D., Oct. 1909

This is a comic real-photo postcard of an event that never took place in Aberdeen. In 1909, many land openings did take place in western and southwestern South Dakota, but all the land in Brown County had been claimed by 1887. In 1909, representatives from Western Canada came to Aberdeen to entice people to homestead in Western Canada, just like Aberdeen did in 1881 to get people to move here.

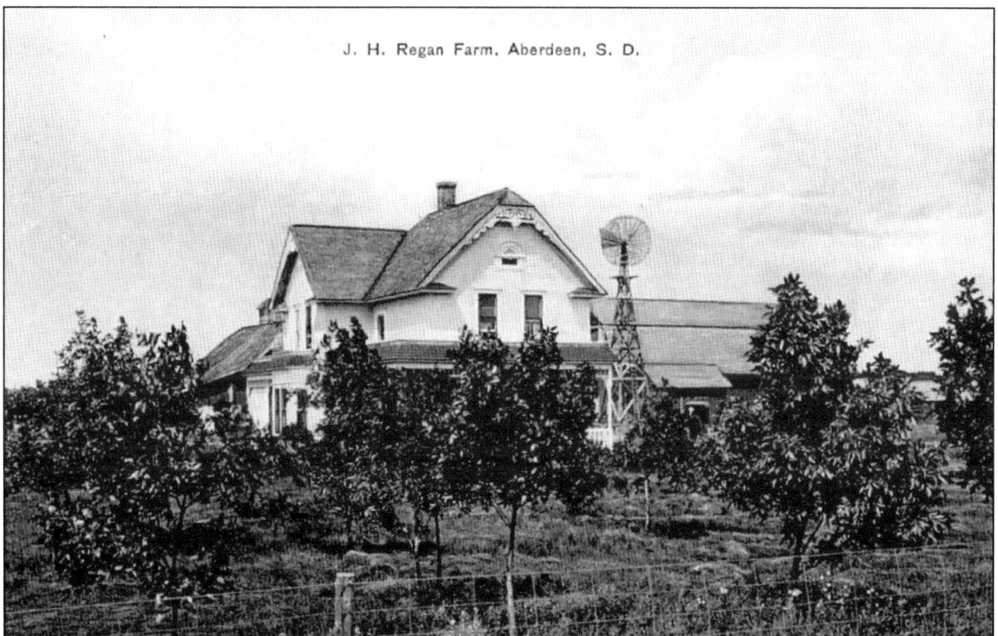

Jas. H. Regan had one of the largest farms in the area. It was located near Bath, South Dakota. He later moved into Aberdeen while continuing to farm.

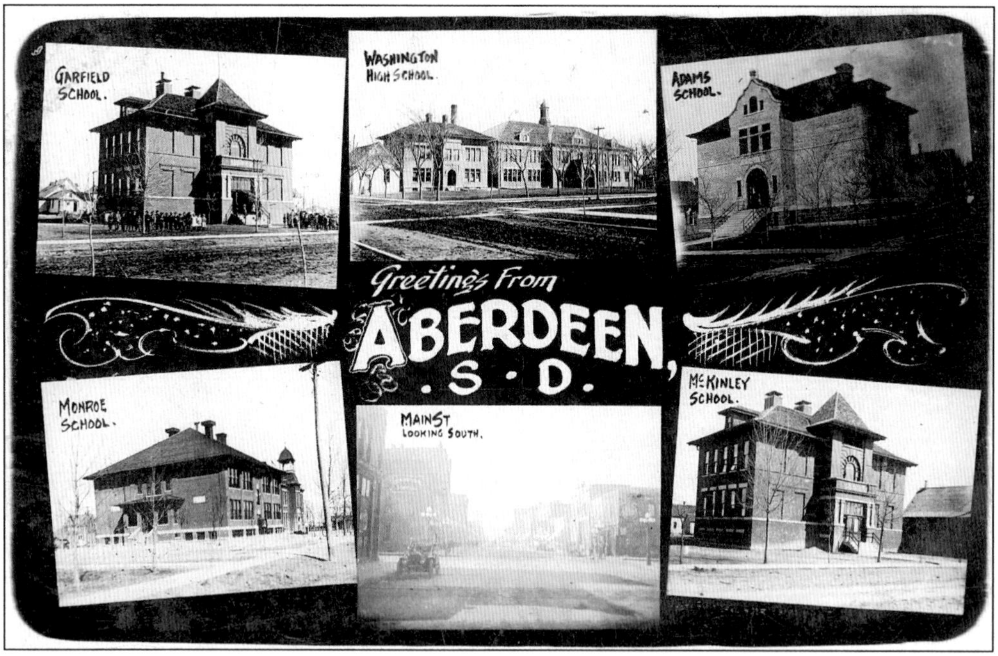

This multi-view of Aberdeen schools is a composite view of images of Main Street looking south. It features Washington High School, and Adams, Garfield, McKinley, and Monroe Schools.

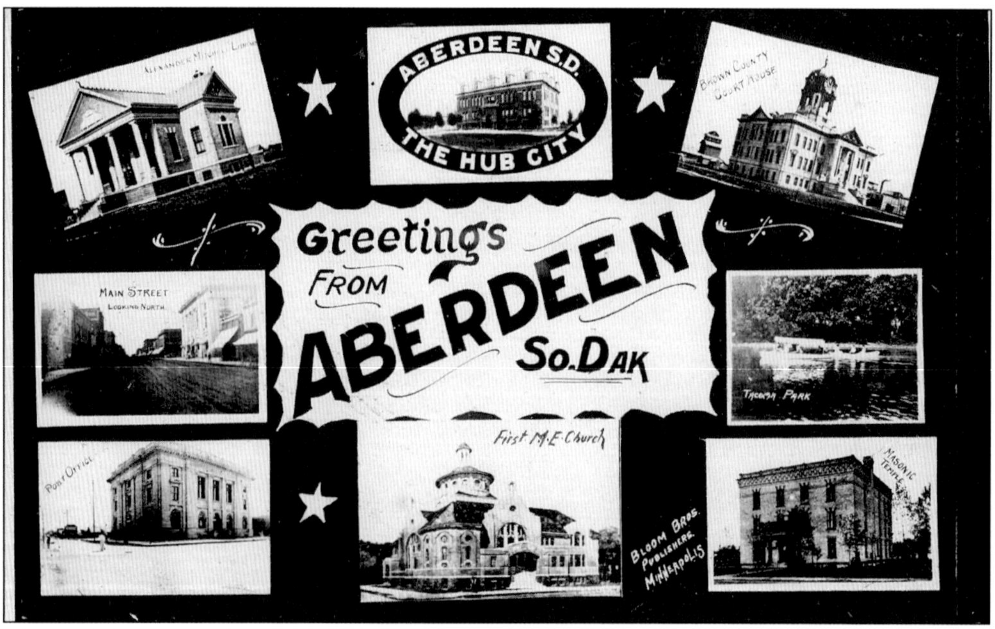

This card features eight great views of Aberdeen landmarks, including the post office, Brown County Courthouse, Northern Normal and Industrial School, Alexander Mitchell Library, Masonic Temple, First Methodist Church, Main Street, and the Tacoma Park recreation area.

This is the third logo for Aberdeen. The first was "Hub City of Dakota," whish was used in territorial times; the second was "Aberdeen, the Hub City," which was also a complete circle; and now the one-quarter circle, "Aberdeen, Hub City of the Dakotas." Aberdeen was also one of the towns claiming to be the Pheasant Hunting Center of America. Both Redfield and Winner claim this distinction. The first pheasants released in South Dakota were actually near Redfield.

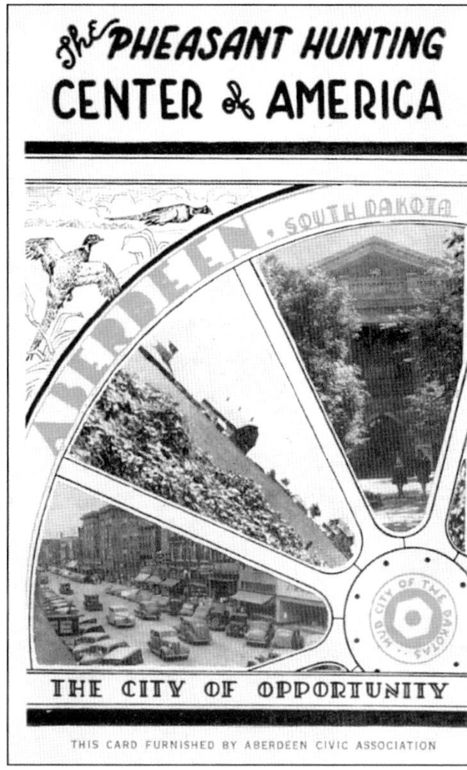

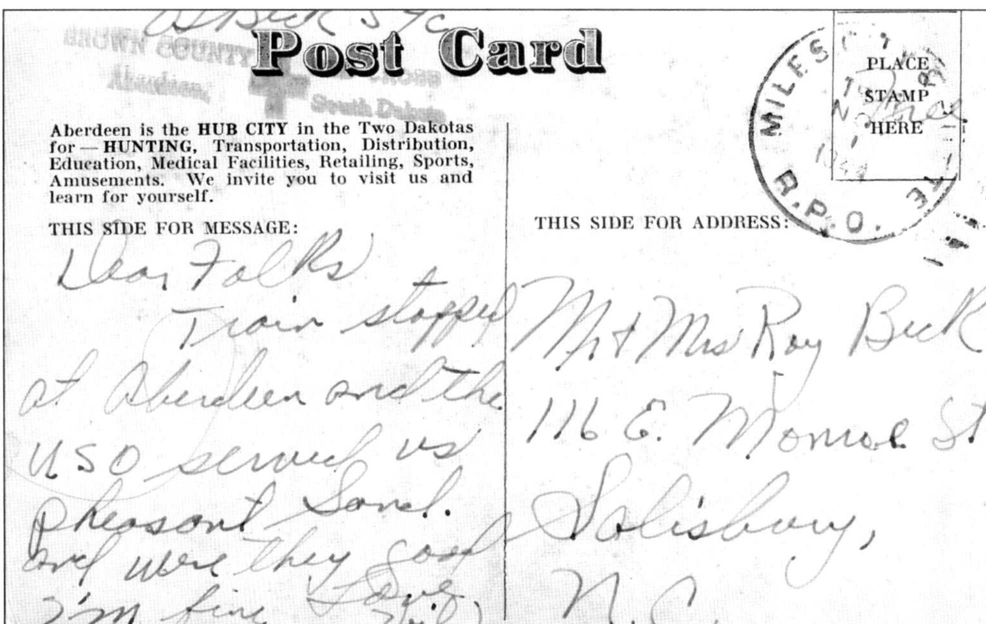

This is the message side of the above postcard. In World War II, servicemen could send their mail for free. A lot of troop trains came through Aberdeen, and when they stopped, the women of Aberdeen prepared and served "pheasant sandwiches" to the troops. They were so popular that many servicemen returned to the area in the years following the war to go pheasant hunting.

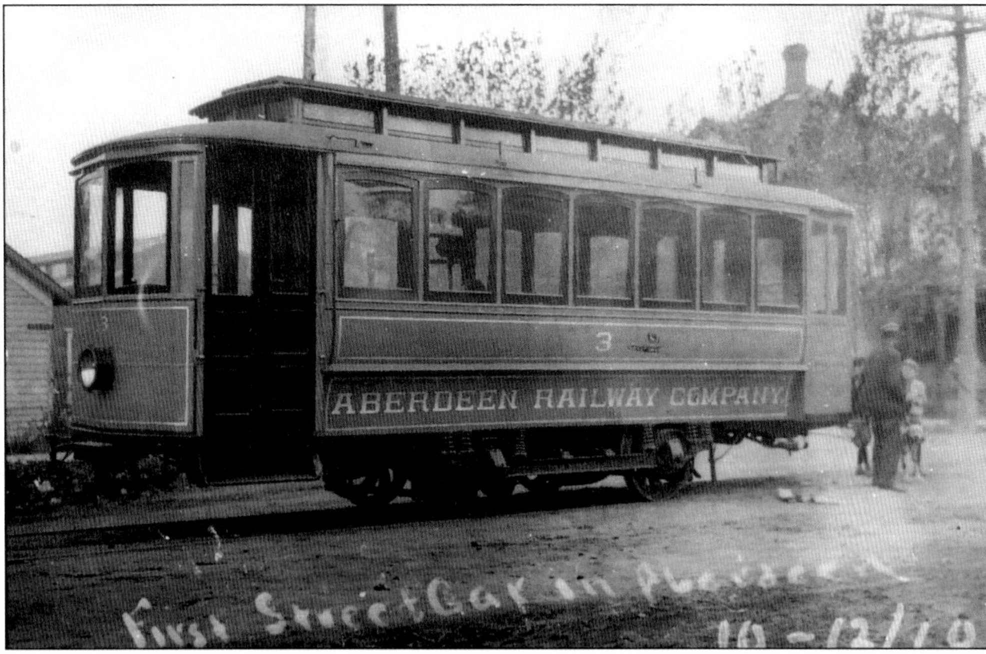

Real photo of the first streetcar in Aberdeen. These cars were very elegant with aisles carpeted in red. A typical car could carry 30-40 passengers with additional riders standing and holding on to hand straps. These hand straps carried advertising from local businesses.

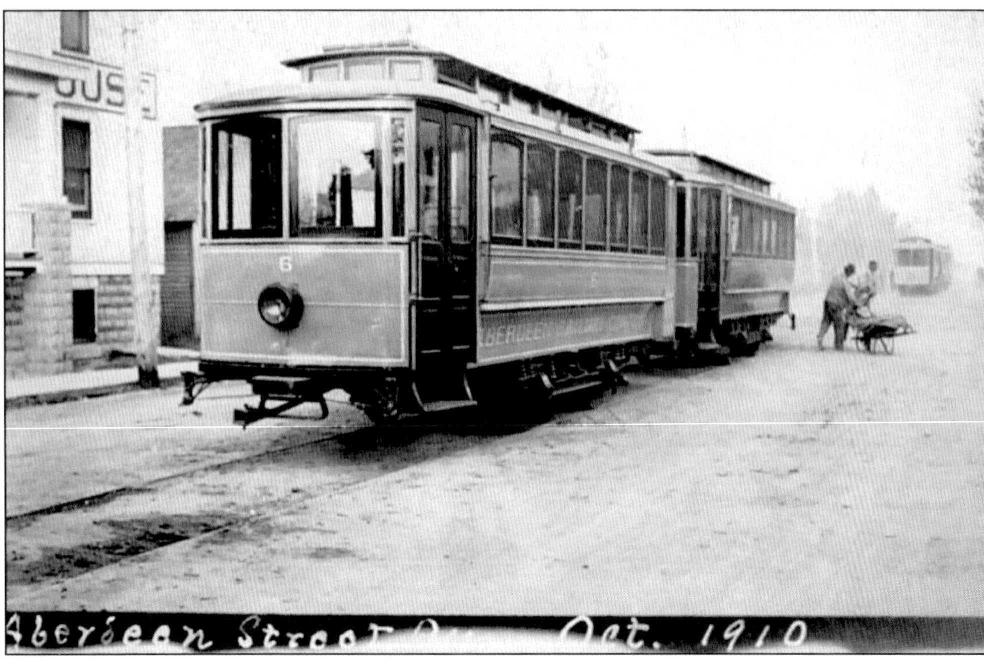

Aberdeen's first streetcars were yellow and the trolley's number was painted on each end of the car. Windows allowed passengers a panoramic view of the route as well as ventilation on a hot day. Entry doors were located on each end of the cars. The early cars had bench type seats running lengthwise, but later models had two seats on either side of an aisle running the length of the car.

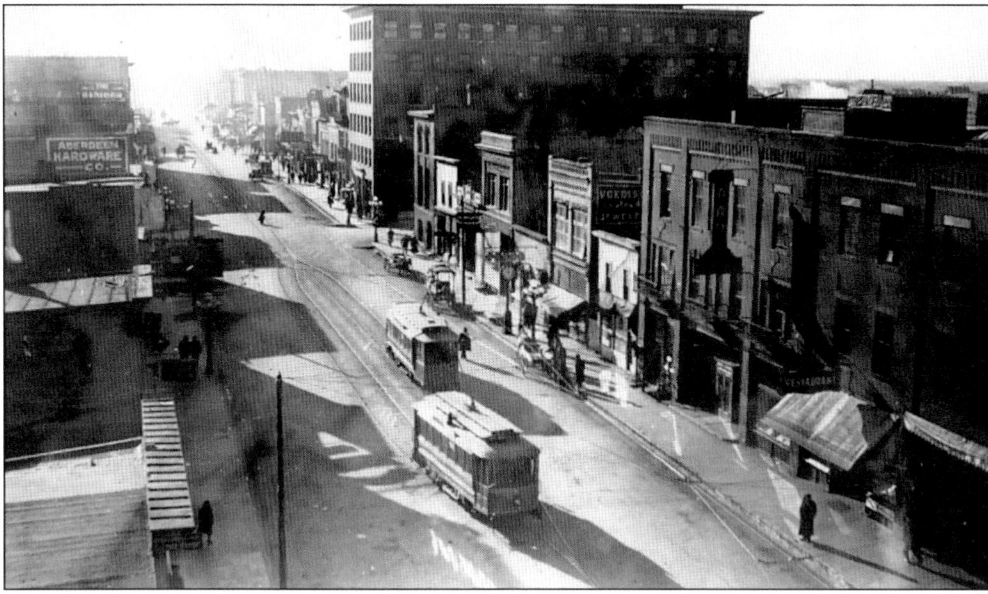

Looking south from the Western Union Building, this is a good shot of the double tracks located on the 100 block of South Main that allowed the streetcars to pass each other. These streetcars were double-ended, meaning they had steering mechanisms and controls on both ends, which eliminated the need to turn around at the end of the route. The driver merely walked to the other end of the car and used the other set of controls to retrace his route.

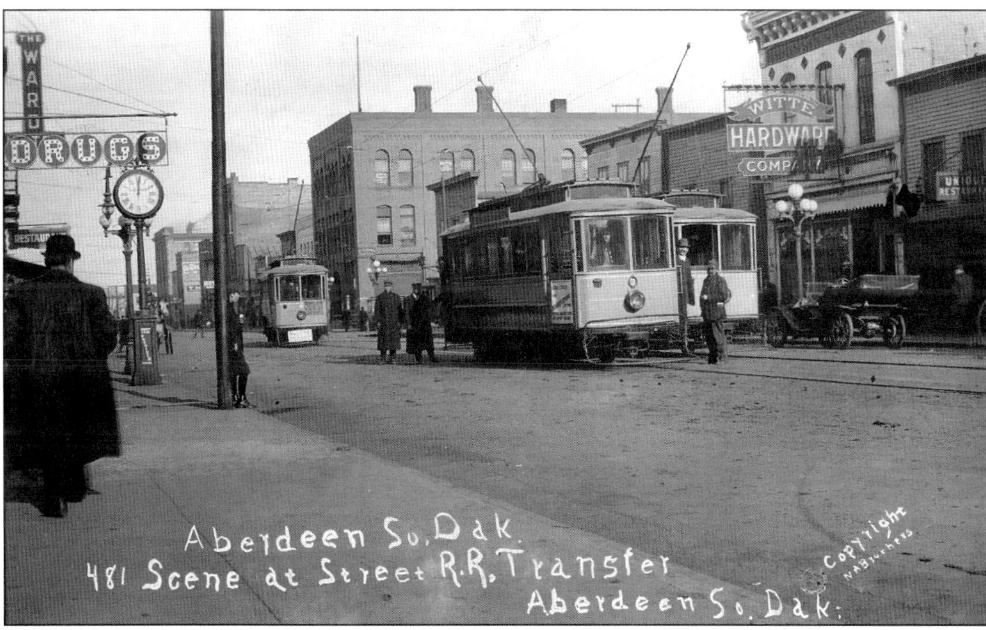

Aberdeen Street Railway cars like these traveled Aberdeen's streets for 12 years. Being on time was vital to the success of the operation, and motormen had to work very hard to maintain their strict schedules. This clock outside Voedisch Jewelry Store served as the official clock for the streetcar schedule. Motormen had to arrive at their stops by a certain time, and if they arrived early, could not depart until the scheduled departure time.

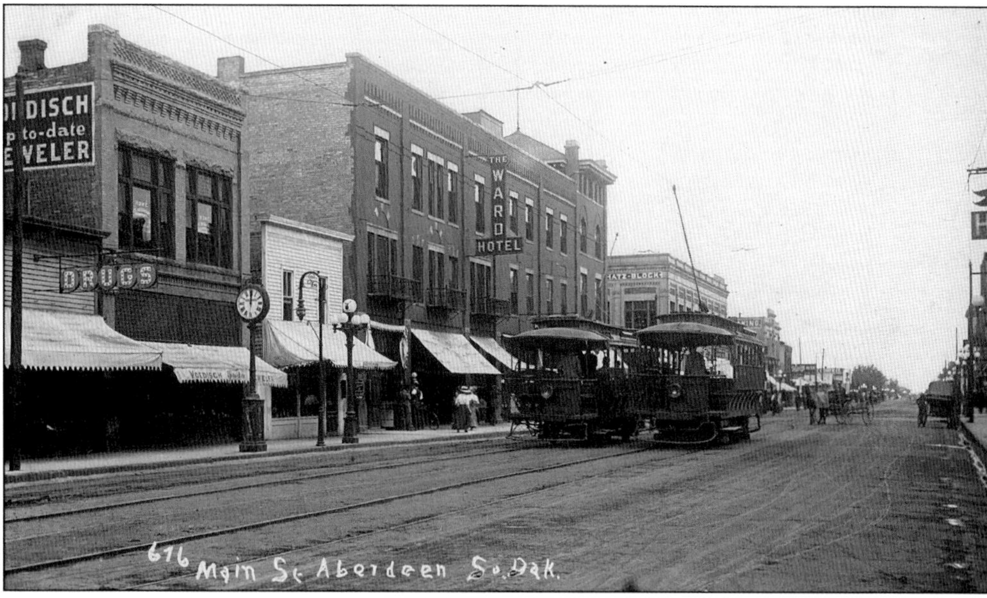

Between 1910 and 1922, Aberdeen citizens could ride trolley cars like these that were part of the Aberdeen Street Railway system. The route included stops at Wylie Park and Northern Normal on opposite ends of town. For one block on Main Street there were two sets of tracks that allowed cars to pass each other as they traveled in opposite directions. The last of the tracks were finally removed in 1965 at the corner of Sixth Avenue and Lincoln Street.

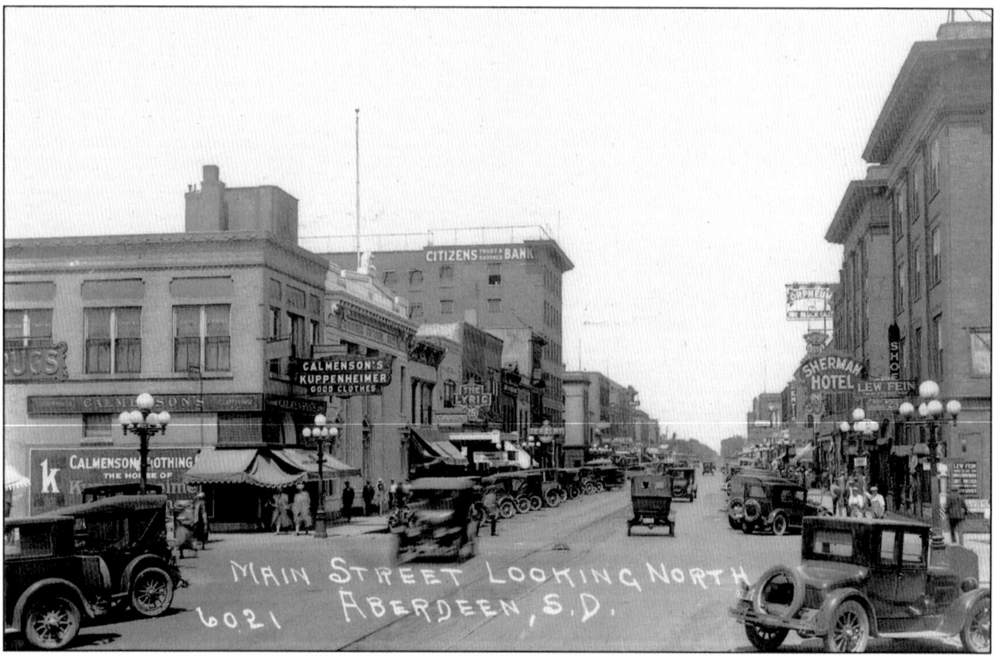

This real photo taken in the early 1920s shows one of the reasons that the Aberdeen Street Railway went out of business—the automobile. Running a streetcar business was very expensive with high labor and maintenance costs, which in the poor economic times of the early 1920s proved to be too much for the company to survive.

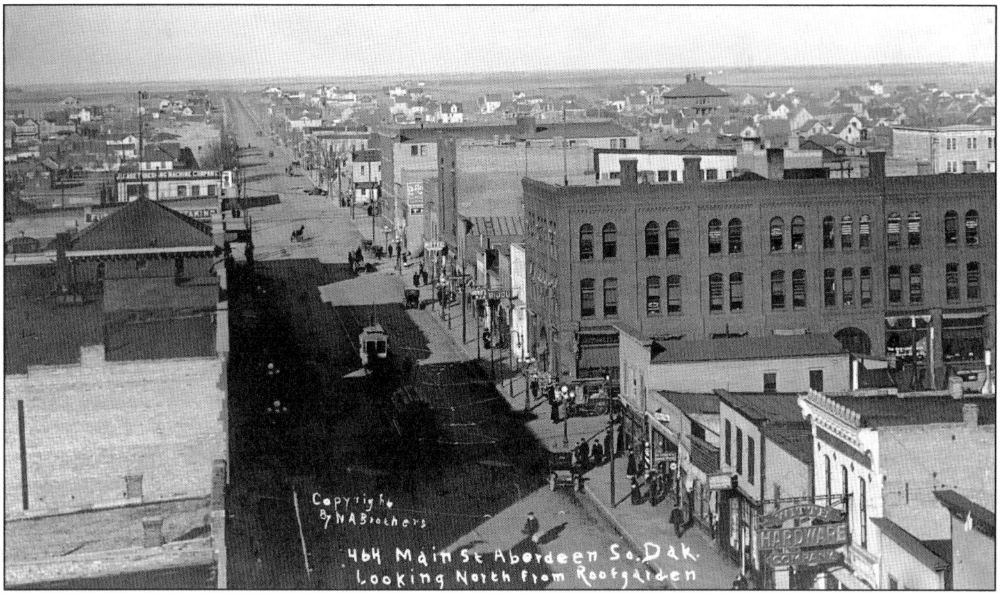

Here Main Street looks north from the Roof Garden. The trolleys of the Aberdeen Street Railway System made their debut on Thanksgiving Day 1910, and ran through July 21, 1922, when service was discontinued. The streetcars ran in each direction every 15 minutes between 6:00 a.m. and 1:00 a.m. The car barn was located near the present day site of Presentation College.

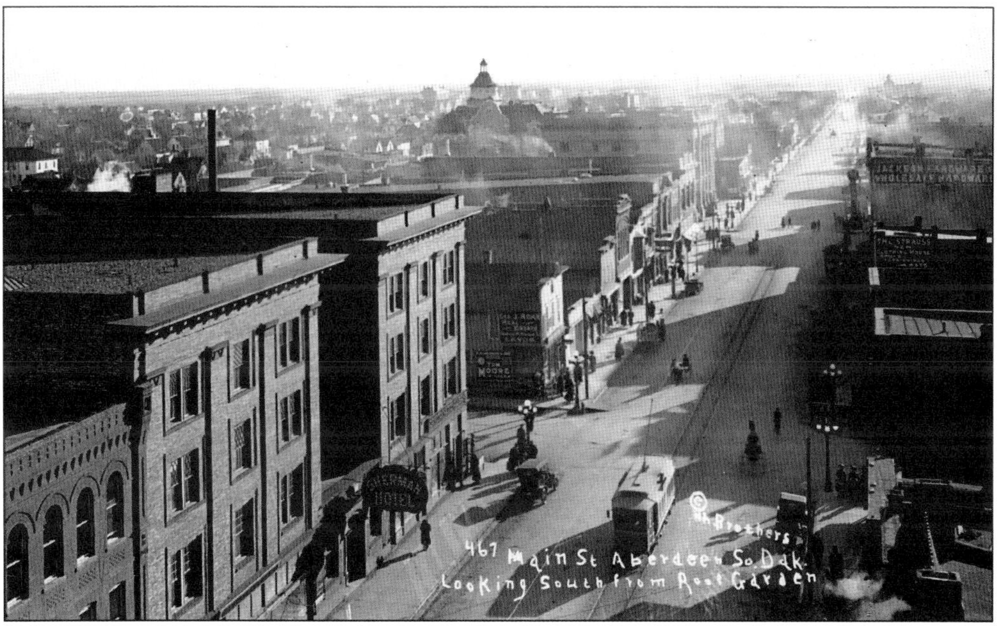

This view of Main Street looks south from the Roof Garden. The Sherman Hotel is the predominant building in the foreground and was located on the corner of Main Street and Third Avenue. By 1913 when this postcard was post marked, Aberdeen had grown south for many blocks. In the far background on the right is a grain elevator located on the corner of South Main Street and Twelfth Avenue.

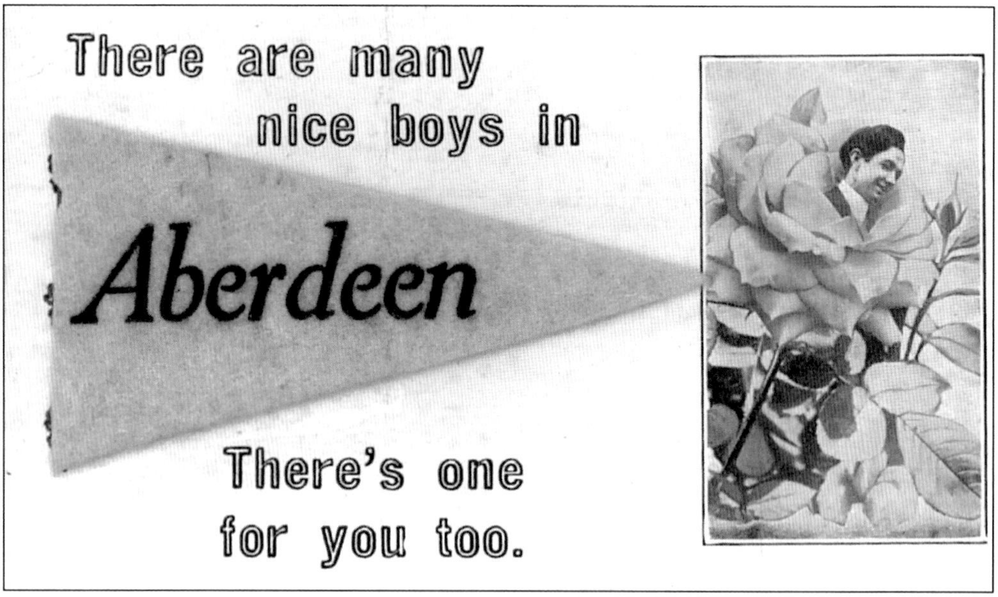

This example of a humorous greeting card features a manipulated image and a felt pendant with Aberdeen printed on it. This message still rings true today.

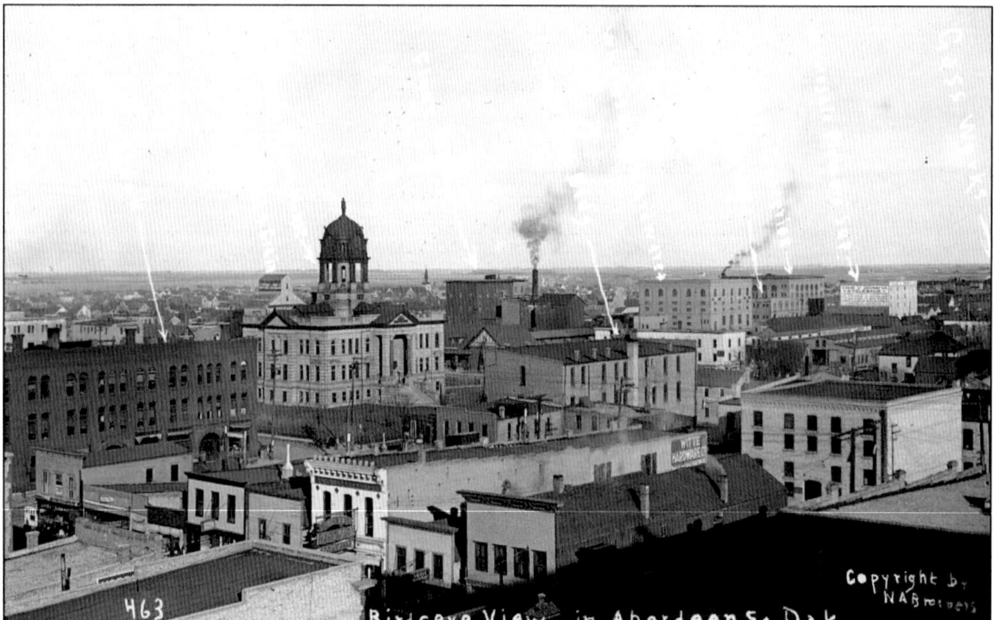

A birds-eye view shows the wholesale district that developed along the tracks of the Milwaukee Railroad. Businesses that were built adjacent to the tracks shown in this view include the Aberdeen Roller Mill, which produced flour under the name Snow White. The mill could produce 200 barrels of flour a day. Also pictured is Jewett Bros. Wholesale Grocery, home of "Indian Girl" brand food products sold throughout the Dakotas and Montana. The Jewetts eventually expanded their business to include wholesale drugs and phased out their grocery line in the 1940s with the advent of grocery store chains.

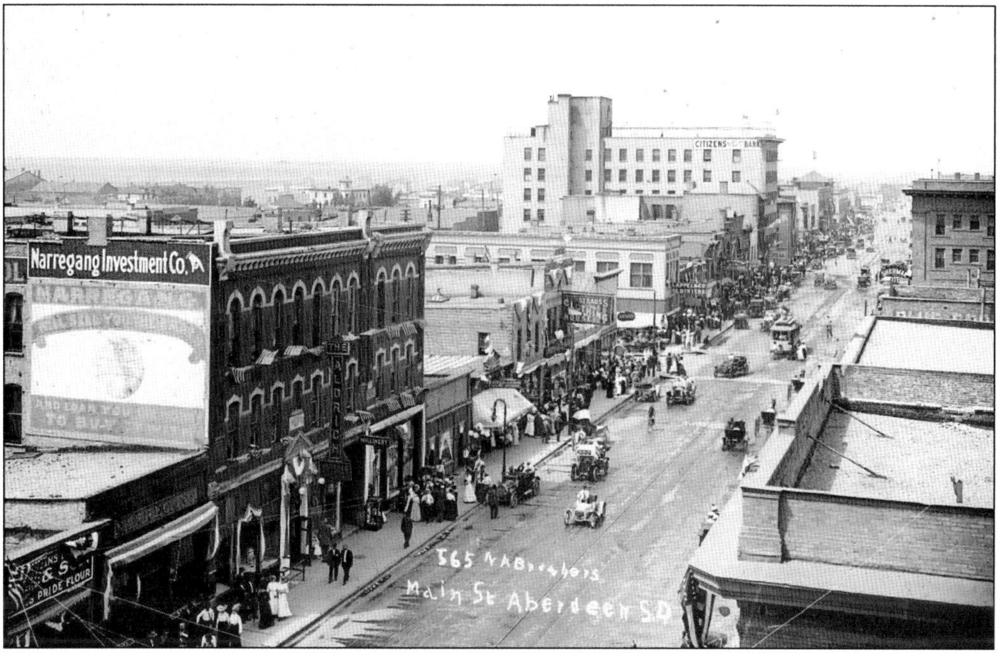

This shot was taken *c.* 1912. Aberdeen buildings are growing upward since prime real estate on Main Street was completely sold out by 1912. The Narregang Investment Co. Building was previously Aberdeen's skyscraper, being three stories tall, but it is now overshadowed by the new Citizens Bank Building's six-story height.

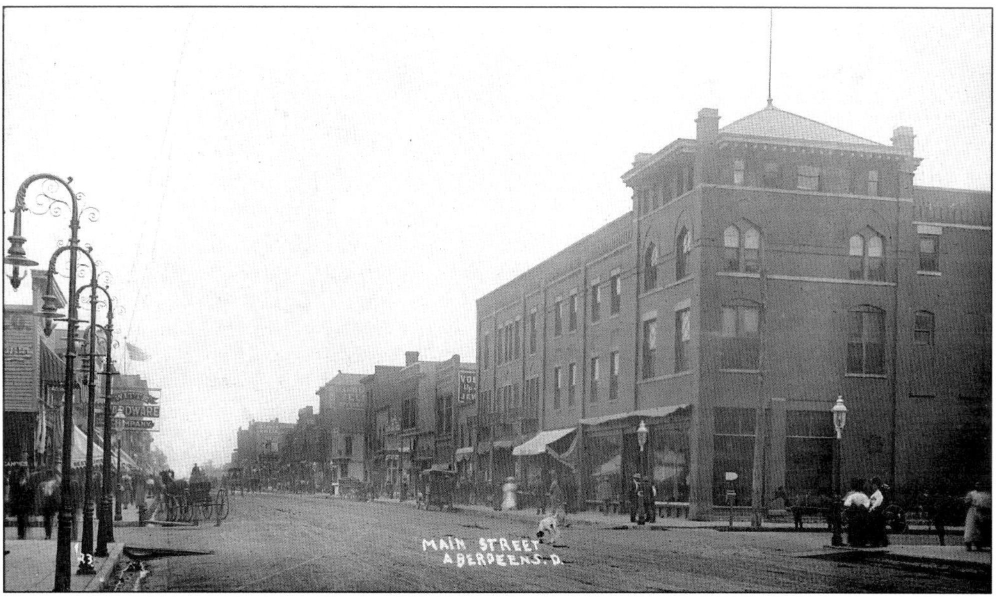

This real photo shows the Ward Hotel in 1910, but what should be noticed are the gas street lamps on the right. Aberdeen's first street lamps were gas-powered and many were in use as late as 1918. In 1914, the Aberdeen Gas Co. was authorized to install 158 streetlights and the company was also to light them at dusk and extinguish them at daylight. Aberdeen had lamplighters whose sole job was to light and extinguish the city's gas lamps.

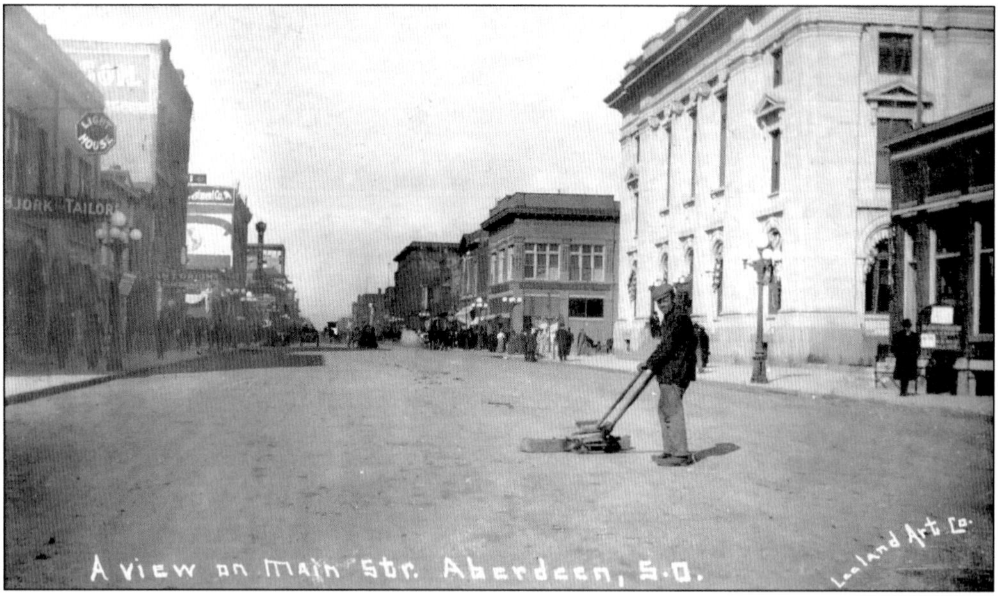

This shot was taken on the 400 block of South Main Street. In 1907, Aberdeen had its first hard-surfaced street when five blocks on Main Street from the Milwaukee tracks to Fifth Avenue were paved with creosote soaked wood blocks, which were installed over a bed of sand and concrete. After the blocks were placed, the street was tarred and covered with more sand. This worker is preparing this section of the street for such paving. These creosote blocks served the city for nearly 30 years.

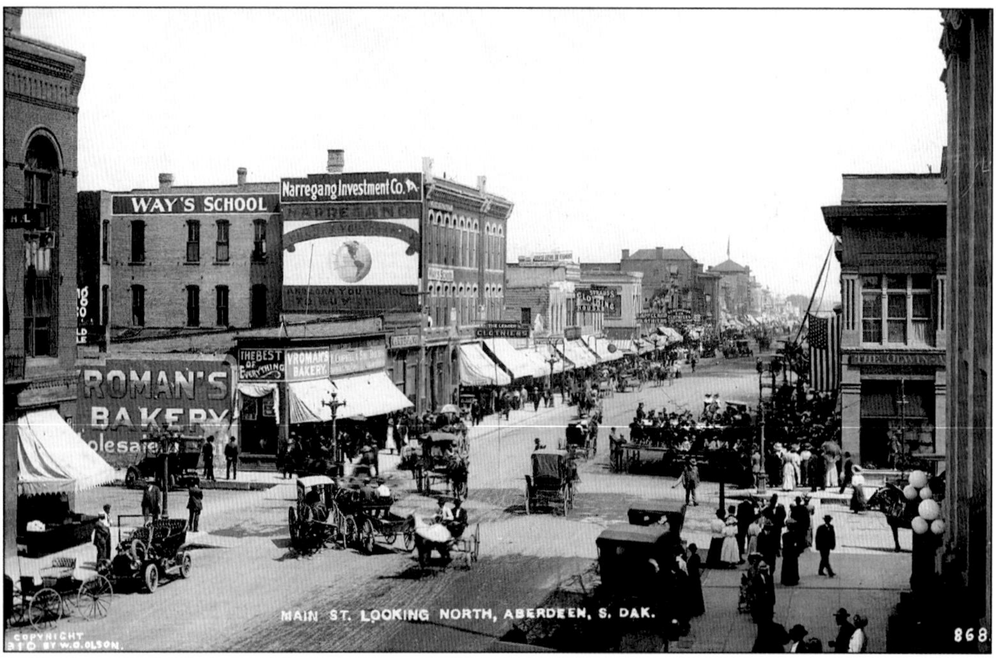

Aberdeen Main Street in 1910, is pictured here showing the intersection of South Fourth Avenue. Way's School, shown on the left, was opened in 1889 by Henry Way and offered double-entry bookkeeping, shorthand, and penmanship in both day and evening classes. Way's School closed in 1910.

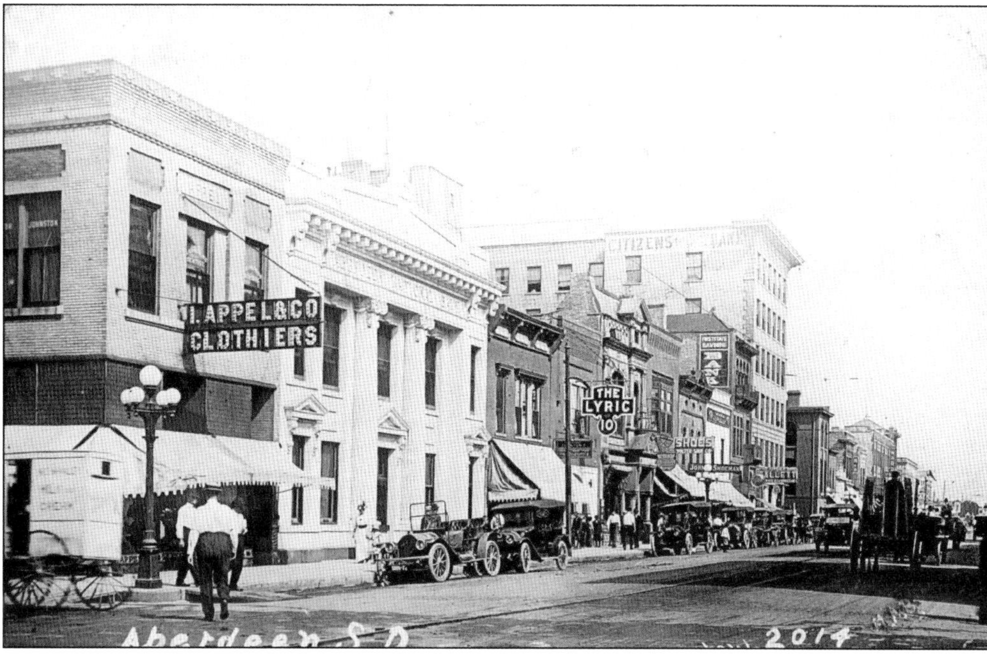

This view of the 200 block of South Main Street shows three of Aberdeen's banks in 1914. Visible are the Aberdeen National Bank built in 1912, the First State Savings Bank built in 1891, and the Citizens Bank built in 1910. This was a "banking neighborhood." The First National Bank was across the street from the Citizens Bank.

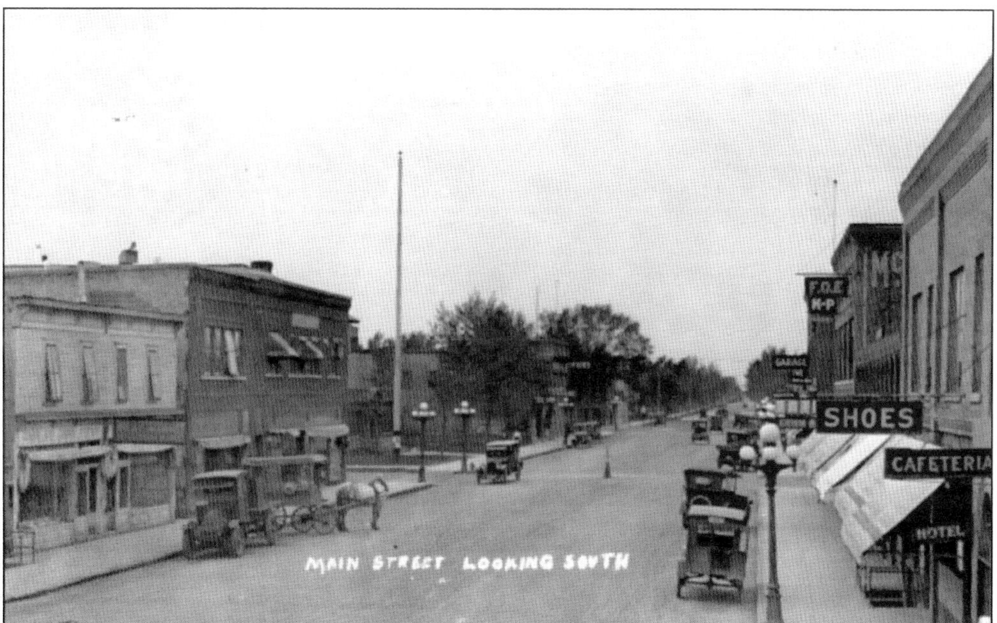

This is the 400 block of South Main Street as it looked in 1920. Visible are The Cafeteria, which was the ground floor business in the Beard Hotel, and Miller's Shoe Co. on the west side. The flagpole on the east side of the street is located in the front yard of the Masonic Temple.

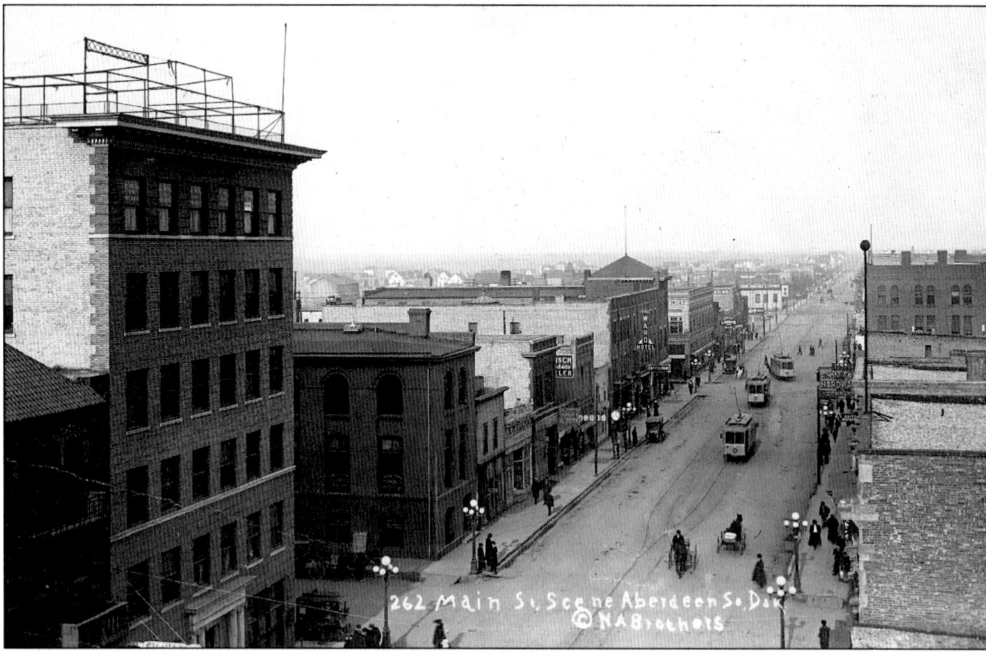

The predominant building on the left is the Citizens Bank Building. Developers hoped to provide Aberdeen with the finest professional office building in the state, and it can be assumed they did just that. The upper floors were filled with medical, dental, legal, and insurance offices. Aberdeen's first woman dentist, Dr. Leona Dix, had her office on the second floor. The IRS also had offices here.

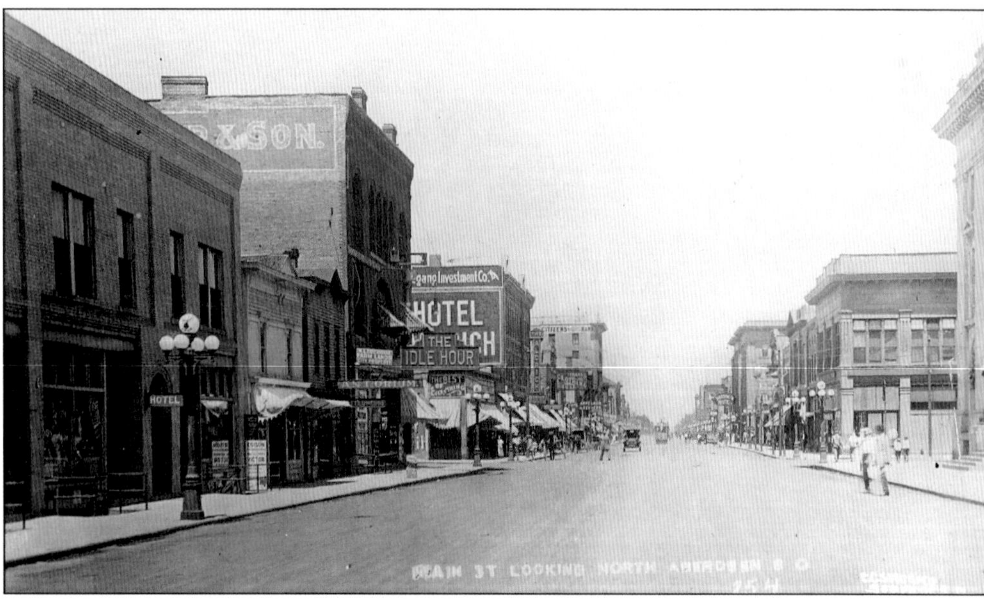

The building in the center on the left is the Jewett Block, built in 1887 on the corner of South Fourth Avenue and Main Street to house the ever-growing wholesale grocery business owned by Harvey Jewett. The Idle Hour Movie Theater next door to the Jewett Block opened on April 1, 1908, to become Aberdeen's second movie theater.

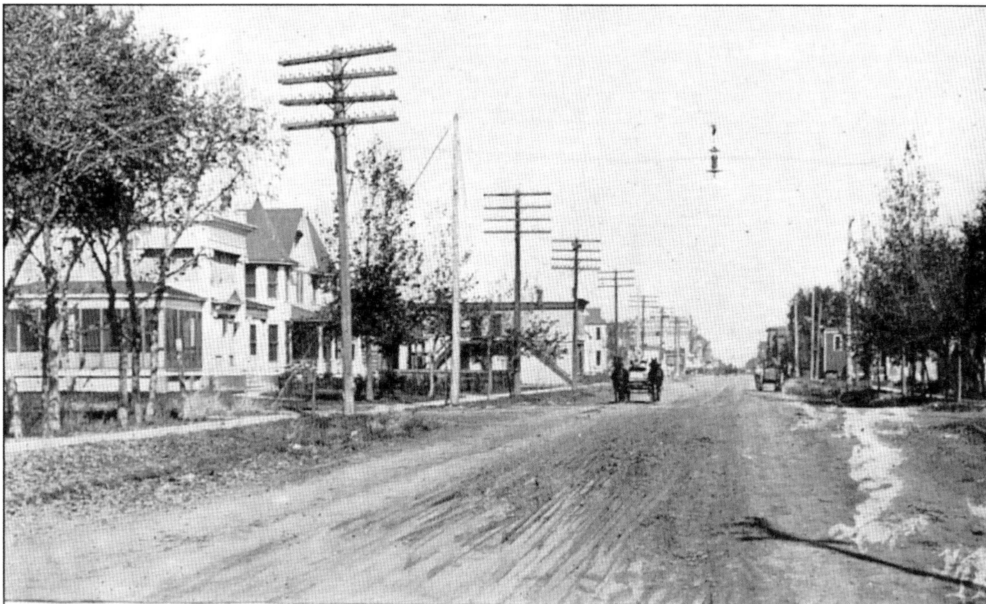

Main Street from M. & St. L. Depot, Aberdeen, S. D.

This view shows the impressive homes on the west side of South Main Street and Eighth Avenue. The first home was built in 1901 for First National Bank President Frank Gannon. The home next door was built for Joseph Suttle, who was the cashier at the First National Bank. Both homes are still standing.

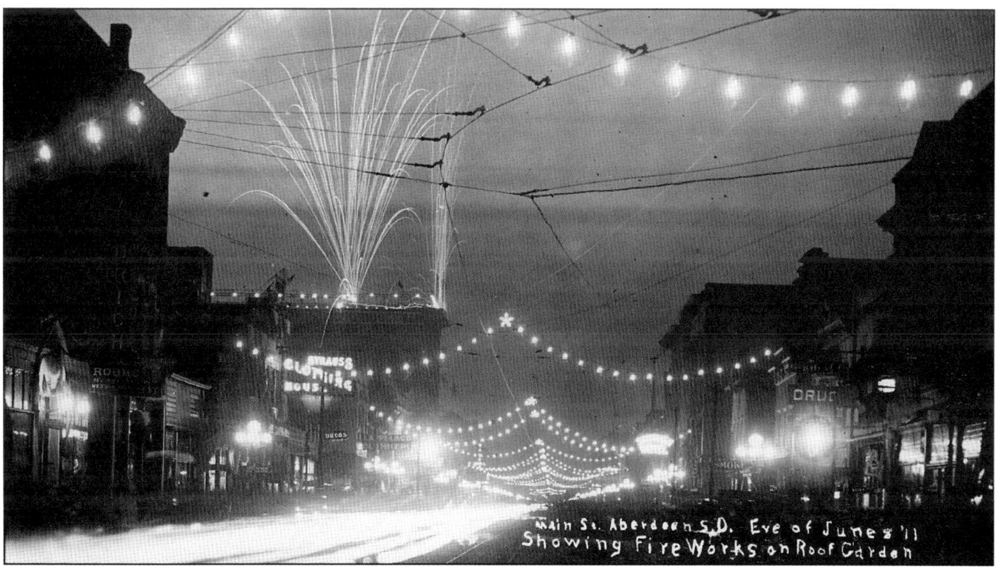

Main Street on the eve of June 8, 1911, was elaborately decorated for the state Elks Convention of June 8-9, 1911. Fireworks were part of the pre-convention festivities and were launched from Aberdeen's new Roof Garden, a gathering place atop the six-story Citizens Bank Building, built in 1910. The Roof Garden featured a dance floor, a stage, and soda fountain in an open-air environment decorated with 150 live rose bushes, 110 natural palms, and 100 ferns, climbing honeysuckles, and grape vines. South Dakota prairie winds caused this rooftop spot to be short-lived.

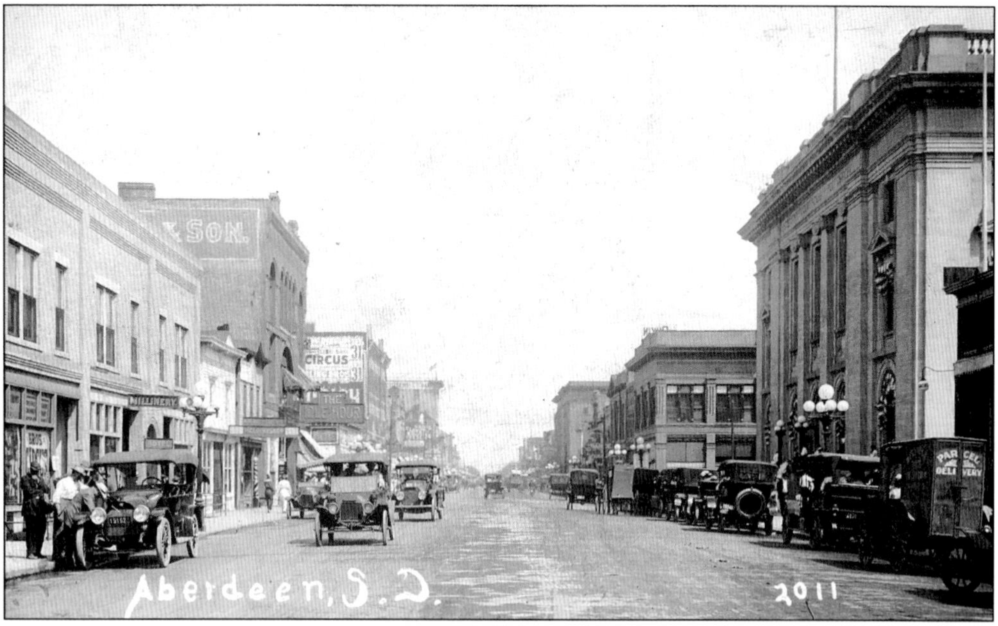

By 1916 when this photo was taken, automobiles had become the popular mode of travel in Aberdeen. George Spaulding opened Aberdeen's first Ford dealership in 1909 and Wallace Parry opened a Dodge dealership in 1914. By 1916 Aberdeen even reported TWO women drivers!

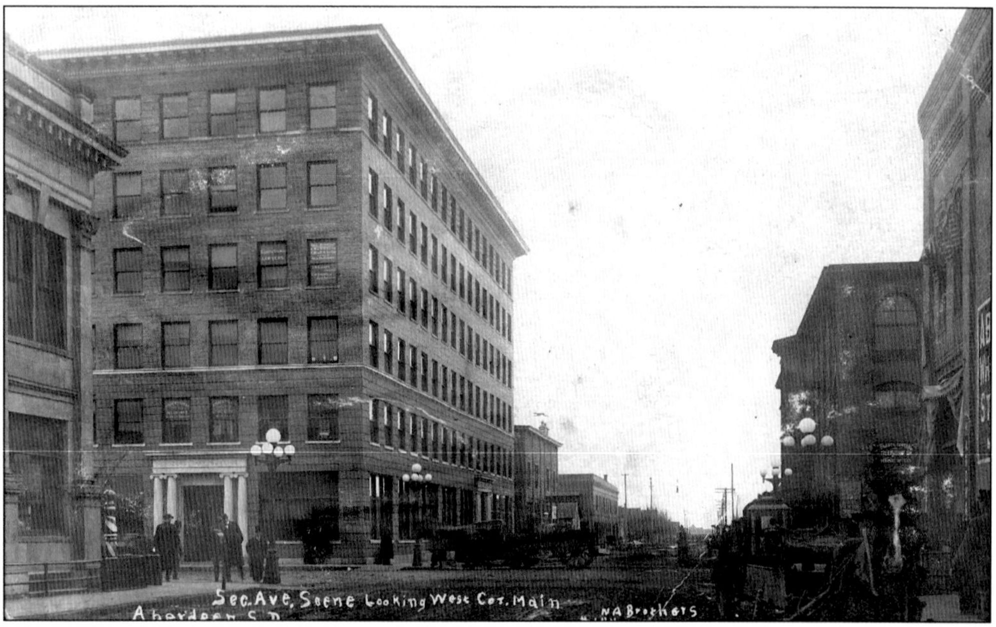

From Second Avenue looking west, this 1910 real photo shows the newly completed Citizens Bank and Trust Building's imposing entrances on Main Street. The Main Street entrance serviced the bank, while the avenue entrance serviced the offices on the upper floors. Aberdeen businessmen J.L.W. Zietlow, W.G. Bickelpahupt, Ole Swanson, and Charles Russell along with former South Dakota Governor Charles Herreid founded the Citizens Bank Company and sold $100,000 worth of bonds to finance the construction of this building.

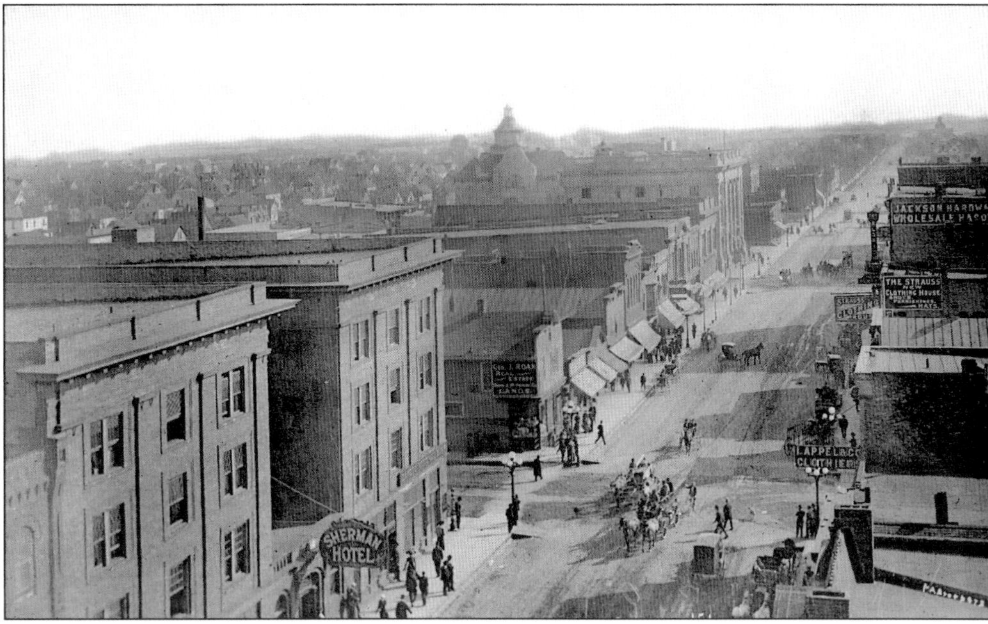

On Main Street looking south from the Roof Garden, two of Aberdeen's premier clothing houses, Appel Clothing and The Strauss New Clothing House, are pictured on the left. The Strauss store moved to this location from its original site in the Sherman Hotel in 1916. Notable in the background is the steeple of the First Methodist Church.

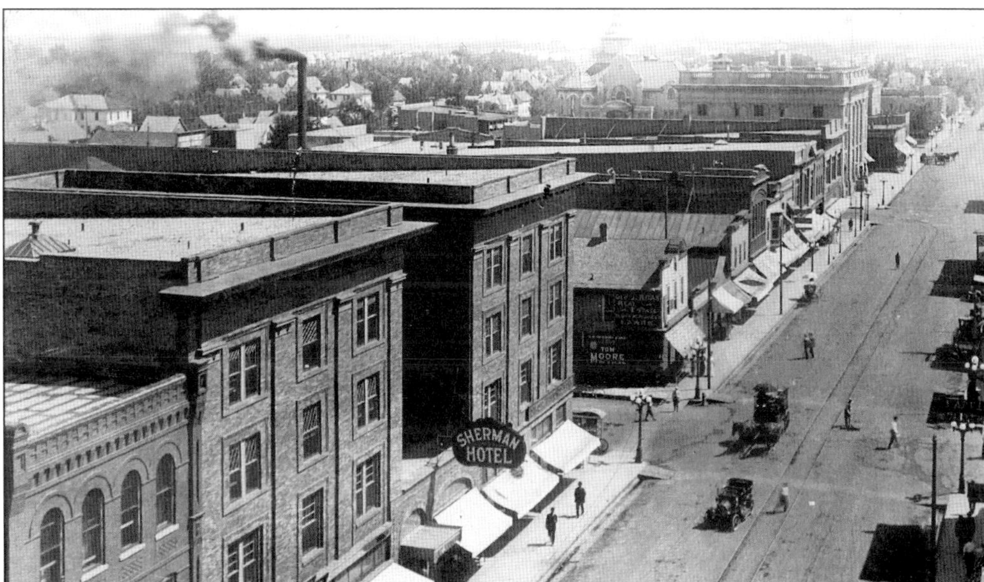

Looking south from the Citizens Bank Building, this photo showing the east side of Main Street *c.* 1920 reinforces the fact that air conditioning was unknown during this period of our history. Notice that all of these buildings have their huge storefront windows protected from the heat of the day with retractable awnings that offered some relief from the afternoon sun. Windows in these buildings were operable and often the only means of ventilation for the tenants on the upper stories.

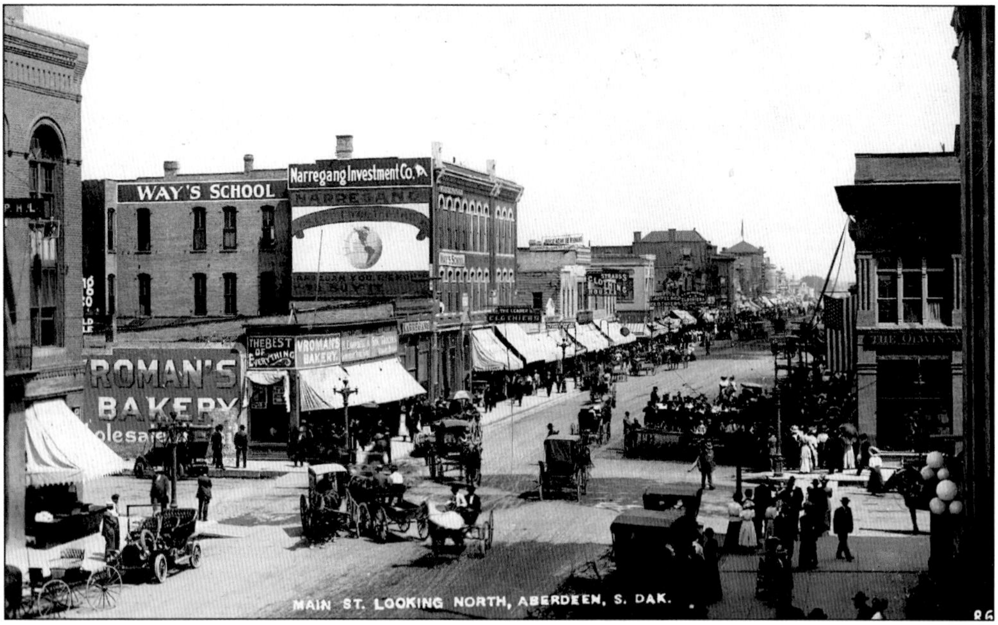

This real photo, *c.* 1909, shows the busy intersection of Main Street and Fourth Avenue. The Narregang Investment Co. building was built in 1887 and was the city's first high-rise building boasting three stories. Narregang was a pharmacist by trade but soon decided that he could make more money in the fledgling town as a real estate and land developer.

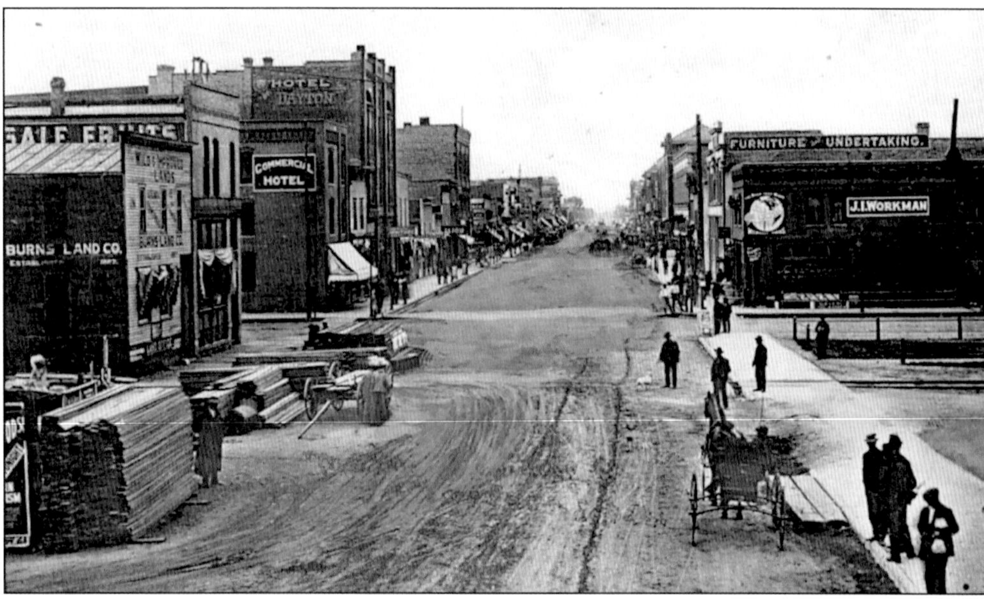

This shot was taken *c.* 1907 and shows the Main Street area near the Milwaukee Depot. The building materials could be for the Aberdeen Wholesale Grocery Co., which was erected in 1907 just south of the Milwaukee tracks next to the Burns Land Co. They distributed the "Hub City" brand of cigars. Also pictured is the Commercial Hotel, which was one of six hotels in the first block south of the Milwaukee Depot. With 13 passenger trains daily, together with even more freight trains, the hotel business was a prosperous one during this era.

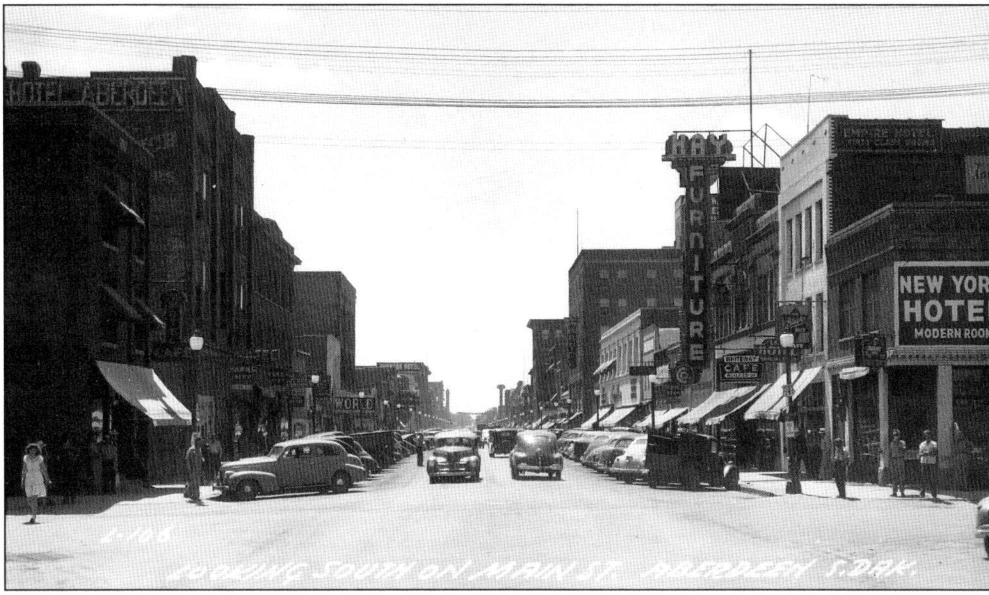

This street scene shows one of Aberdeen's oldest Main Street sections as it looked in the 1940s. The New York Hotel boasted reasonable rates and rooms with hot and cold running water. This building housing Hay Furniture was built in 1903 by J.B. Moore to house a furniture and undertaking business. The Hay family purchased the building in 1932 and moved their furniture business to this location. The building, torn down in 2002, was the oldest building in South Dakota in continuous use as a furniture store.

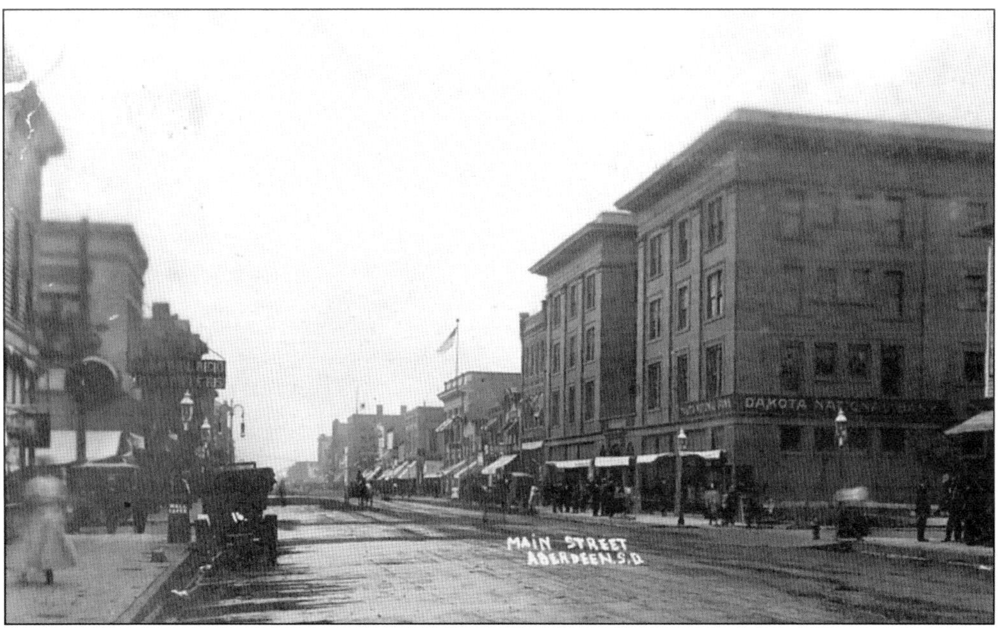

The Sherman Hotel was built in 1907 and opened on November 13, 1908. One of the first ground floor tenants was the newly organized Dakota National Bank. In 1918, this bank moved up the street to occupy space vacated by the Dakota Central Telephone Co. The Dakota National Bank was absorbed by the First National Bank after the financial crash of 1929.

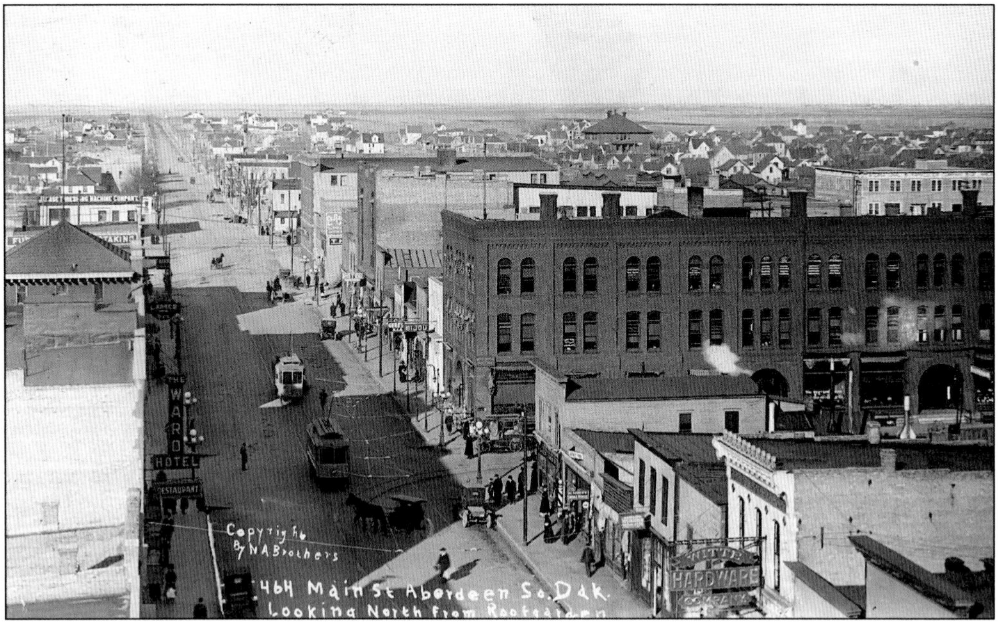

The long building in the center of this photo is yet another of Aberdeen's early banks. It was built in 1888-1889 to house the Northwestern National Bank that reportedly had a capital worth of $150,000. According to newspaper accounts, this new bank promised to be one of the strongest and best managed institutions in the west. That statement proved false when they liquidated its assets on January 15, 1892, and closed its doors due to the area's depressed farm economy.

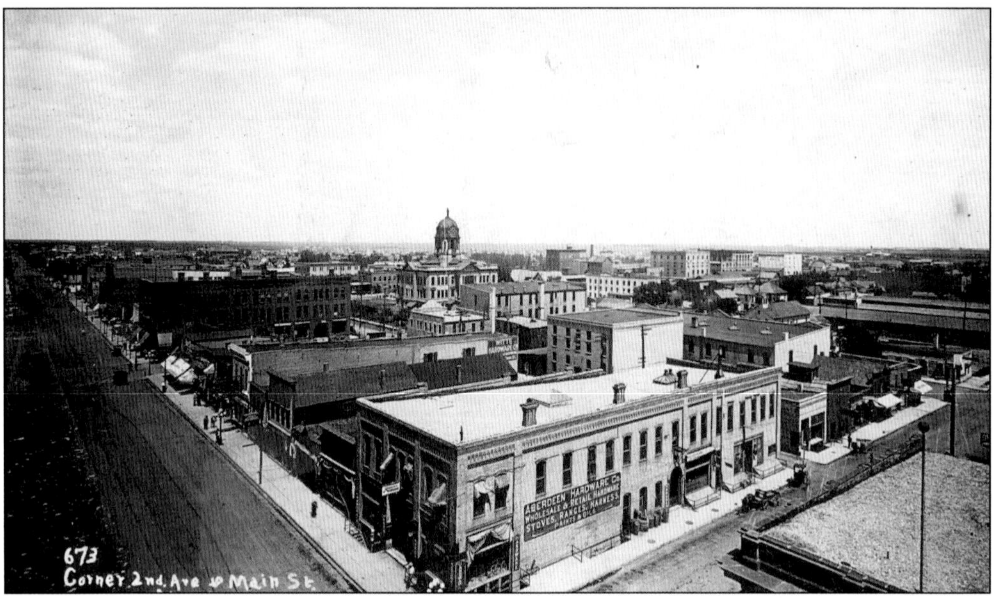

The Aberdeen Hardware Co. occupied space in this imposing building on the corner of South Main Street and Second Avenue for many years. The building provided four retail spaces on the main level as well as numerous office spaces on the second floor. Rental spaces were also available in the basement, which was accessible from entrances off the sidewalk. One basement tenant was Iver Haugen who ran one of Aberdeen's many billiard parlors.

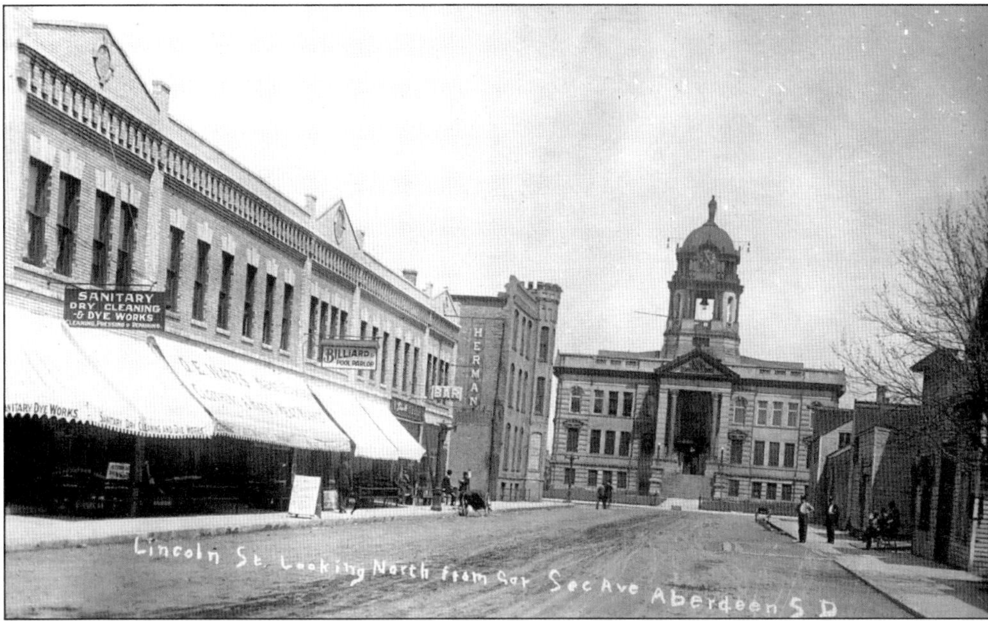

This is an unusual view of Lincoln Street, *c.* 1910. Today, only the courthouse and the long building on the left remain. The Clark Title Co. Building has replaced the Commercial Club, which was formerly between these two. All the buildings on the right are now a parking lot.

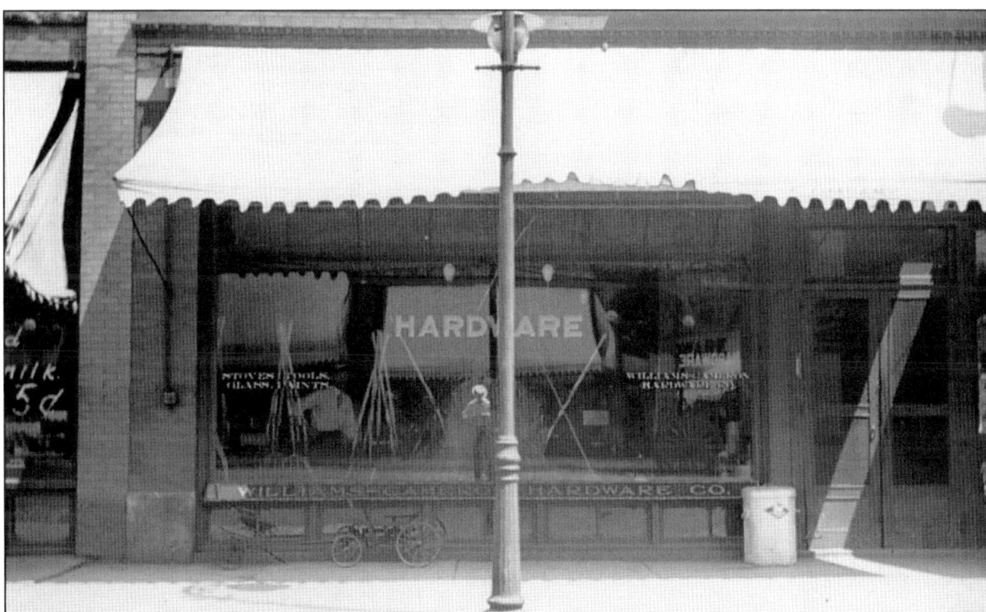

The Williams and Cameron Hardware Store was built in 1907 at 315 South Main Street and was first known as the Champlin Block. H.S. Williams and James Cameron operated their hardware business from this location *c.* 1910-1920. The upper floor of the building, a large open area, once housed the Rainbow Ballroom. In the 1950s, it was one of the temporary locations used by the Alexander Mitchell Library until its new building was completed.

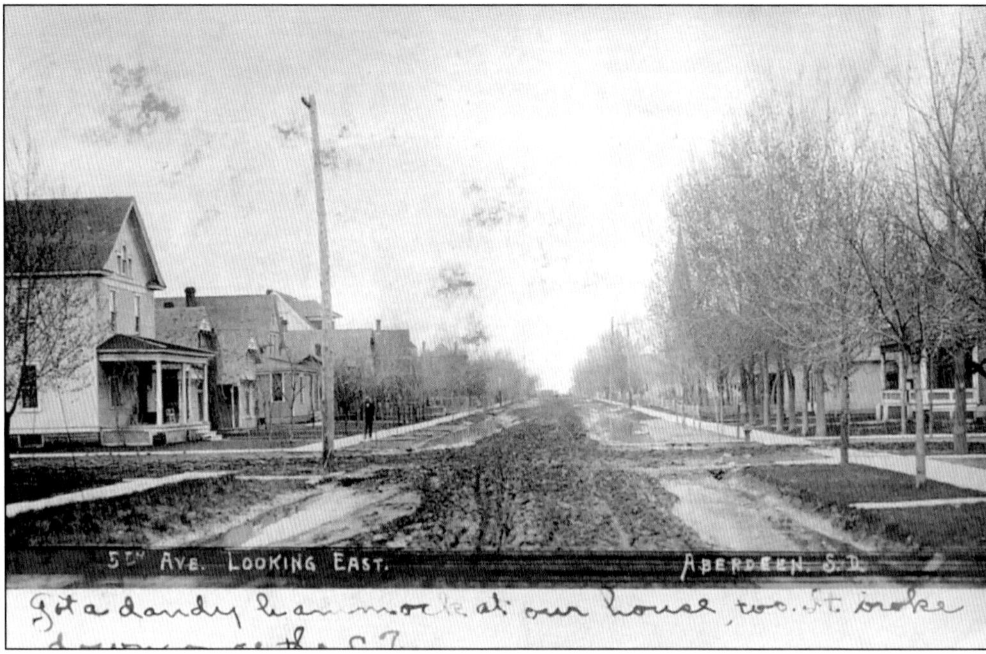

This shot shows the intersection of South Washington Street and Fifth Avenue looking east. The homes on the left are still standing today. The steeple of the First Evangelical United Brethren Church is barely visible in the trees on the right. This steeple, built in 1887, towered 100-feet above the street and was visible for miles around Aberdeen. For many years it was the highest structure in Aberdeen.

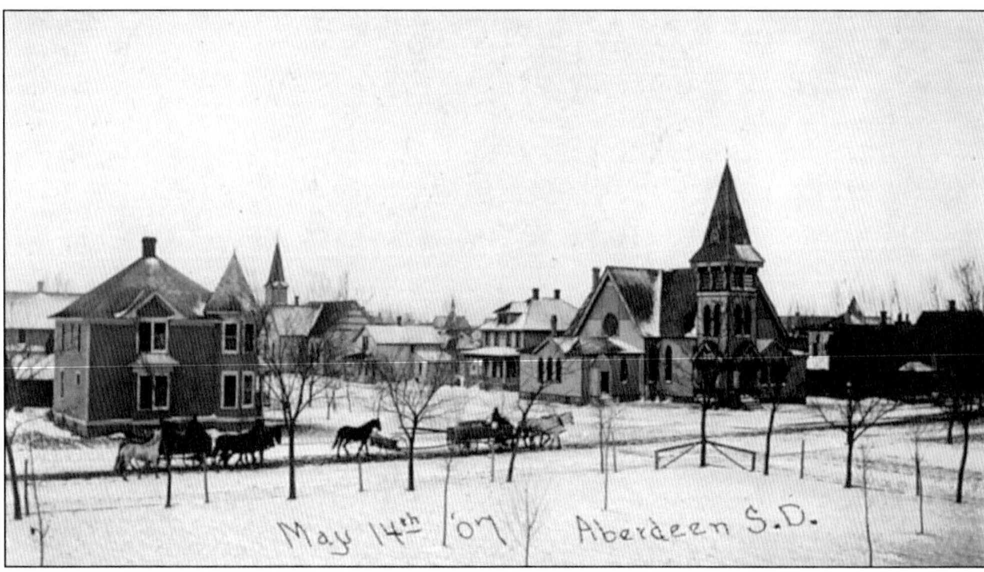

Aberdeen Methodists built this church in 1886, on lots the congregation purchased at the corner of Third Avenue and Jay Street for $425. In 1909, the Methodist congregation sold this building to the Aberdeen Zion Lutheran congregation for $5,750. It was home to the Lutherans until 1953. The house on the left was built by Orrin Schram and still stands today. The spire in the background is atop the Bethlehem Lutheran Church. The horse-drawn carriages are headed west on Third Avenue.

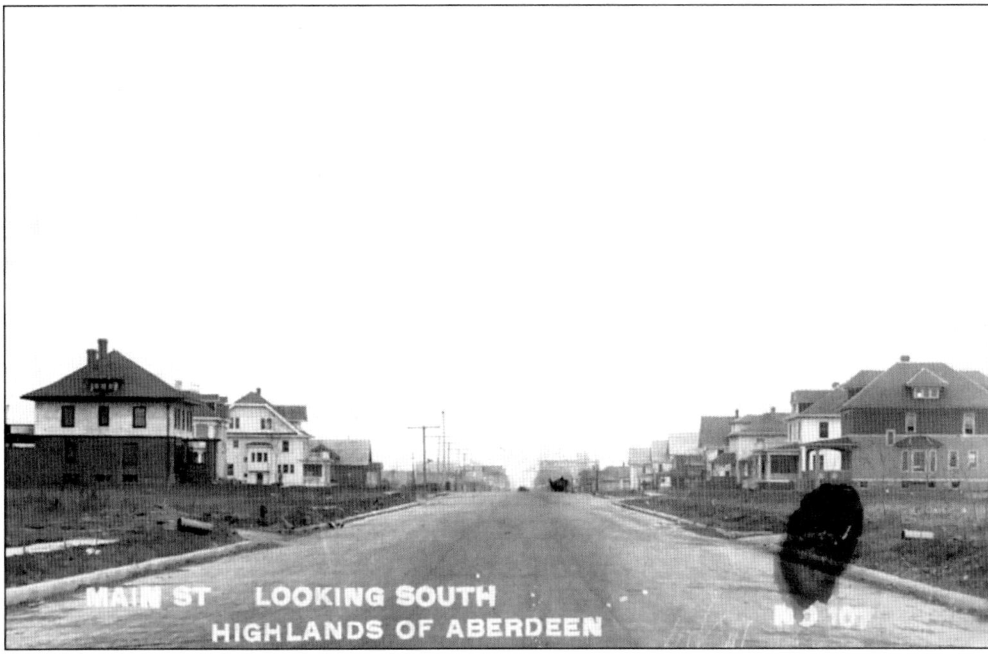

The area north of the Milwaukee Depot was developed much later than the area south of the tracks. In February of 1910, the Highlands Company began selling lots in this undeveloped area, which reportedly is 7-9 feet higher than the surrounding areas, thus the name, The Highlands.

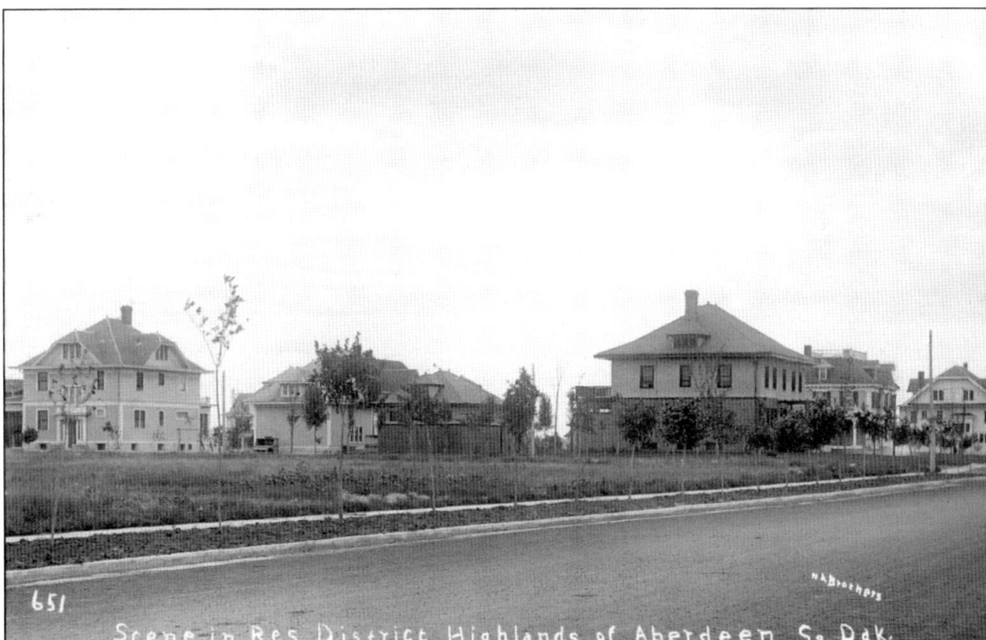

Many of Aberdeen's prominent businessmen purchased lots in the new Highlands development and built grand homes, some of which are pictured here. An auction was held for the sale of these lots and of the 275 offered, 225 were sold in the first 2 hours and 15 minutes they were made available. Prices ranged from $225 to $400 per lot.

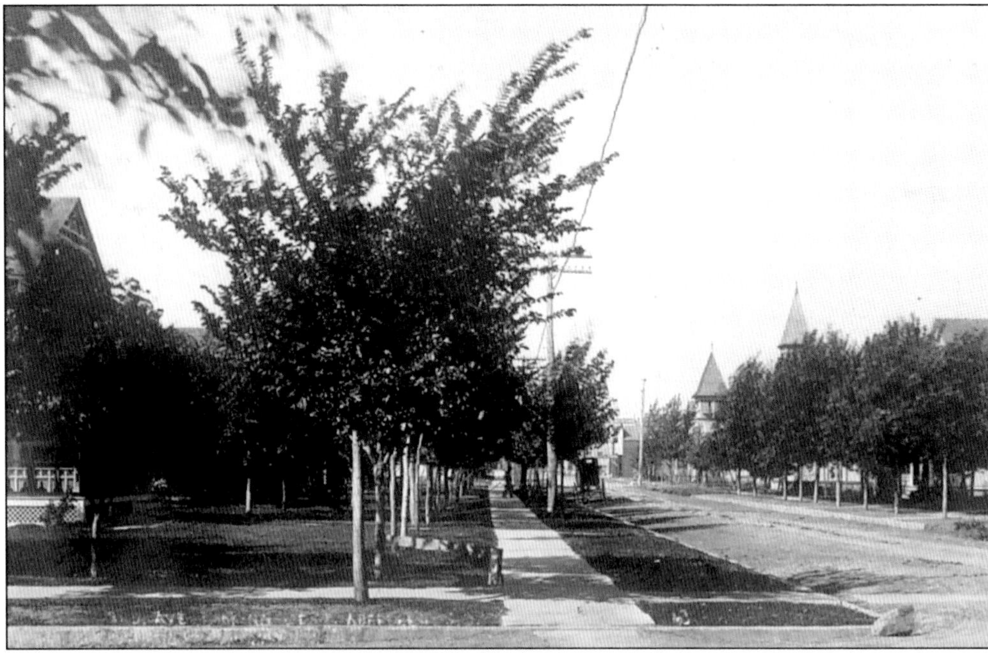

By 1909 when this photo of Third Avenue looking west was taken, Aberdeen's residential area had spread well away from the Main Street business district. This shows an established neighborhood well-shaded by maturing trees.

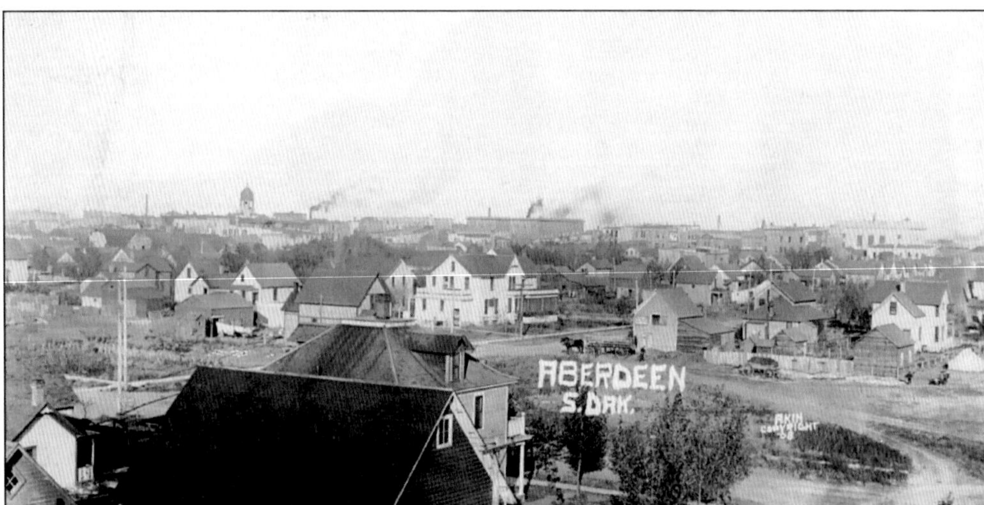

Aberdeen was a railroad town from the beginning. Here is a 1909 photo of a neighborhood built by workers on the various rail lines near the wholesale district north and east of the Brown County Courthouse,which is visible in the background.

Five

Our Schools

The Aberdeen pioneers didn't just open up new businesses and build homes, they also built churches and schools. The earliest of bond issues were for schools, including the only high school in the county until Northern opened a high school for Brown County residents. The college later also added an elementary school. In Aberdeen, all of the schools were centrally located in the different neighborhoods and the high school was in the center of town. Aberdeen is now building a new high school to open in the fall of 2004, on the southeast edge of town. Aberdeen can be proud of its educational system.

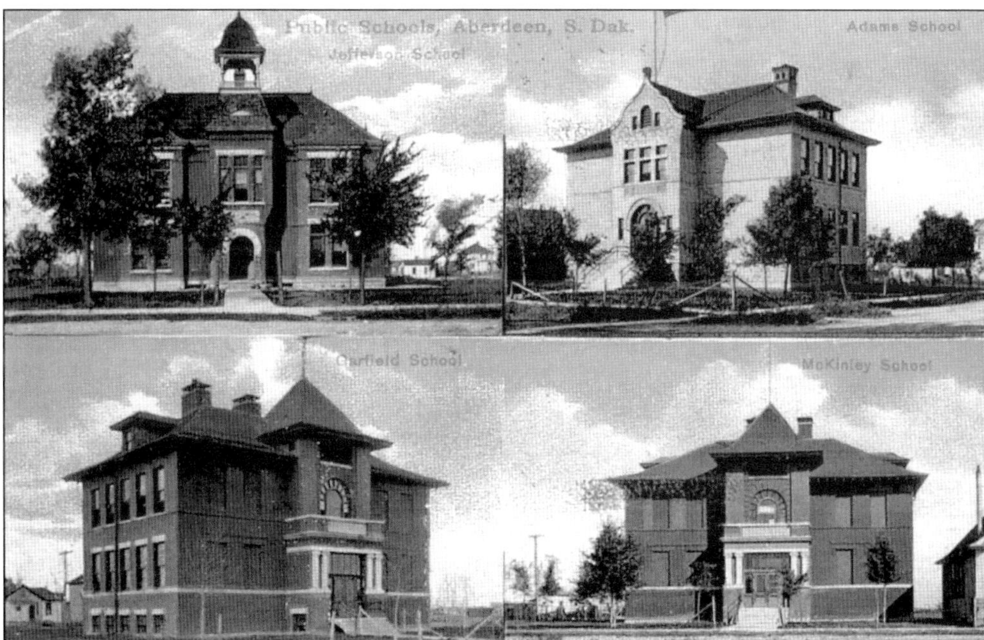

The first schools in Aberdeen were all named after presidents. Garfield was president during the land rush of the 1880s. McKinley was very popular because he had visited Aberdeen in 1898 and that helped with his popularity in the surrounding area. Washington, Jefferson, Adams, and Lincoln were popular school names all over the country.

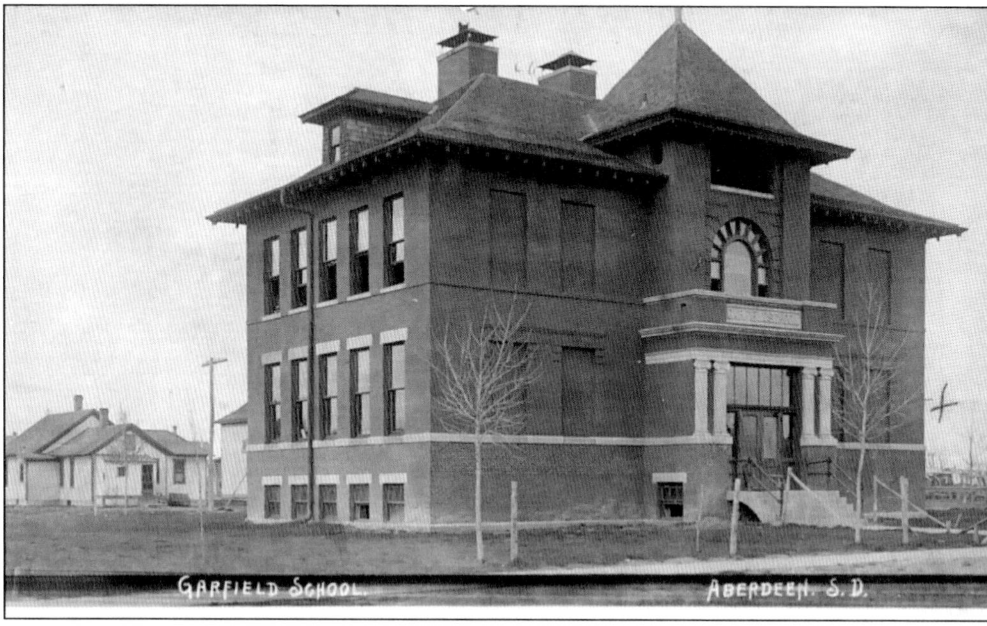

This school was named after President Garfield and was located on the corner of Eighth Avenue and South Arch Street. In 1910, Emma Meier was the principal and the teachers were Josephine Holmes, Kitie Johnson, and Alice McKenna. It was used as an elementary school until the early 1960s, it was then torn down and now is a very nice neighborhood park.

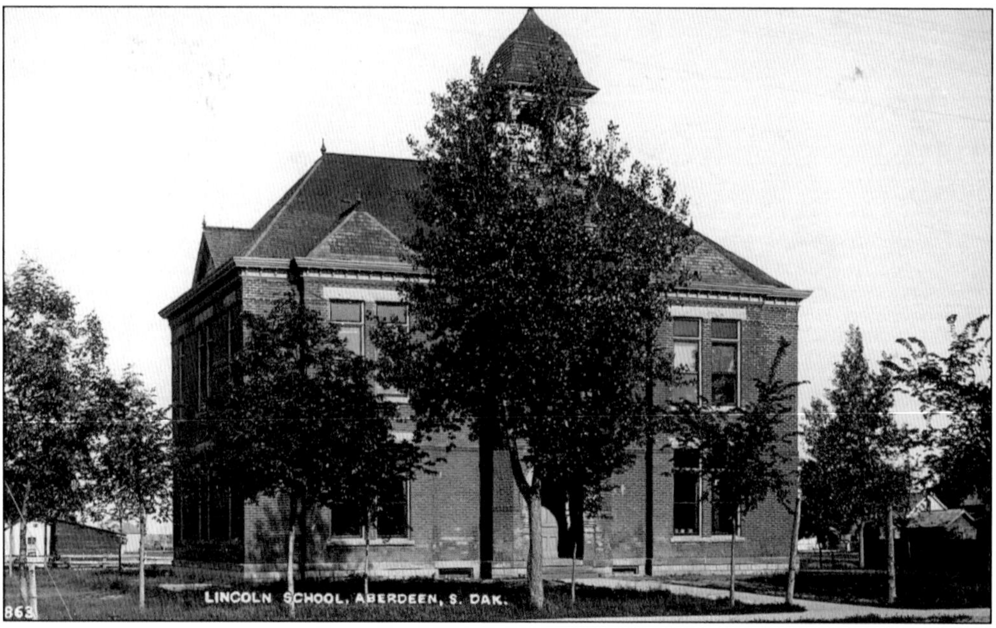

This is the original Lincoln School that was located on the corner of Third Avenue SE and Jay Street. In 1910, Luella Hightshoe was principal, and the teachers were Edith Pierson, Mayme Porter, Laura Bruce, and Mrs. Myrtle Wright Foster. The original Aberdeen High School was next to it. When the new Central High School was built in 1910, Lincoln School was rebuilt on the corner of Sixth Avenue SW and Tenth Street.

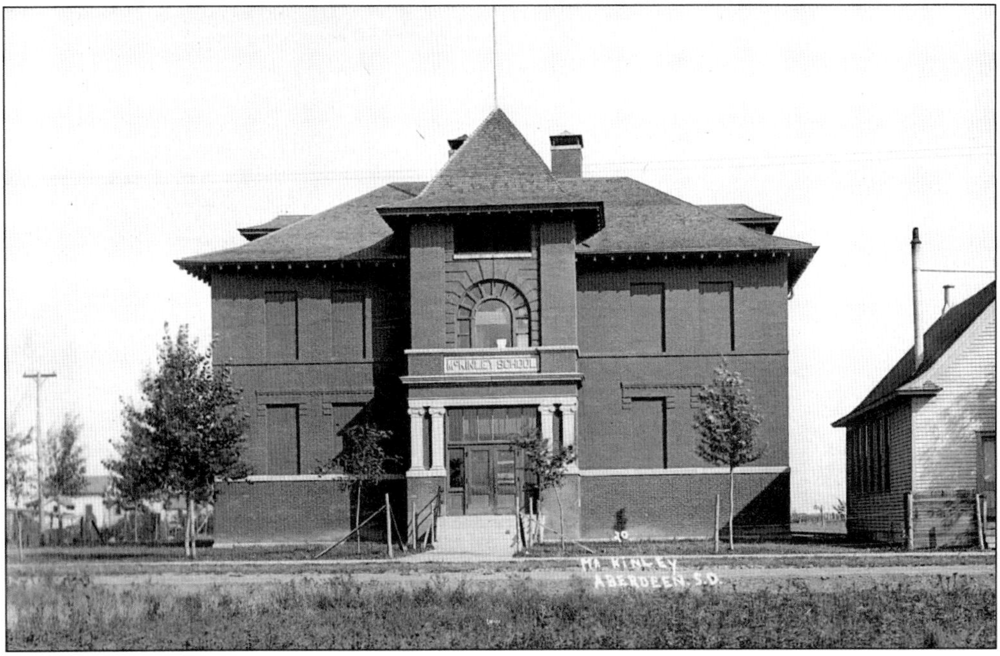

McKinley School was named after the popular President McKinley who was assassinated in 1901. It was located at 621 Third Avenue NE and was torn down many years ago. In 1910, the principal was A.A. Gaylord and the teachers were Bertha Anderson, Nina Anderson, Clara Searles, and Ethel Dunn.

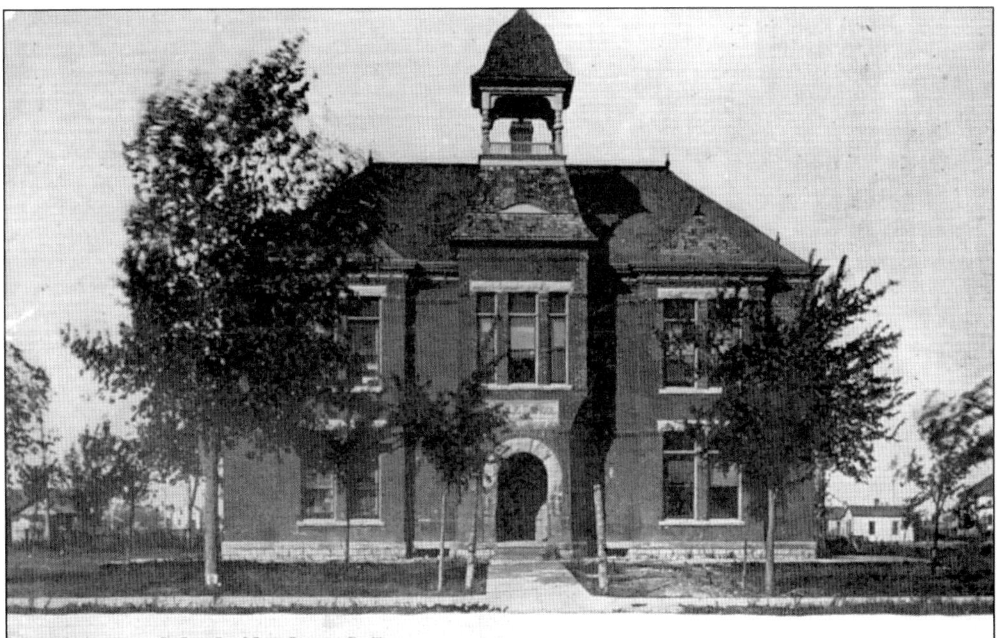

Jefferson School was located at 409 N. Washington. Years later, Monroe Junior High School was built next to it. Jefferson was demolished to make room for a school gym. In 1910, Mary Arntz was principal and the teachers were Inez Sims, Clara Washburn, and Myrtle Edgington.

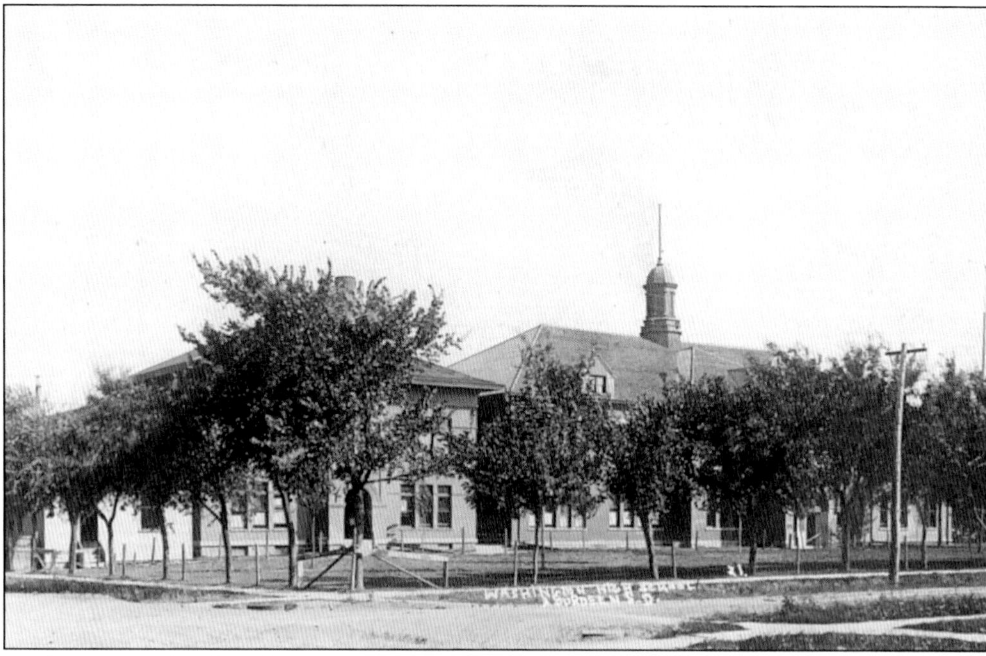

Washington High School became part of the new Aberdeen High School when it opened in 1910. Washington High School was located at the corner of Third Avenue SE and Kline Street, next to the Lincoln Elementary School. Washington building is still part of the Central High School.

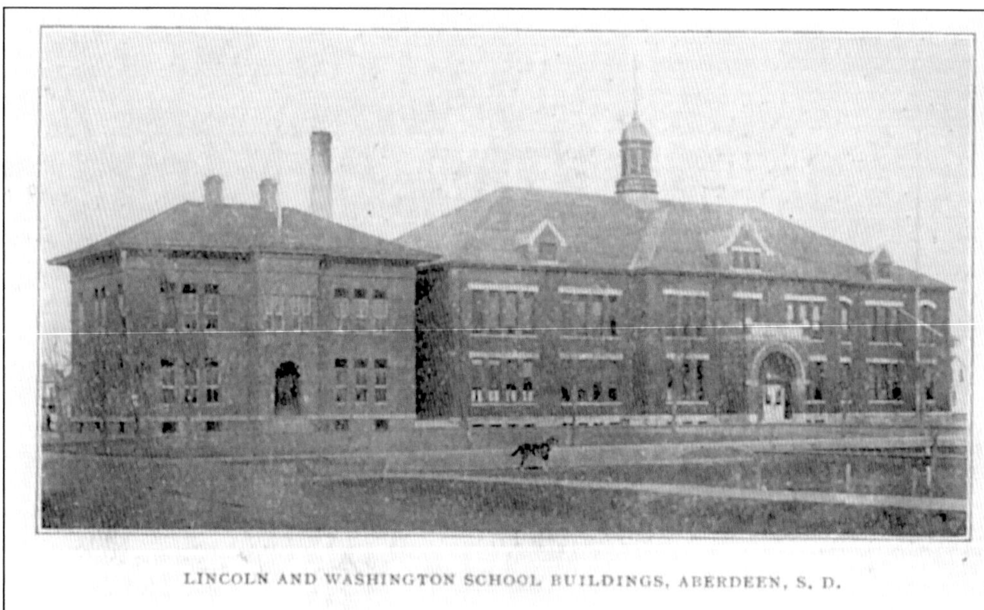

This is a pre-1907 undivided-back postcard of the elementary and high school before any trees were planted.

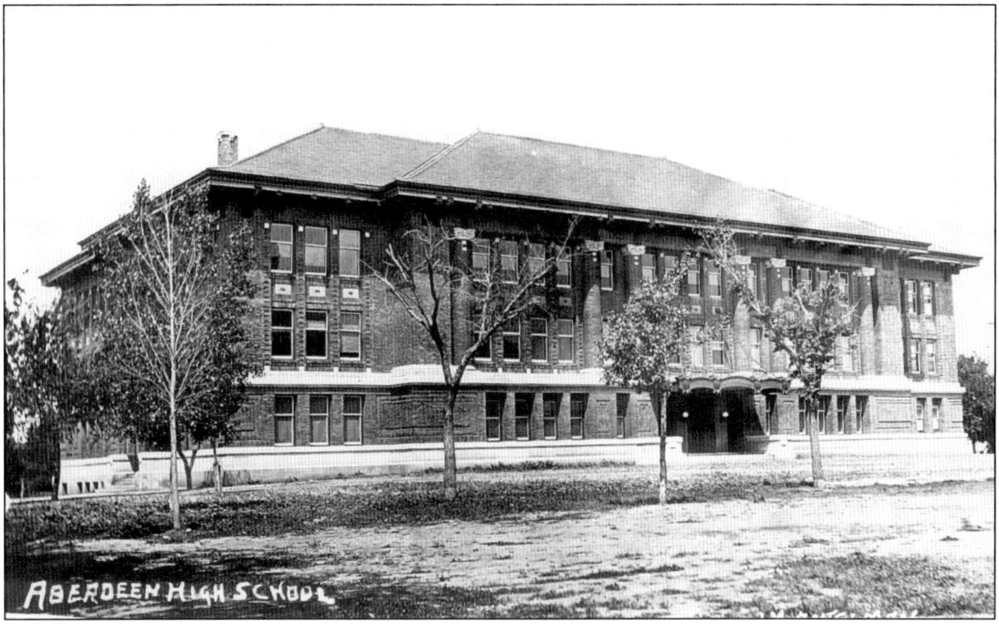

The new Aberdeen Central High School was opened in 1910. A silver trophy was presented to Professor Kirk, the principal, by the class of 1910. Aberdeen's new high school will open for the school year 2004-2005 and this same trophy will be further engraved and presented to the principal by the class of 2005.

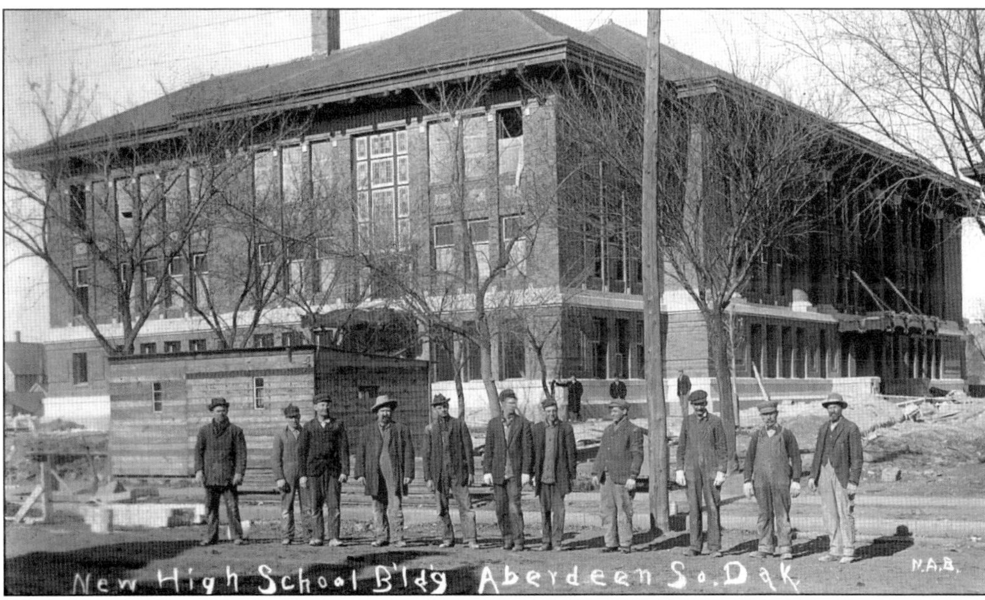

"Aberdeen Will Have the Finest High School Building in State," was the headline carried by the June 7, 1911, *Aberdeen Daily American*. According to the article, "Aberdeen citizens have spent freely to make this one of the most complete high schools in the west . . . the building is built with all the advanced ideas of modern education . . . to give every boy and girl the best possible preparation for life's work." The $180,000 school boasted 23 classrooms with a capacity for 690 students.

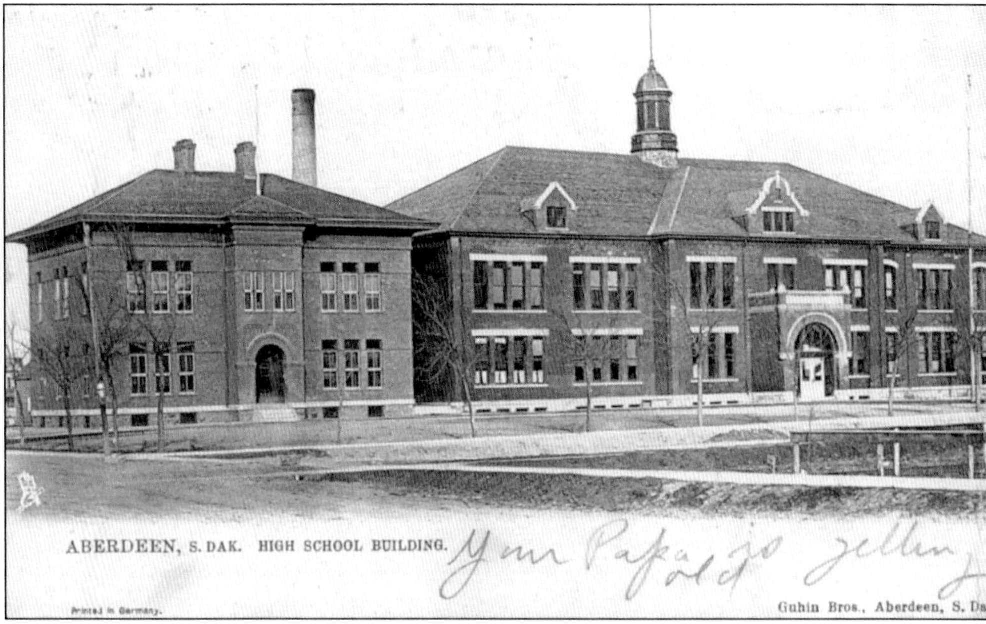

This postcard view of the Lincoln and Washington School Buildings was distributed by the Guhin Bros. Booksellers as part of an excellent series of postcards made by Raphael Tuck & Sons as part of the pre-1907 series number 2216 titled "Aberdeen, S. Dak."

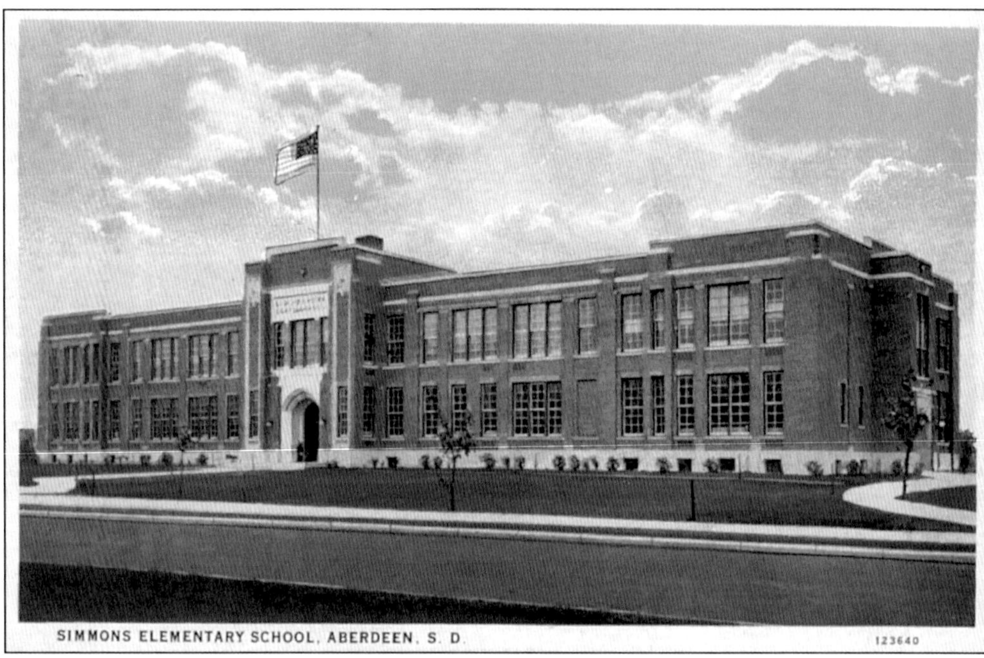

Simmons School opened in 1928 with elementary students using the first floor and the junior high using the second floor. In 1955, it became just a junior high school when Simmons Elementary was opened one block south. It was named after John C. Simmons, an Aberdeen pioneer who came here in 1882. He donated the land that the school and Simmons Field now sit on, and by having a school in this area, it helped develop the other land Mr. Simmons owned around it.

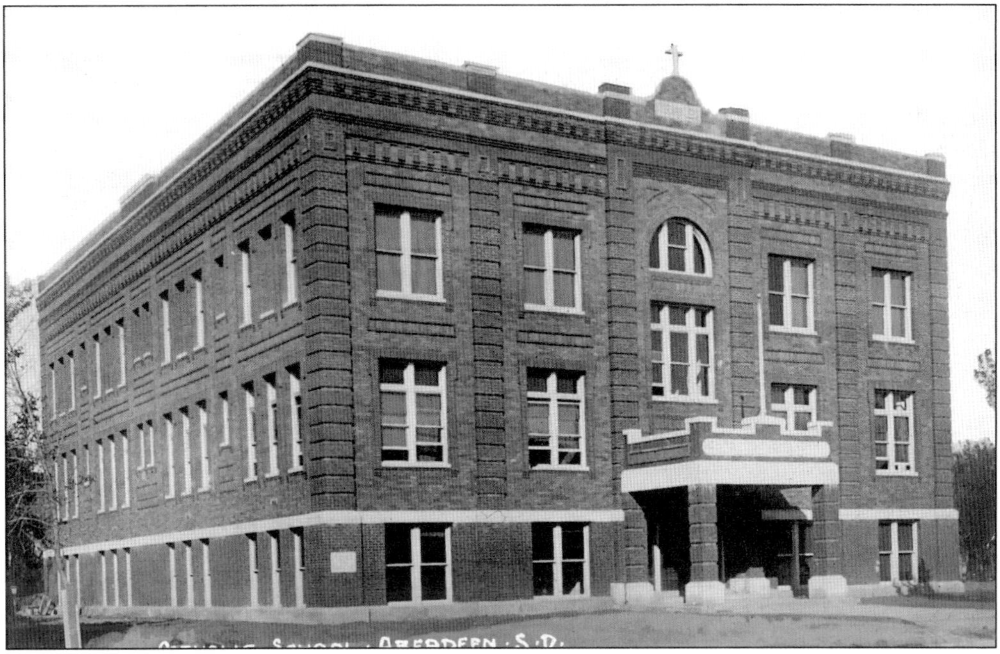

The Catholic School was built on the northeast corner of Arch Street and Third Avenue SE. It was completed in 1914 at a cost of $80,000 with loans obtained from B.C. Lamont and Isaac Lincoln. It is still in use today as a Catholic Middle School.

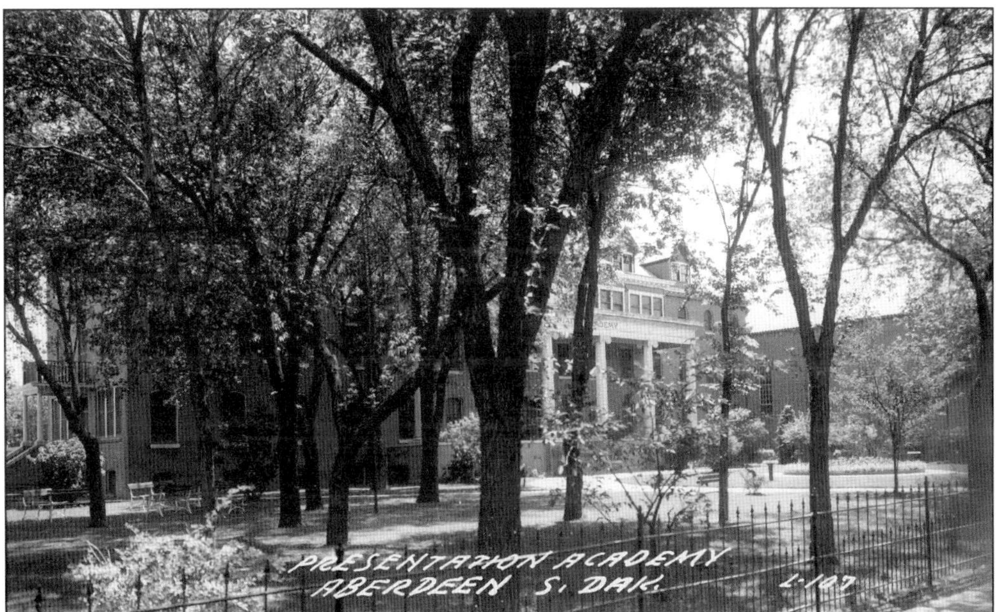

The Presentation Academy was located at 307 South State Street next to St. Luke's Hospital and was conducted by the Presentation Sisters. This was the forerunner of Presentation College. The above school replaced the one built in 1888 that had been referred to as "the box" because of its design. The Presentation Sisters came to Aberdeen, Dakota Territory, in 1886 at the request of Father Haire.

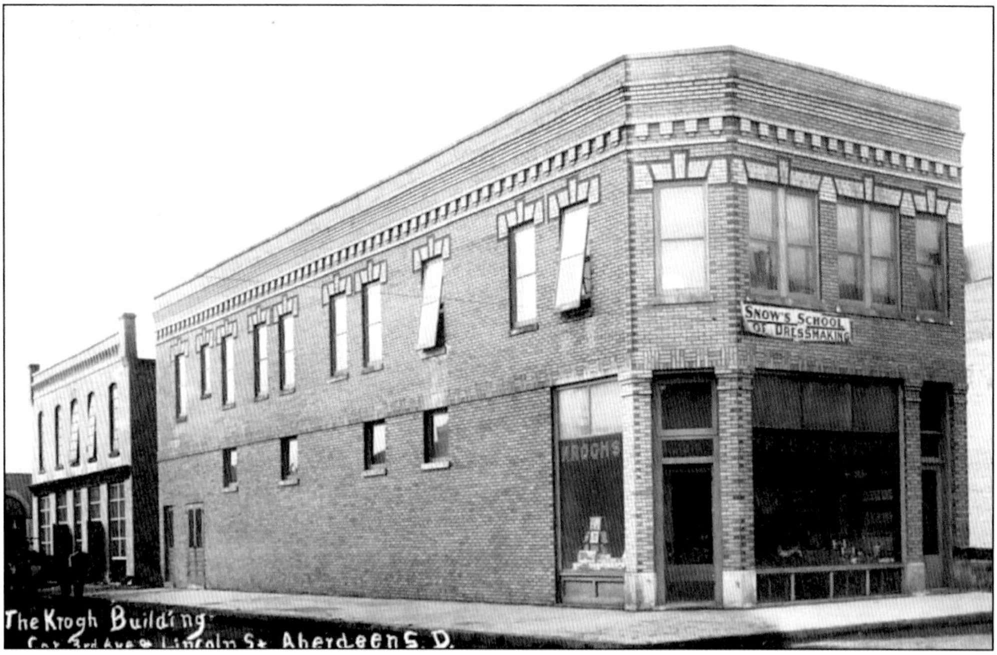

Snow's School of Dressmaking was located at 24 Third Avenue SE. It opened in 1909 and was run by Kathryn Conners and Marion Kimball. A few years later it moved to 702 S. Main Street and was then owned by Minnie Fiene who operated it out of her home.

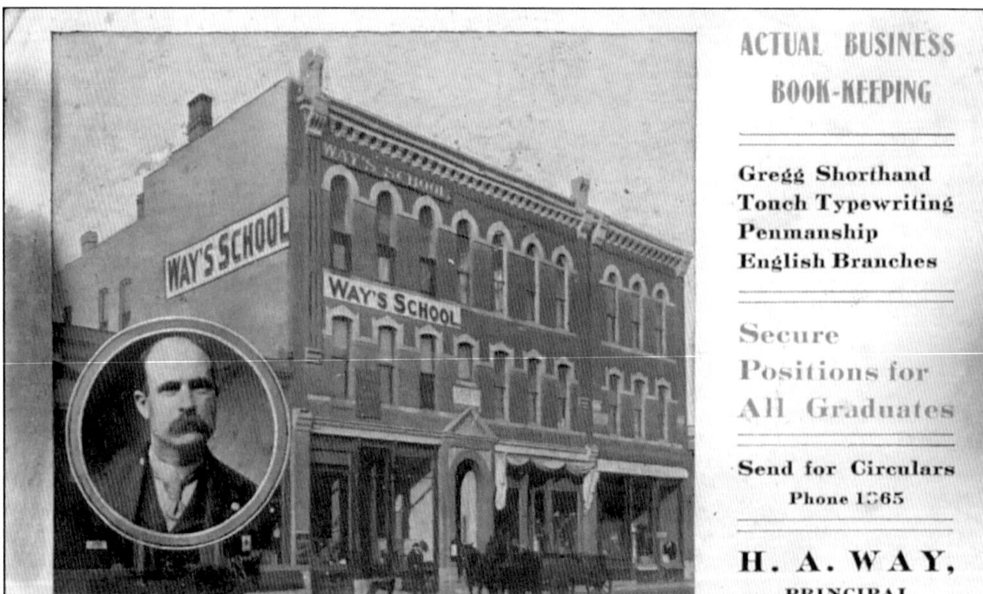

In the early 1900s, Aberdeen had two business schools for occupations that didn't require going to college. They were Way's School and the Granger Business School. By 1917 we also had the Aberdeen Business School and later the Aberdeen School of Commerce.

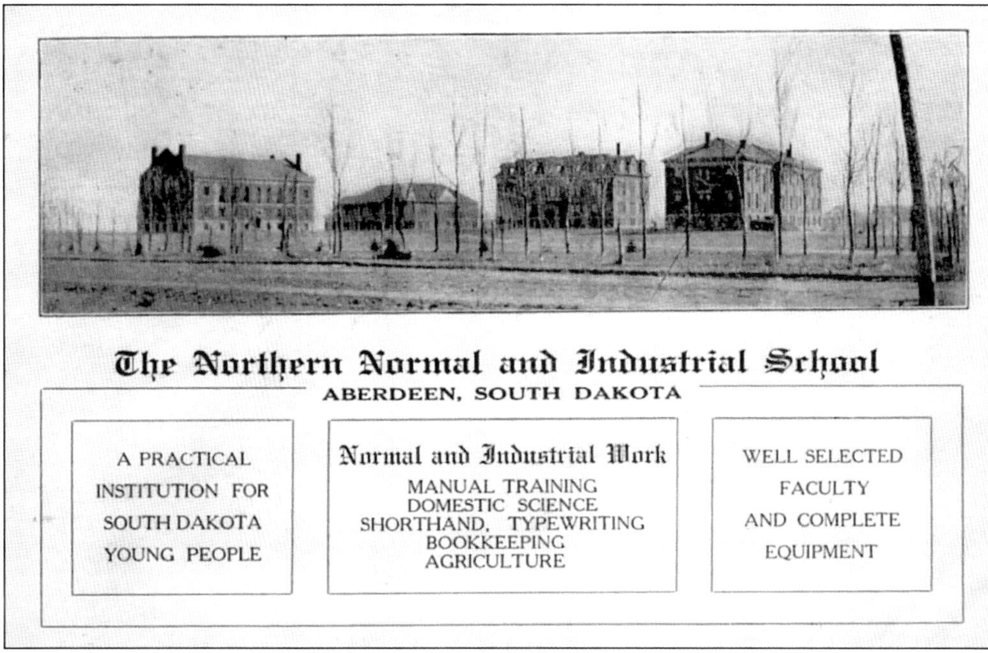

This is an early advertising postcard for the Northern Normal and Industrial School that opened in 1902. The name was changed in 1937 to Northern State Teachers' College, and in 1964, the "Teachers'" was dropped from the name. It is now known as Northern State University and they have just celebrated their 100th anniversary.

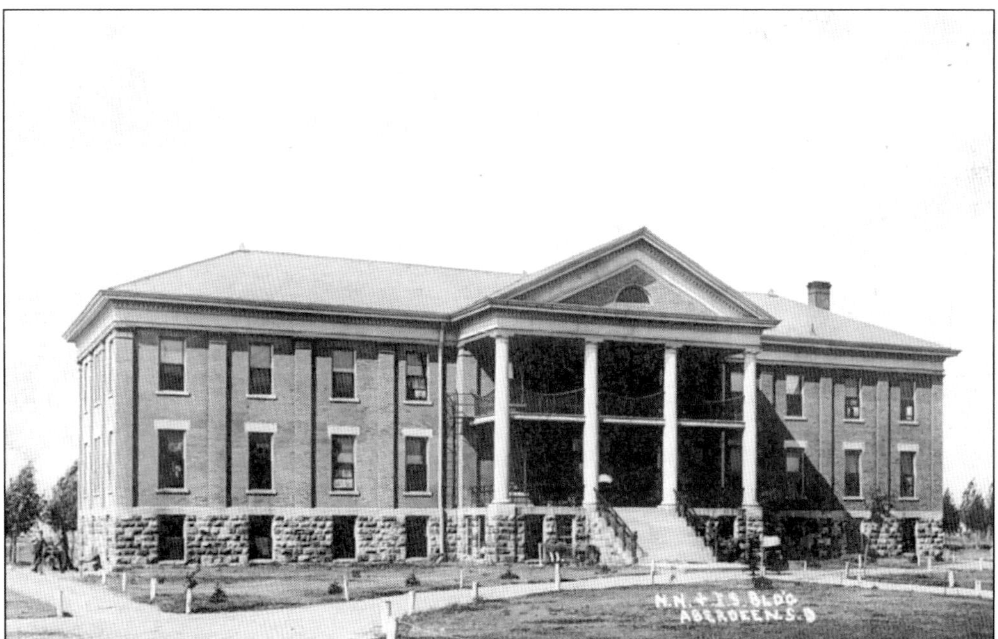

This building was one of the first completed in 1902 of the Northern Normal and Industrial School as the Ladies Dormitory. It is now known as Graham Hall, named after Lydia A. Graham, an early music, piano, and voice teacher. It is currently being used for offices.

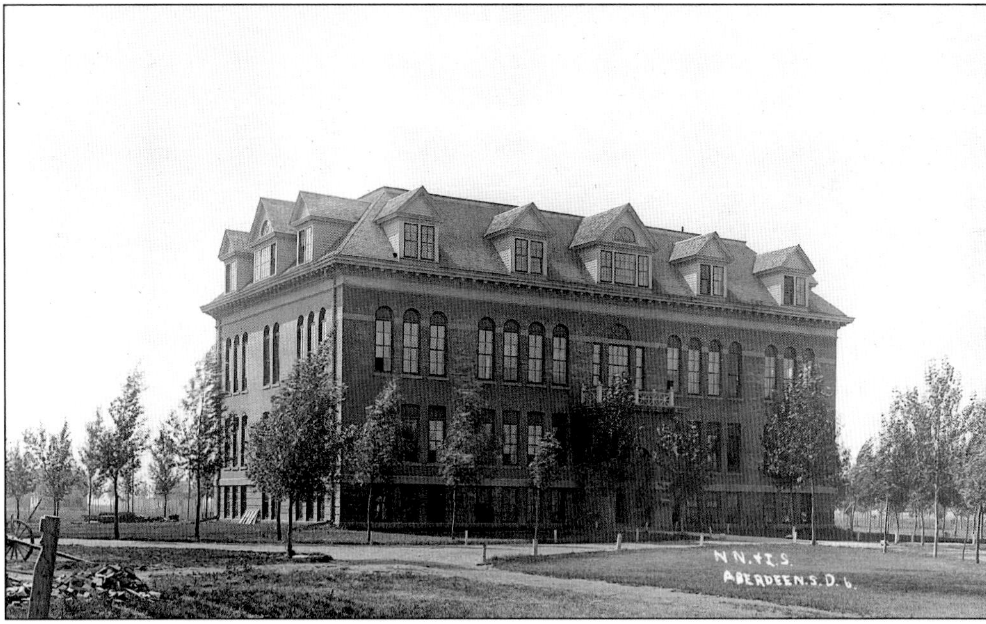

Another of the original buildings, completed in 1902 at Northern Normal, is the Central Building. This building housed the classrooms, which suffered the misfortune of burning to the ground the night of February 1, 1960.

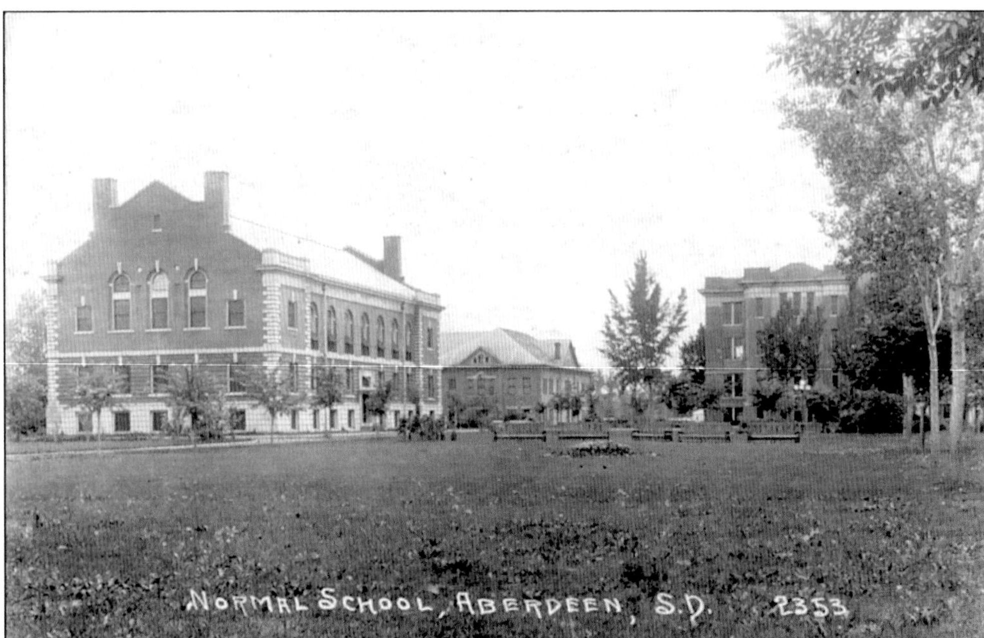

This is the Administration Building and Business Office on the left, with the Ladies Hall in the center and the Industrial building on the right.

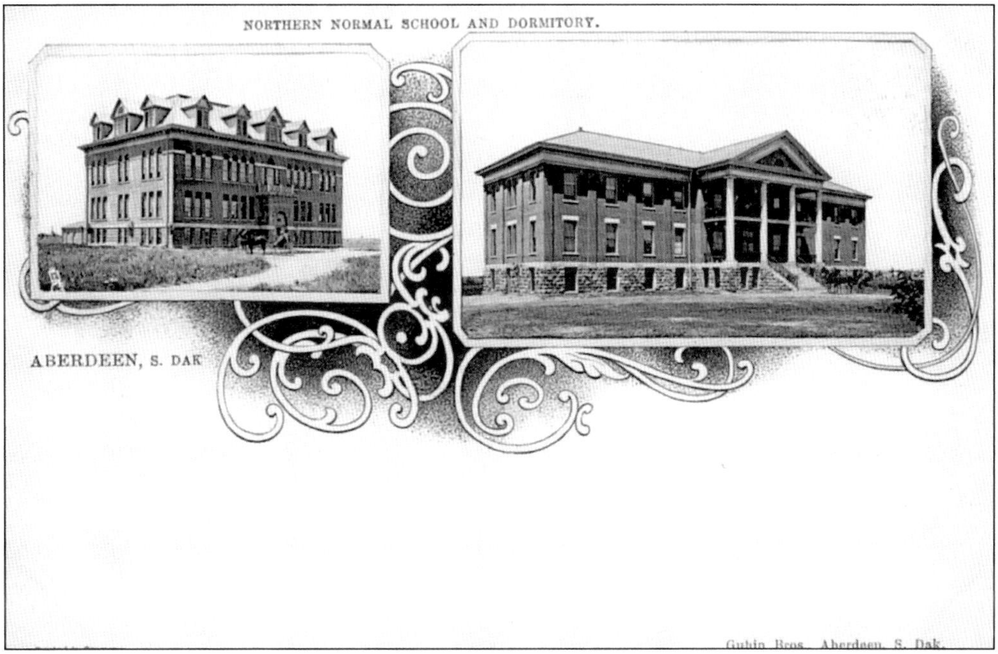

This is one of a series of eight postcards from a 1905 souvenir folder distributed by the Guhin Bros. Booksellers as part of the Raphael Tuck & Sons postcard series number 1086 titled "South Dakota." This shows the first two buildings built in 1902 at Northern Normal.

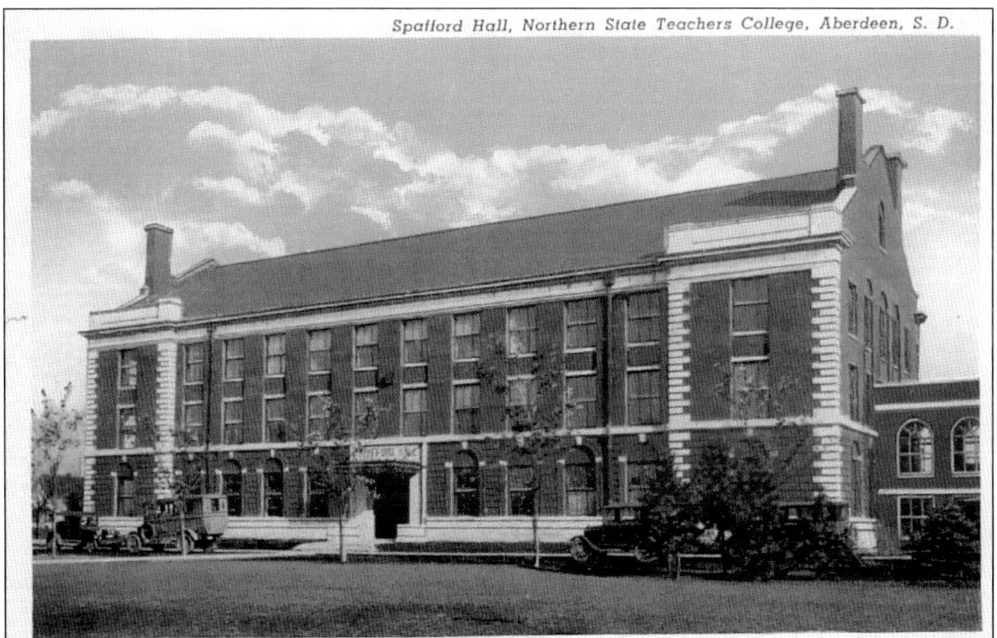

Spafford Hall was dedicated in 1927, in honor of Dr. Frederick A. Spafford, an educator, scientist, and patriot, according to the cornerstone. He was from Flandreau, South Dakota, and was the 1927 president of the South Dakota Board of Regents.

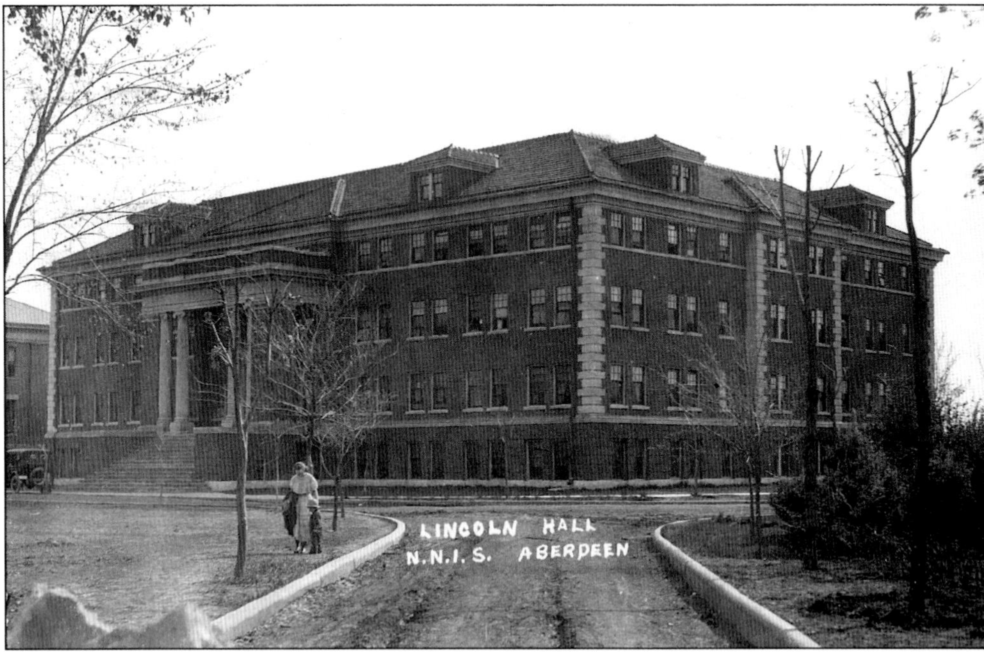

Isaac Lincoln was a prominent Aberdonian pioneer and was very instrumental in obtaining funding for the creation of a college in Aberdeen. This building was built in 1917 in his honor, before he died in 1921. It is just north of Graham Hall and is situated between Graham and Briscoe Hall.

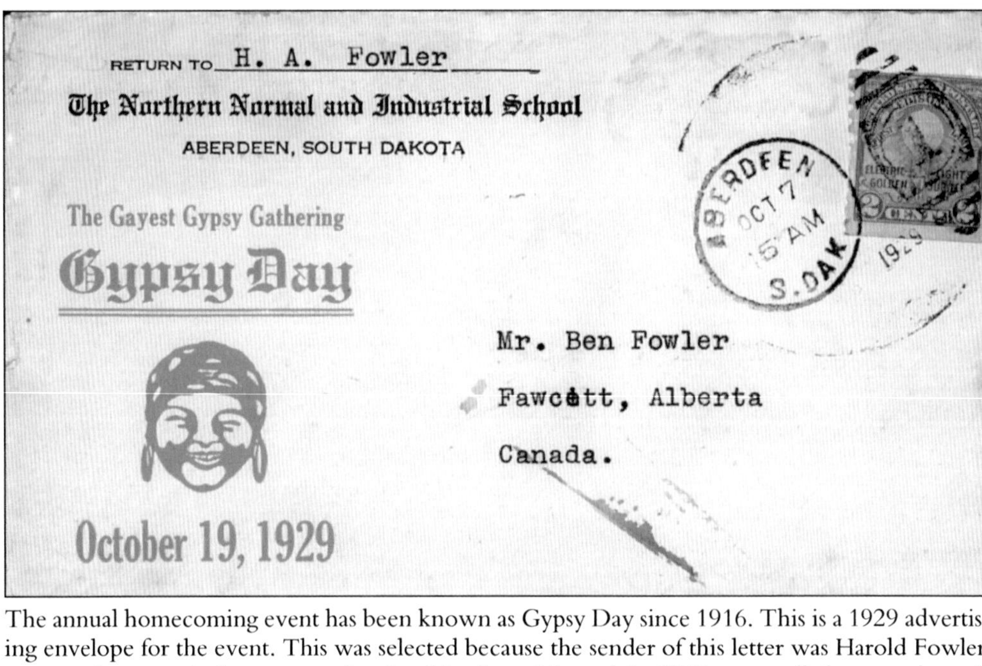

The annual homecoming event has been known as Gypsy Day since 1916. This is a 1929 advertising envelope for the event. This was selected because the sender of this letter was Harold Fowler, a man who started elementary school at Northern Normal in 1912, went all the way through school there, and then to the college. He went to work in the Business Office while a student and worked his entire life there, retiring in 1985 after spending 73 years at the same place.

Six

Parks and Recreation

Before television, people actually had active lives, and even knew who their neighbors were. Visitations with friends, neighbors, and relatives were a common occurrence. Local, state, and national events were discussed, as well as gossip. Families and groups socialized together and this was accomplished by going to our local parks and recreation areas. In the early days, not everyone had an automobile, and besides, the roads were so horrible that any adventure had to be close by or be accessible by inexpensive transportation like the trolleys and trains. Through the generous donations of different Aberdonians, we had many parks and recreational areas in and around town. People gathered together, and people had fun. The following are places that they went.

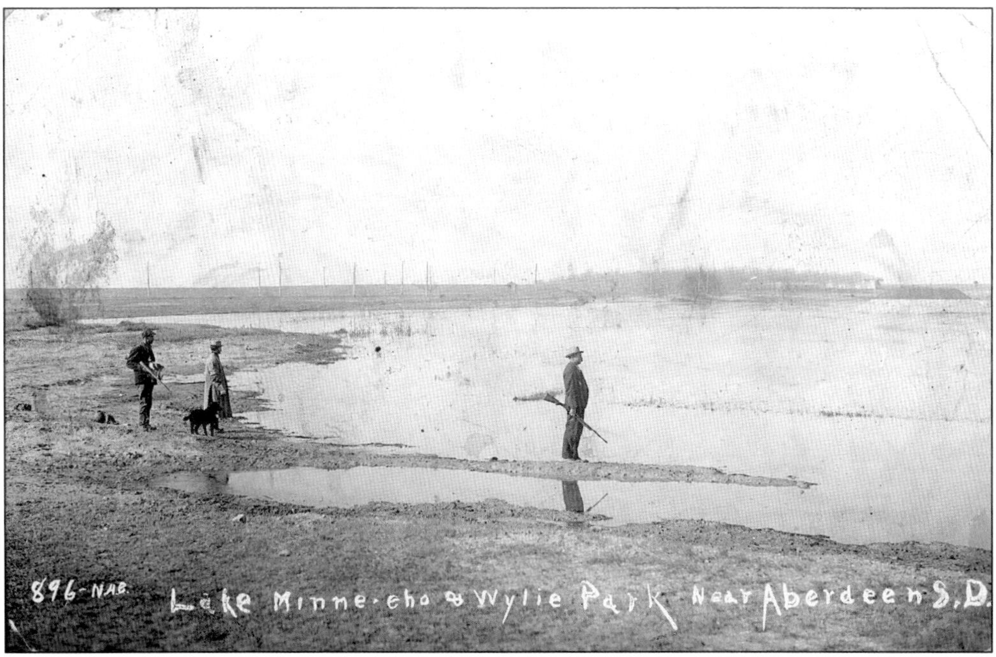

The land for Wylie Park was purchased from Alva N. Aldrich in 1910 and named in honor of his father in law, James H. Wylie, an early pioneer of Aberdeen, Dakota Territory. Wylie was the proprietor of the Wisconsin House. This postcard shows duck hunters standing on the shore of Lake Minneeho, which is still the official name of Wylie Lake.

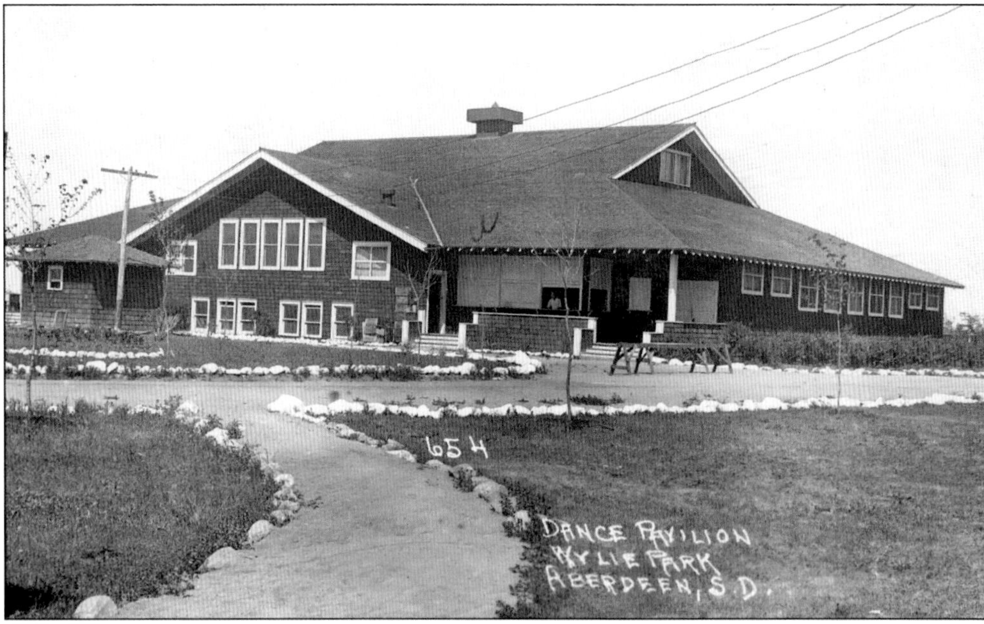

The Wylie Park Dance Pavilion has been used as a favorite recreational spot for Aberdonians since 1911. It was remodeled in 1919. While Aberdeen had trolley cars, they made continuous round trips on weekends and evenings. It was a very popular spot when live music was in its heyday. It is still in good repair and it is used a little today, but not like it has been.

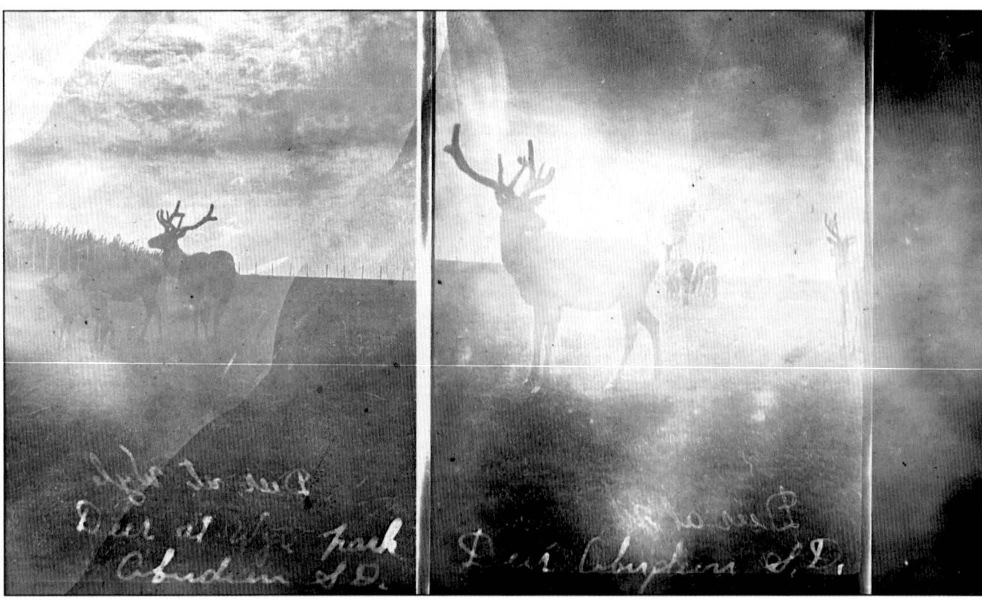

In this *c.* 1910 homemade real photo postcard. The animals labeled as deer at Wylie Park are actually elk. There are still elk and deer at the zoo at Wylie Park today, which many generations of children have enjoyed. You will note the problem many people had in writing backwards on negatives in order to make postcards.

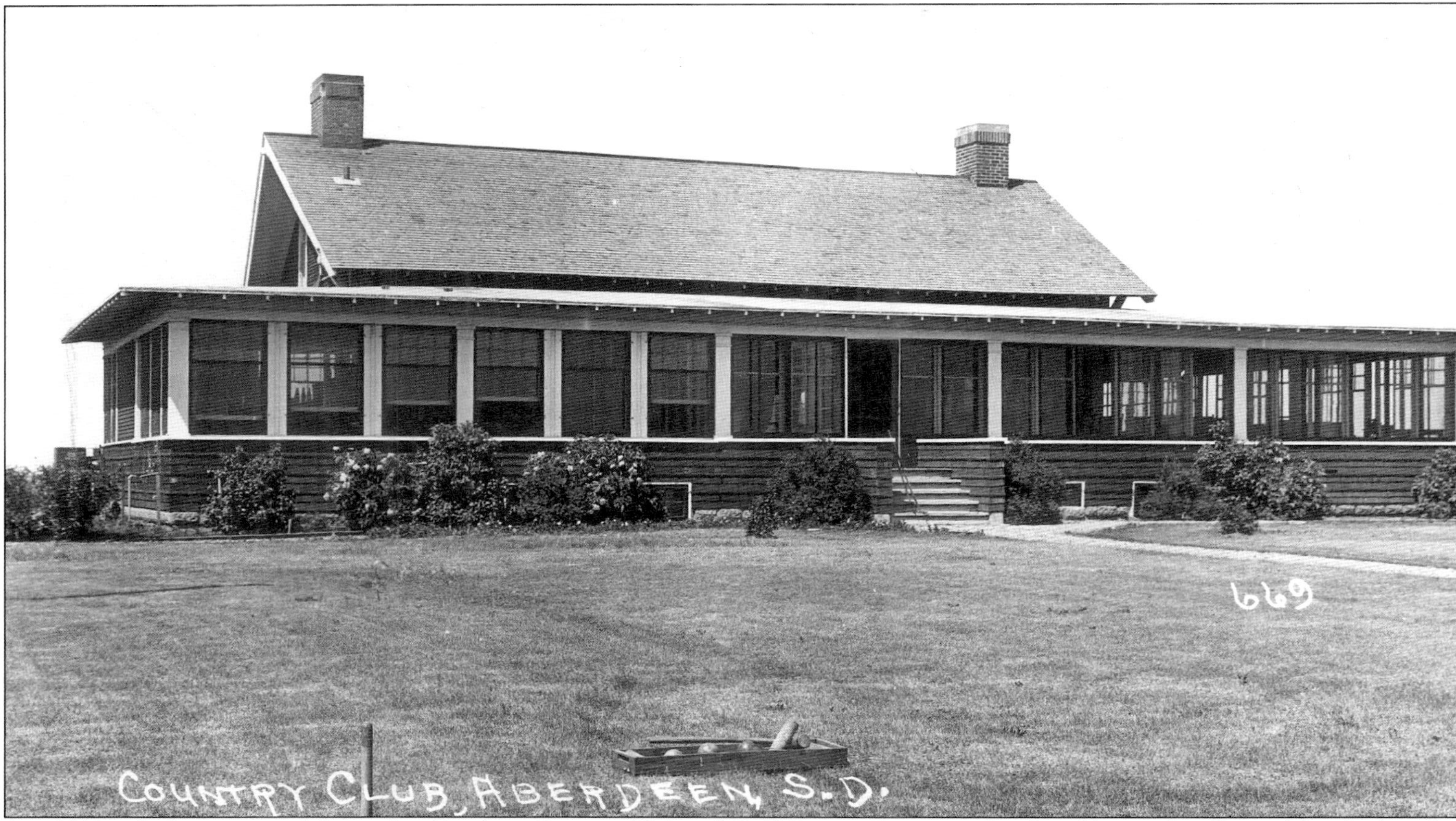

A *c.* 1912 real photo postcard shows the Aberdeen Country Club and Golf Course. For many decades, this was the elite social gathering place and had one of the finest dining establishments in the area. Starting in 1928, it was home to the Dakota Open Golf Tournament, which is the longest running tournament in the Dakotas. This building was demolished in 2002 and an entirely new housing development and 9-hole golf course will be built.

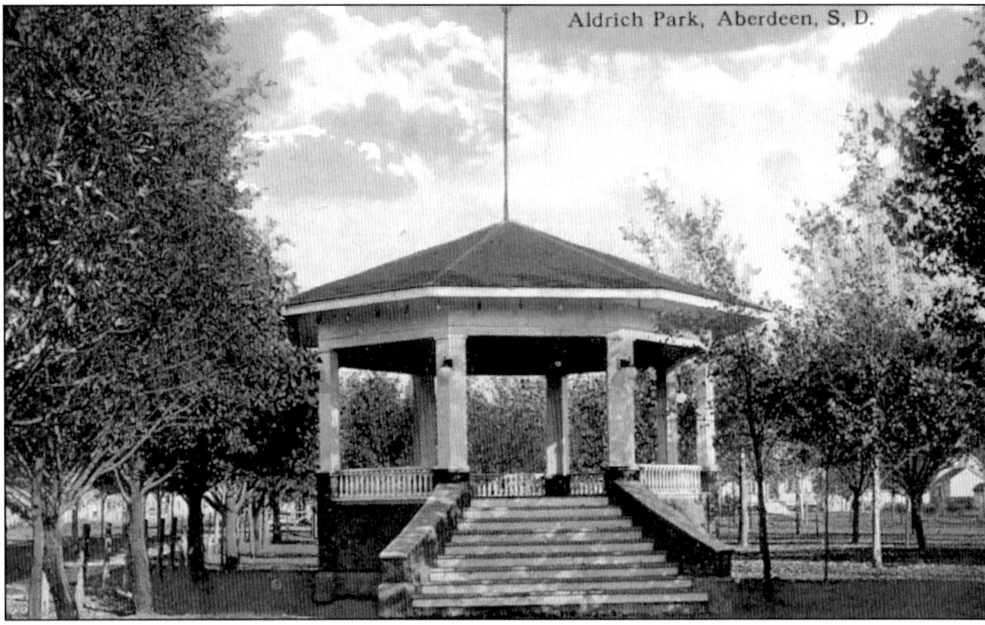

Upon this site was the original Brown County Courthouse in Aberdeen until the new courthouse was completed in 1904. No photographs of the original wooden courthouse are known to exist. The park was created in 1912 and named after Alva N. Aldrich, a prominent Aberdonian and city mayor. This bandstand was built in 1914 and still stands today.

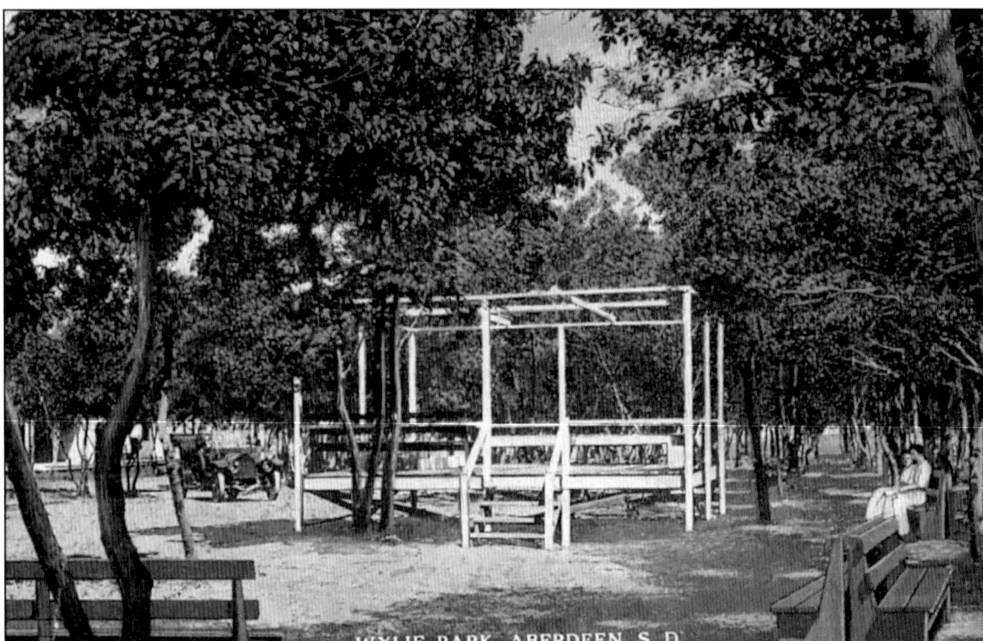

Wylie Park has always been a very popular picnic and gathering place. It is now a big tourist attraction because of the addition of Story Book Land and the Land of Oz area. The camping area, with new showers and a convenience store, has been expanded over the past few years, making it a nice place for tourists to stay.

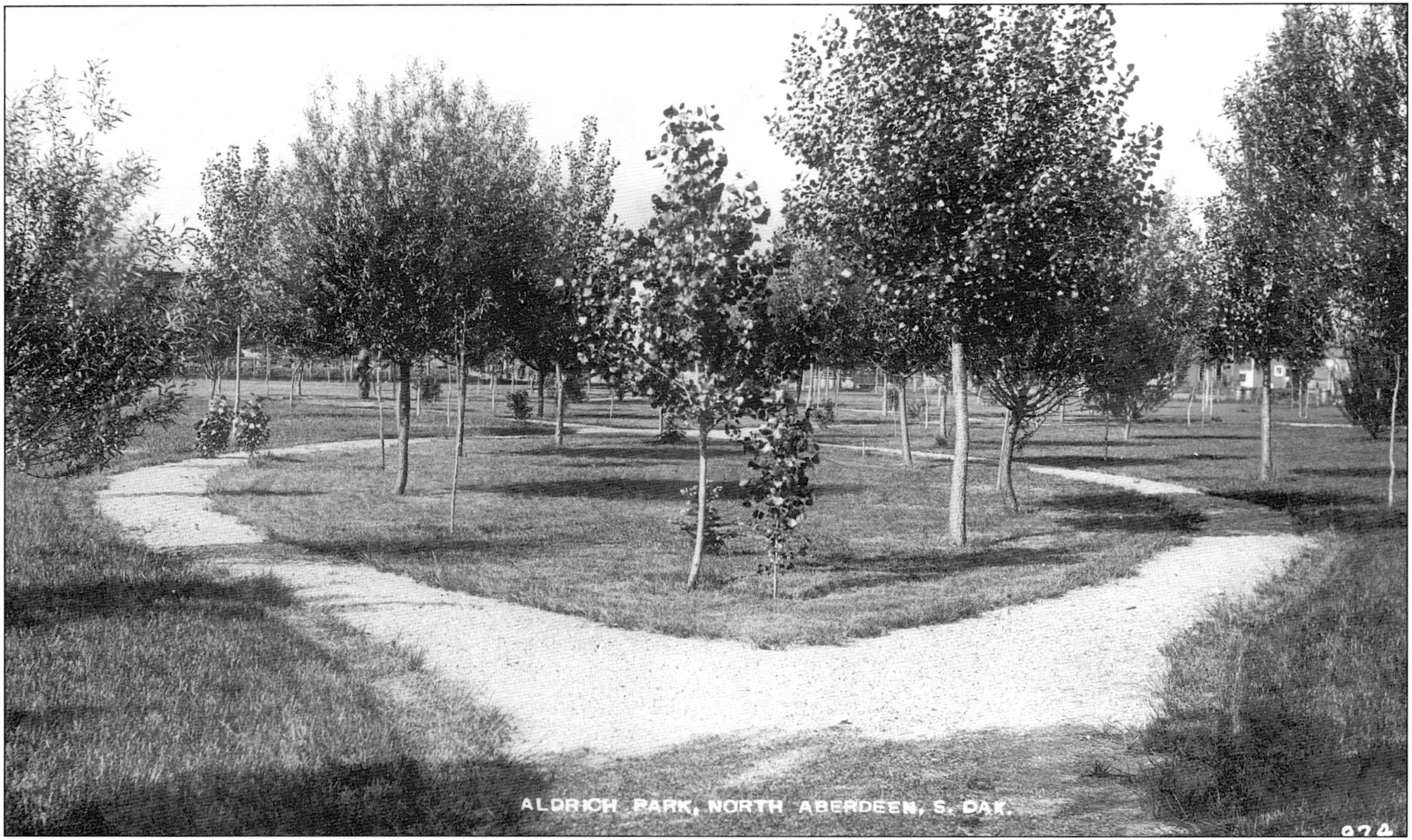

This is another view of Aldrich park. A monument was erected here in 1935 to Maud & Kate, the two mules who had worked for the city for 31 years. I am not aware of any other monuments to mules in existence.

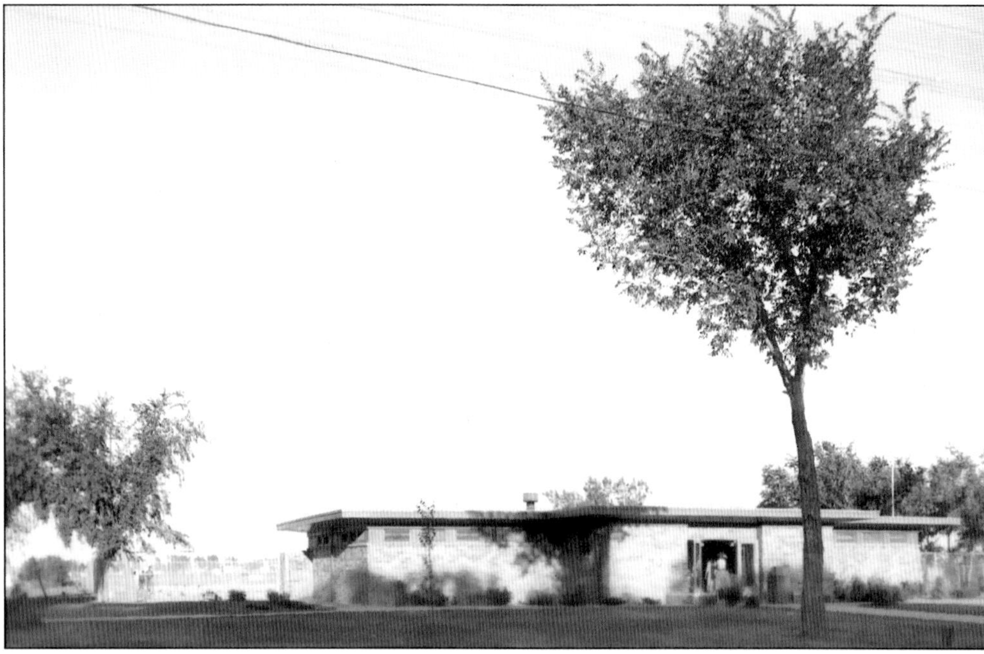

Two views of the Municipal Swimming Pool at 1209 South Dakota Street. It was built in 1957 and is still in use. It is now commonly known as the South Side Pool, since the opening of the pool at the Holgate School. The bottom picture shows the three diving boards that were later removed for insurance liability reasons. The pool is still a fun place on hot days.

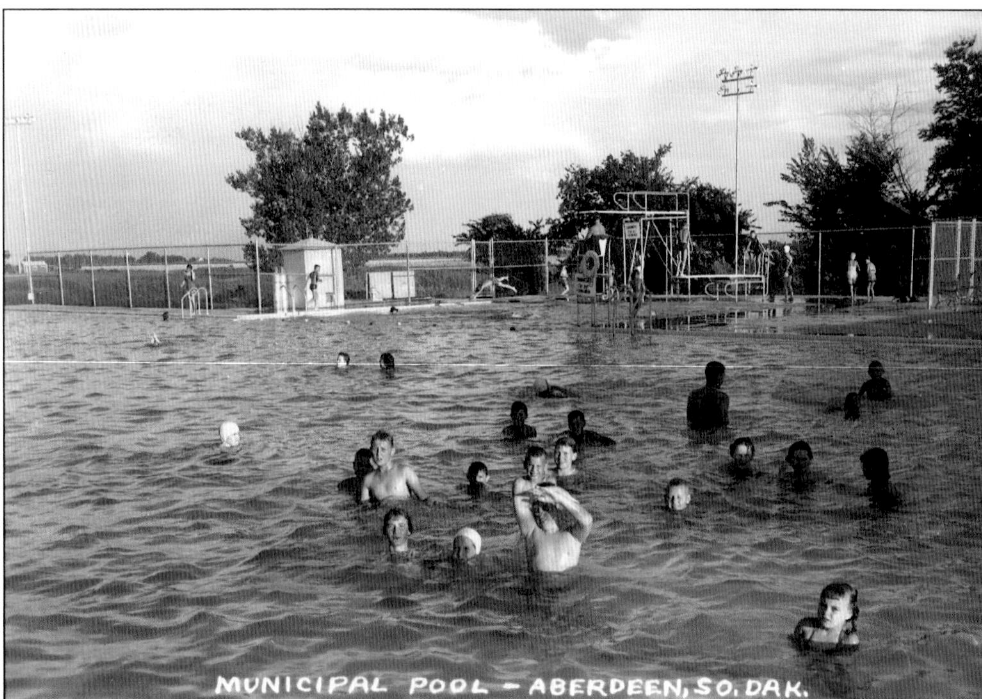

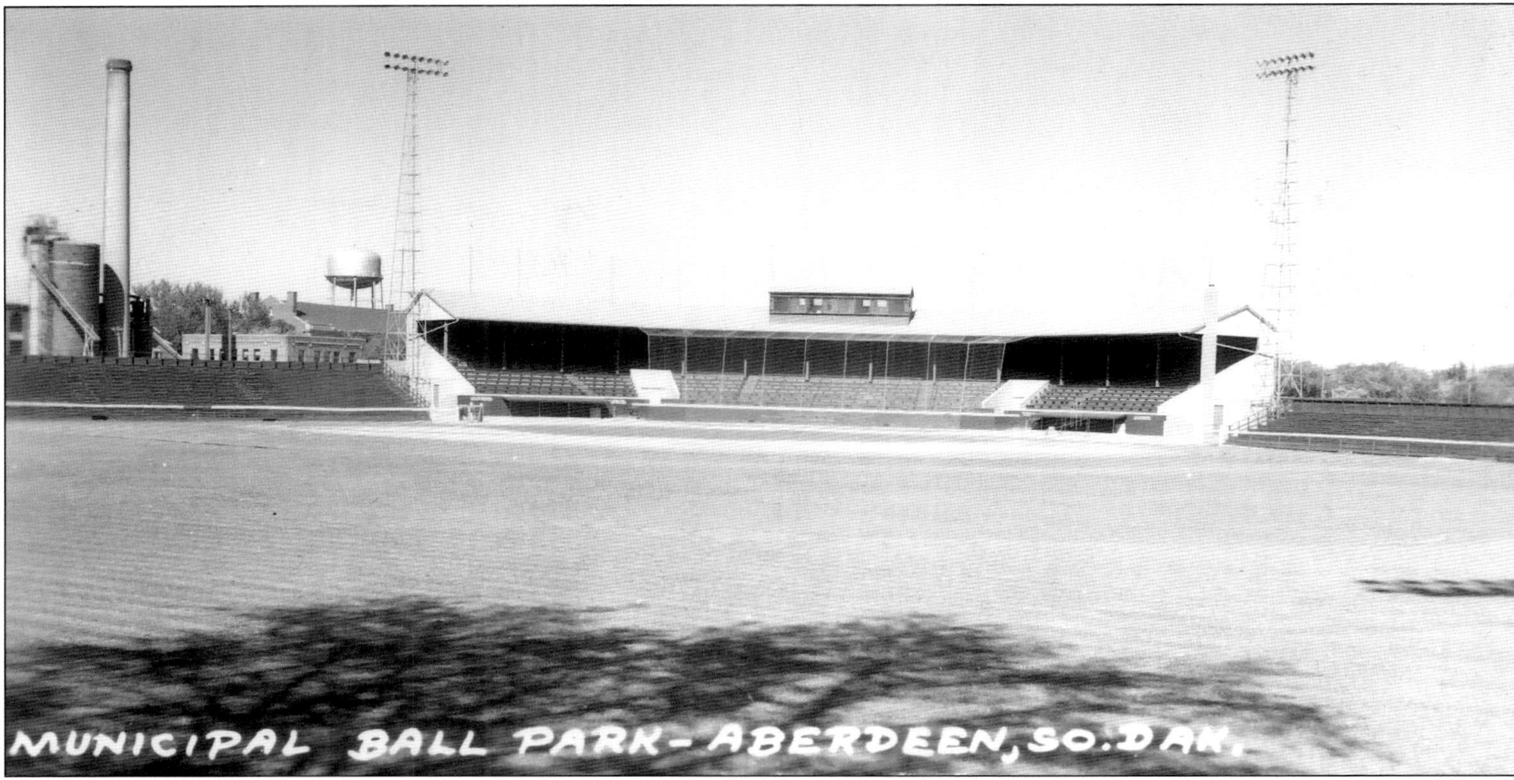

Aberdeen has always had baseball, beginning with the Aberdeen Baseball Association of the 1880s where L. Frank Baum, author of *The Wizard of Oz* was involved, to the semi-pro teams of the 1920s and 1930s when Hall of Famer Al Simmons played here, to Abe Pred's teams of the 1940s and 1950s, then the American Legion Smitties baseball where the 1965 World Series of Legion was played in Aberdeen. From 1947 to 1971, Aberdeen had the Pheasants, a minor league team originally a farm team for the St. Louis Browns who became the Baltimore Orioles. Cal Ripken Jr. was a bat boy in 1964, the same year his father, Cal Ripken Sr. was manager and Hall of Famer Jim Palmer was a pitcher. Lou Piniella was on that same team. The first stadium burned down in 1951, and was quickly replaced with this stadium, which was demolished to make room for the Barnett Center at Northern State University.

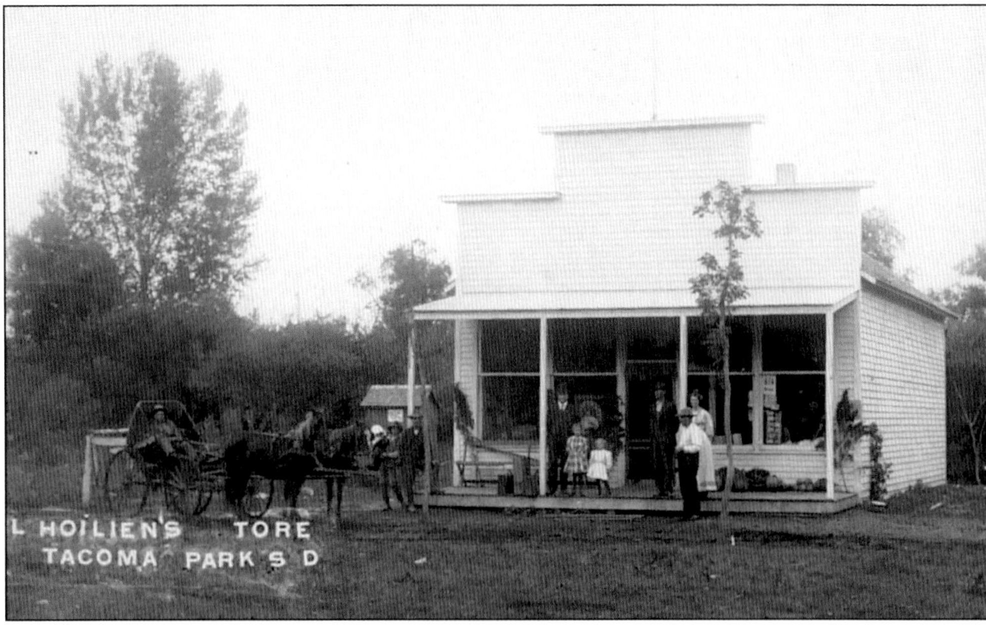

The trains from Aberdeen made frequent 12-mile round trips to Tacoma Park. It was about 16 miles by automobile. Tacoma Park was a summer resort town with lines of small cabins on both sides of the river. They even had a post office from 1914 to 1951. This is a *c.* 1915 picture of Hoilien's Store.

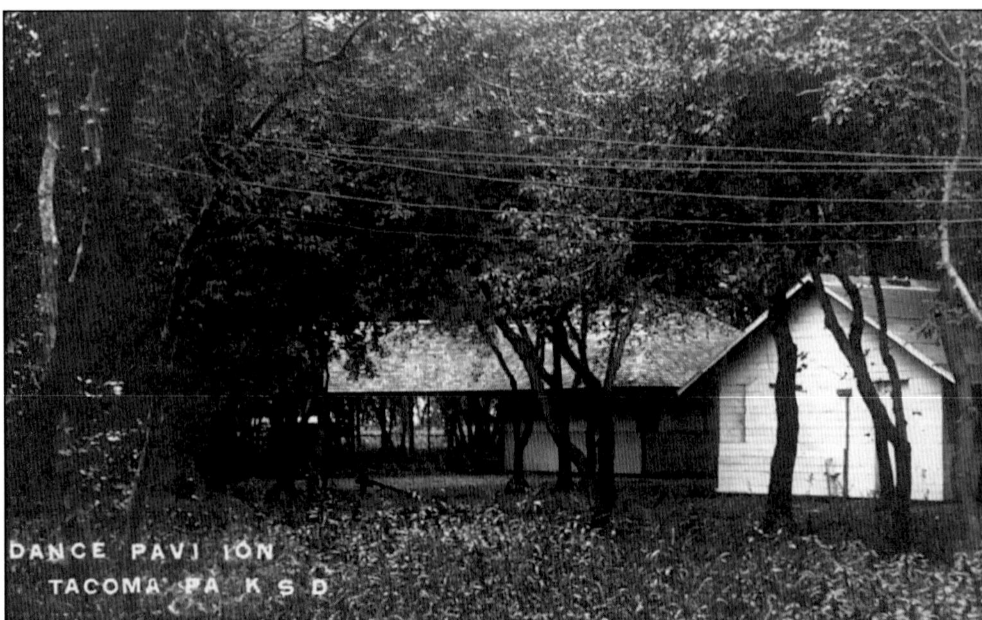

Tacoma Park and live dancing music went hand-in-hand from the early 1900s until the 1960s. The other dance pavilions in the area were the Richmond Lake Ballroom, Wylie Park, atop the Citizens Building for awhile, and the Ward Hotel Ballroom.

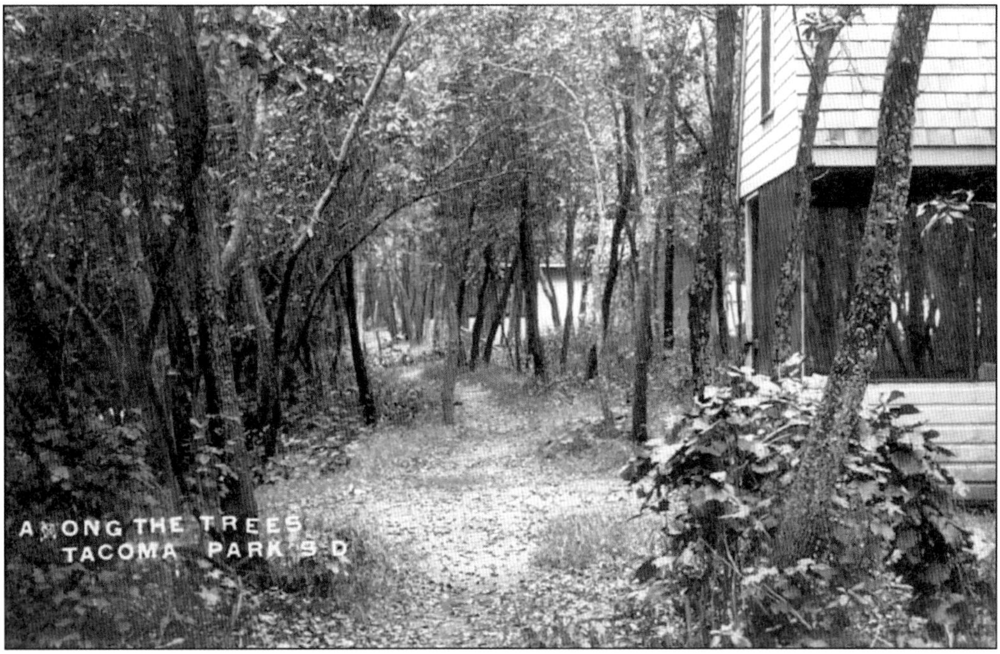

Tacoma Park had a lot of summer cabins in an area that had more trees than the rest of the county. Richmond Lake and Mina Lake were not developed as of yet.

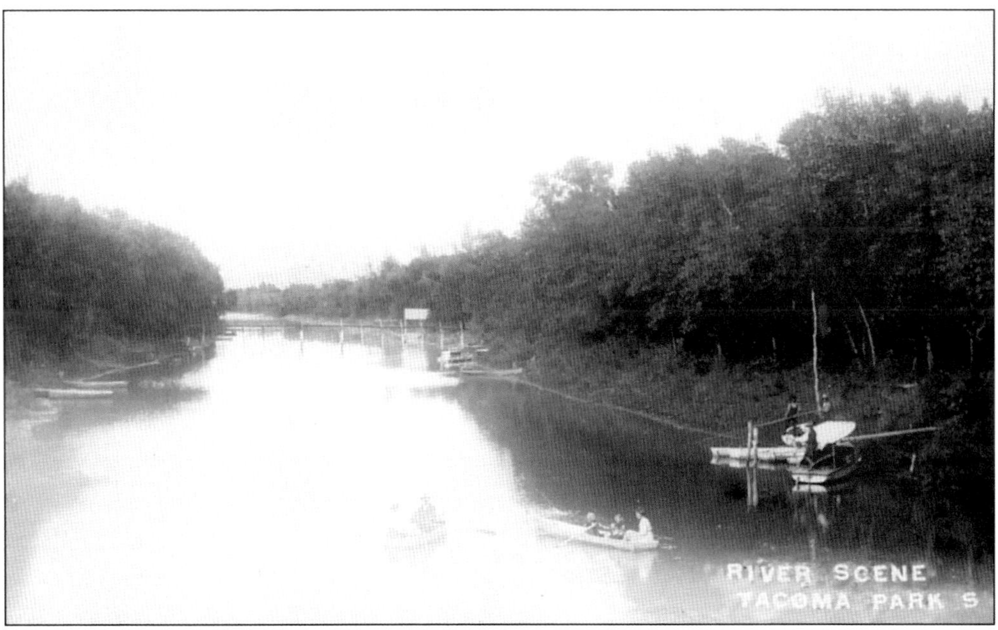

Fishing has always been good along this part of the James River that goes through Tacoma Park. All of the current maps show this as the James River even though it has never been legally changed from the Dakota River, the name it was given by the U.S. Government in the 1860s.

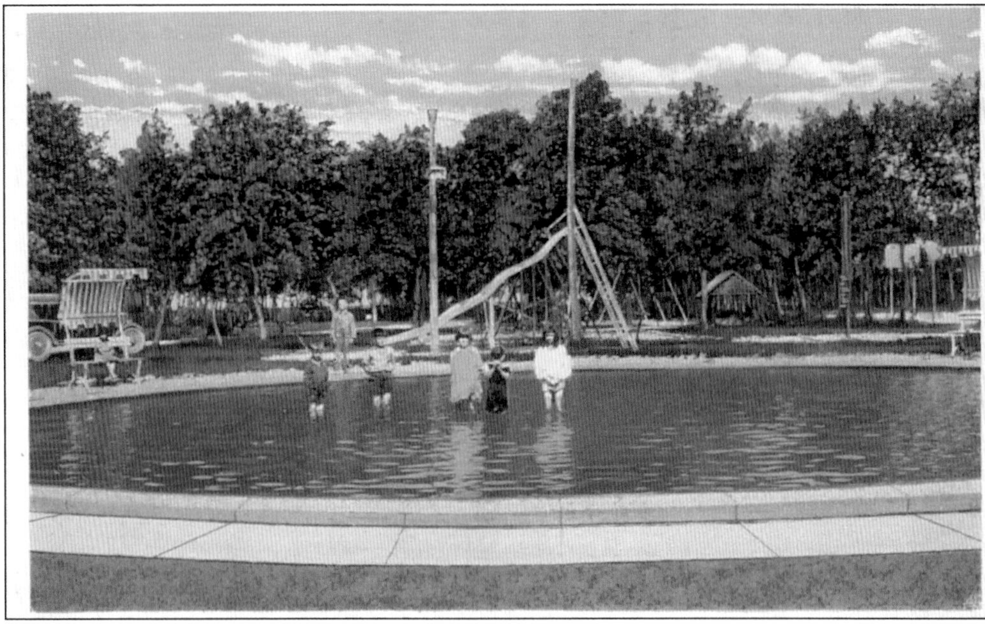

This is the kid's swimming pool at Melgaard Park. It has been one big sand box for years now. Andrew Melgaard donated this land for the park in 1909, when there was nothing south of Twelfth Avenue except the college and the Simmons House. It was used a great deal, but now all of the screened buildings and most of the picnic facilities are gone.

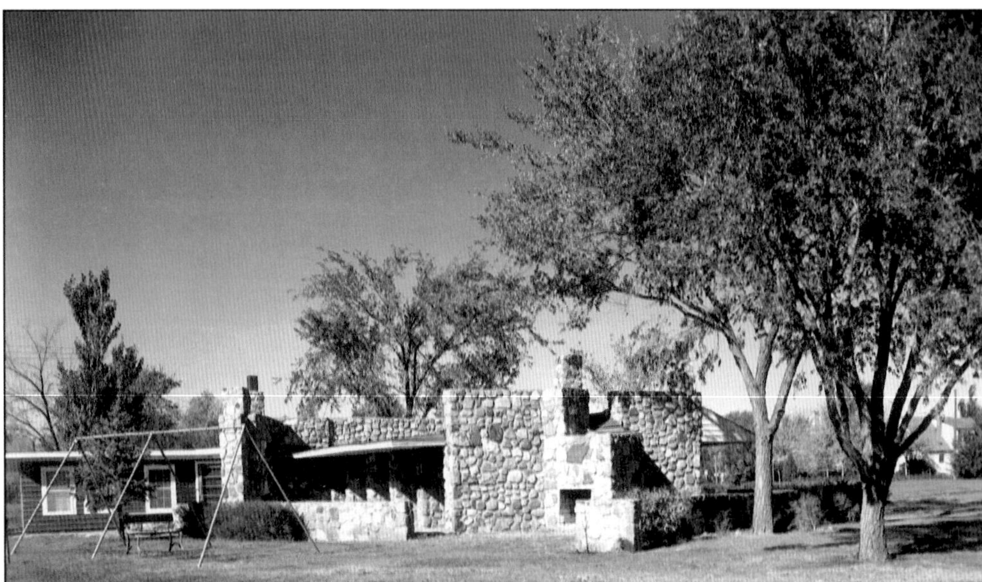

The park was named in honor of Sophus H. Anderson, Aberdeen's superintendent of city parks from 1916 until his death in 1945. He lived in the house in Melgaard Park all that time. Anderson Recreation Park was erected in 1938 and was a W.P.A. project. It was frequently used during the winter as a warming building for ice skaters on the Bog. It has been greatly expanded and serves various senior citizen activities and the senior nutritional programs.

Seven

Railroads of the Hub City

Aberdeen owes a lot to its railroads. We were a railroad town. There were so many tracks coming in and out of town in many different directions that it looked like spokes of a wheel with Aberdeen at the hub. Consequently our nickname as the "Hub City," was started in Dakota territorial times. This chapter shows some of the highlights of early railroading in Aberdeen. But we must never forget the hundreds or even thousands of Aberdonians whose lives depended on the railroads; not only the railroad employees, but also the hotels, the restaurants, and the businesses in the wholesale district. Aberdeen was a railroad town, and proud of it.

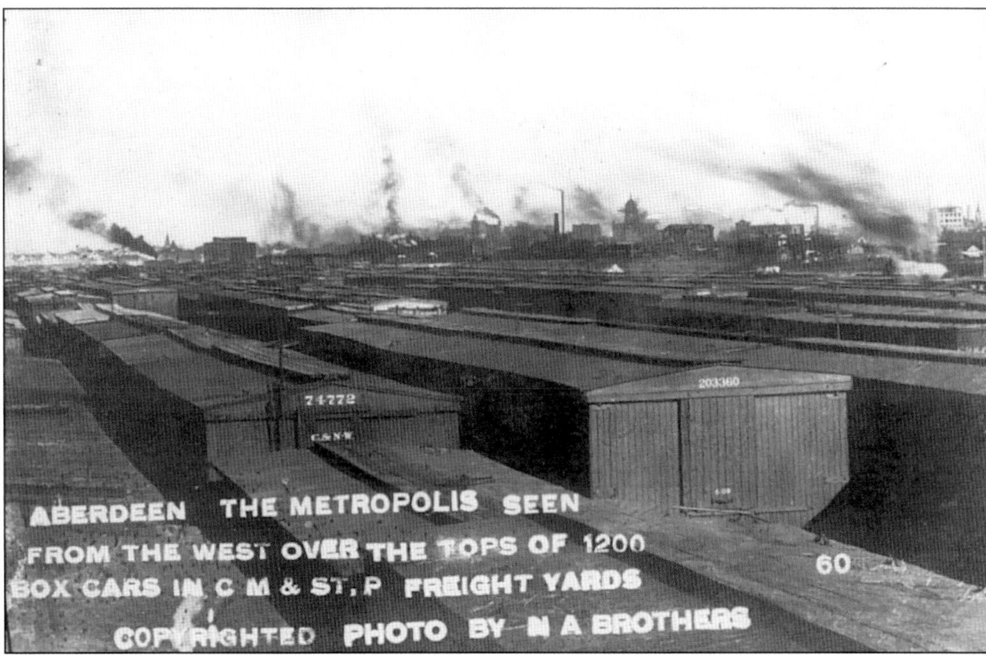

The Chicago Milwaukee & St. Paul Railroad built a freight yard in 1907 to relieve the congestion near the main depot. The yard was located one mile east of the city, and its six sets of tracks, if spread end to end, would run for three miles. This expanded freight area could accommodate up to 400 cars at one time. When the railroad bridge was completed over the Missouri River in 1907, train routes from Chicago to Tacoma, Washington, became possible.

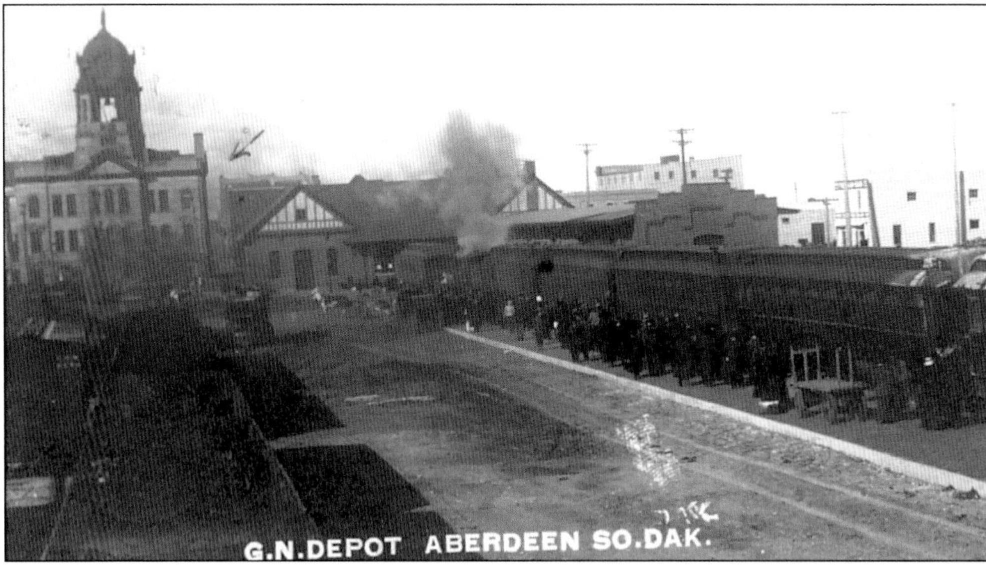

This postcard is dated November 13, 1909. The arrow pointing to the courthouse indicates the place where Emil Victor, a drifter, age 19, was hung for murder at 8:00 a.m., November 16, 1909. The message states that they were building the scaffold on the north side of the courthouse at this time. Victor had brutally murdered four people near Stratford in a robbery attempt that had gone bad. This was the first and only public execution in Aberdeen.

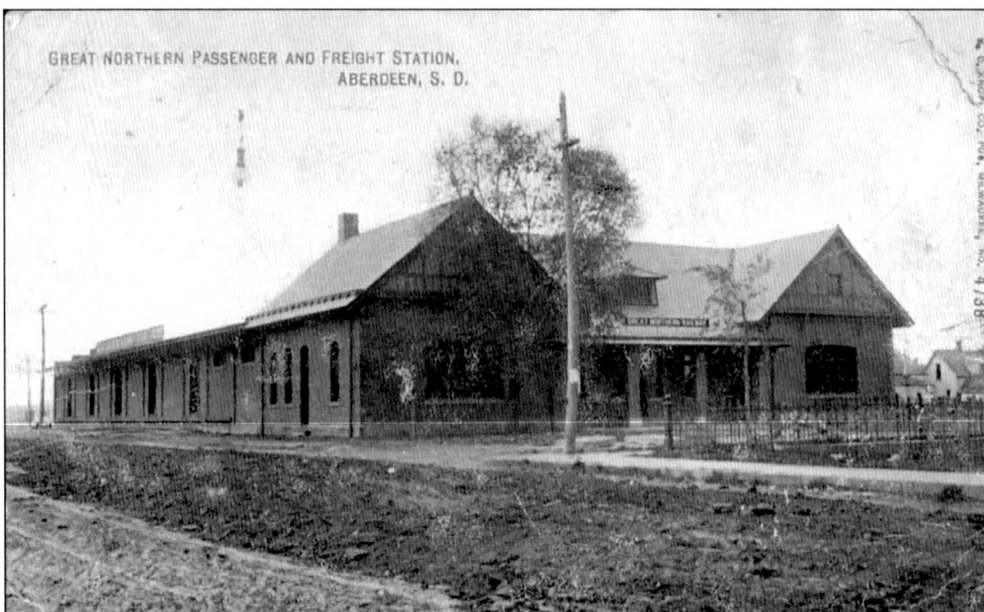

This structure was completed in 1907 for the Great Northern Railroad. Many Aberdonians boarded Great Northern trains bound for Tacoma Park, a popular resort area northeast of Aberdeen. A ticket on that route cost 50 cents and the ride lasted about 30 minutes. The Great Northern ran two passenger and two freight trains through Aberdeen each day. This depot was sold in 1982 to a group of attorneys who renovated it to house their offices.

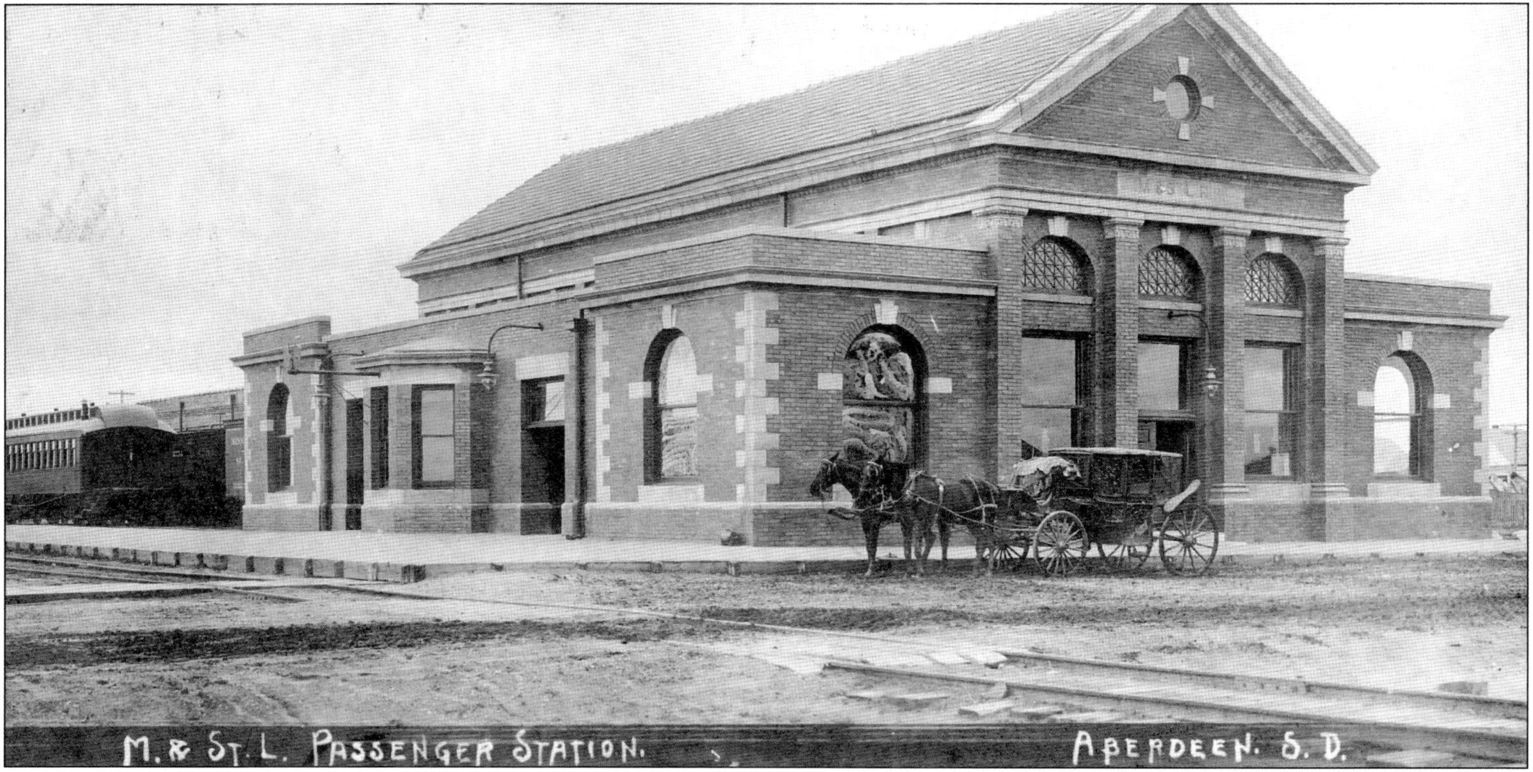

The Minneapolis & St. Louis Railroad was the last railroad to reach Aberdeen, arriving in 1906. The line serviced an area from Watertown to Leola, and later to the Long Lake area north of Leola, carrying both passengers and freight. Until this time, a daily stagecoach had gone between Aberdeen and Leola, the last stagecoach still used in this area. This railroad depot was constructed in 1907 on the southern end of Aberdeen's Main Street at Eleventh Avenue, well away from the hub of the city. The fare on this new train was two cents per mile. This depot was sold in 1960 when the Chicago Northwestern Railroad purchased the Minneapolis & St. Louis Railroad and maintained only freight service to the communities formerly served by the rail company. In the 1960s and 1970s, it was converted into a bar widely known as the Depot Club. In the late 1980s, it was purchased by Randy Grote and several businesses are located there.

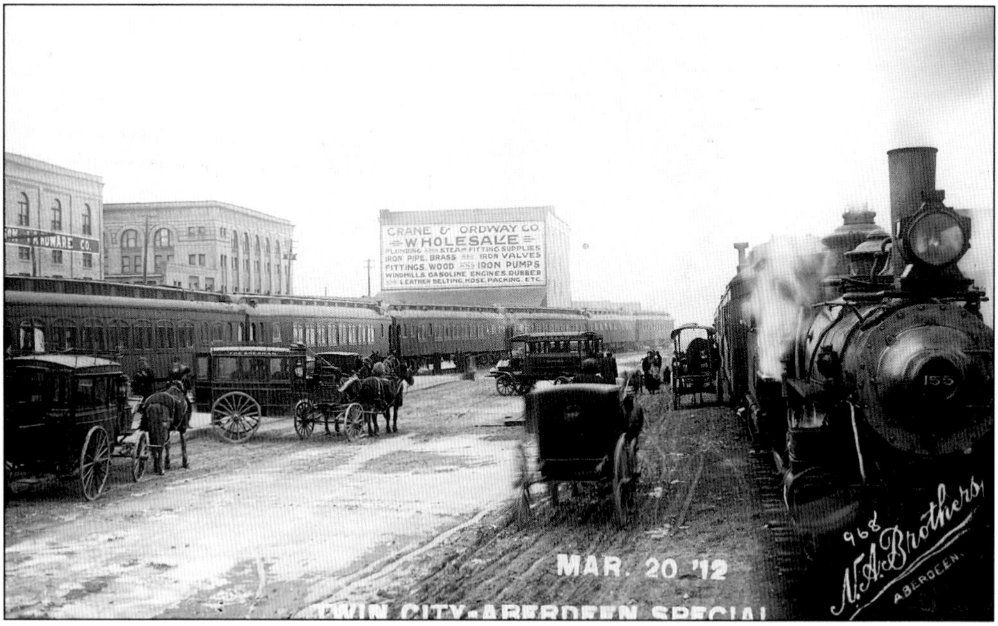

This Milwaukee Railroad Twin City—Aberdeen Special passenger train is shown in the wholesale district that developed east of the Depot. Coaches would meet these trains to transport passengers back to local hotels. Shown in this picture is a coach from the Sherman Hotel.

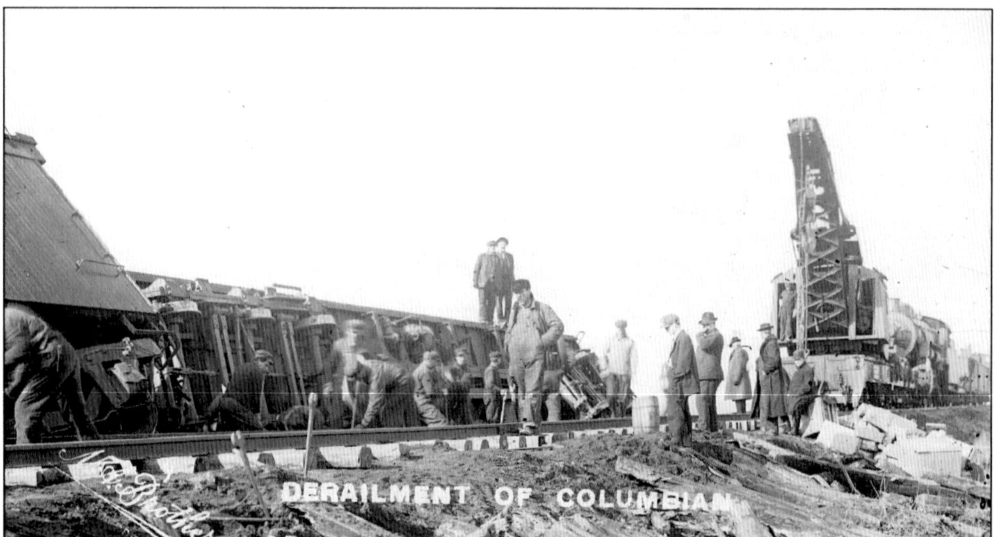

Thirteen passenger trains arrived and as many departed Aberdeen's Chicago, Milwaukee and St. Paul Depot in the early years of the 20th century, one of which was the Columbian. On April 12, 1913, the eastbound Columbian was derailed at the Minneapolis & St. Louis crossing west of Aberdeen. As a result of the wreck, two cars of fresh fish, the baggage, the express, and mail cars overturned into the ditch. The engine and passenger cars remained on the track, so there was no loss of life in the accident. The train eventually pulled into Aberdeen nearly 12 hours later than scheduled.

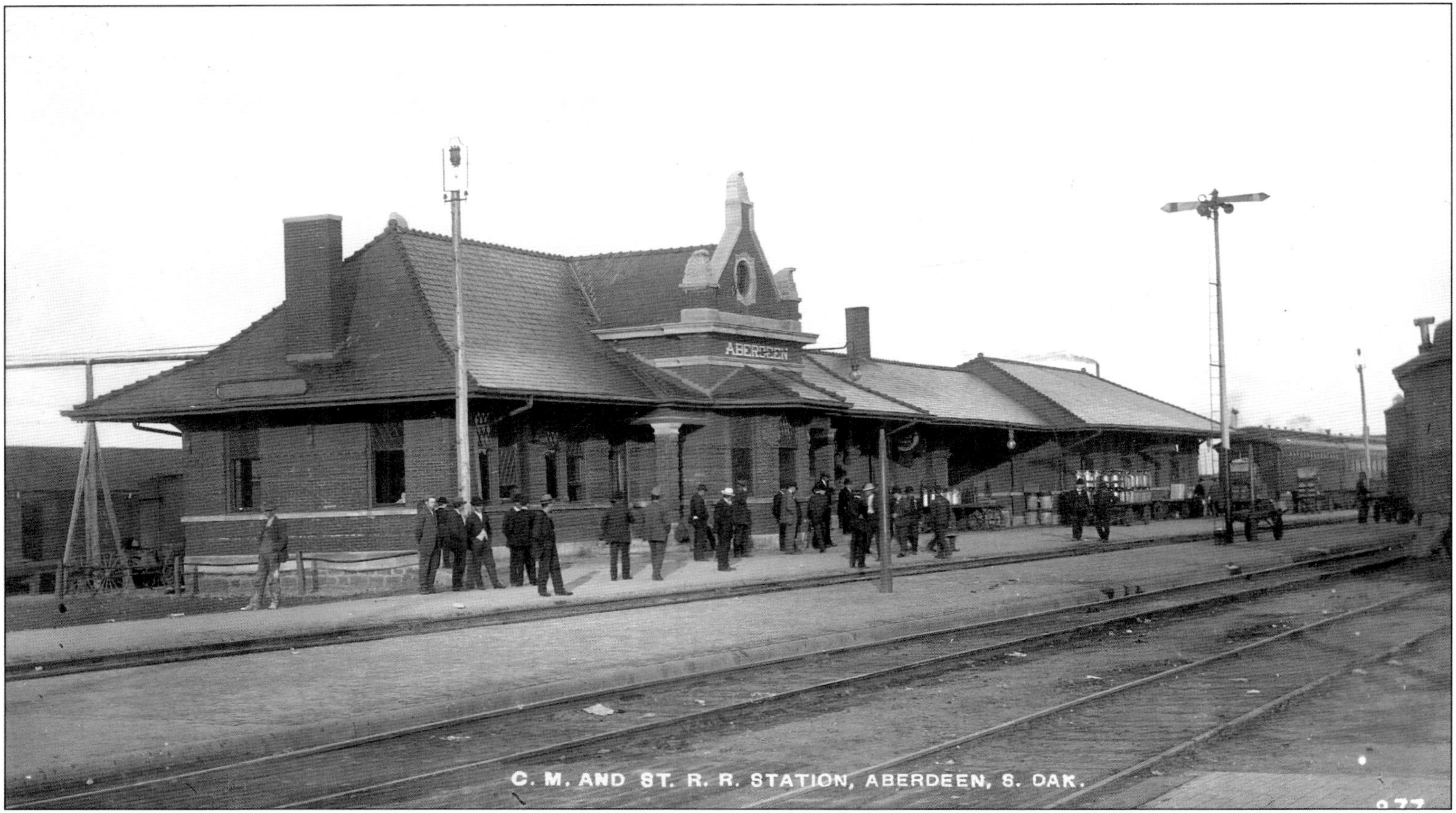

This brick and stone depot was built for the Milwaukee Railroad in 1904 for $35,000 to replace its wood frame depot, which the line had outgrown. The building was 182 feet in length and housed a ticket office, kitchen, pantry, lunchroom, toilets, and two large waiting rooms (one for men, one for women). Space in this depot was devoted entirely to passenger services. The offices were housed in the old depot that had been moved to the new rail yard and remodeled as part of the 1904 construction project.

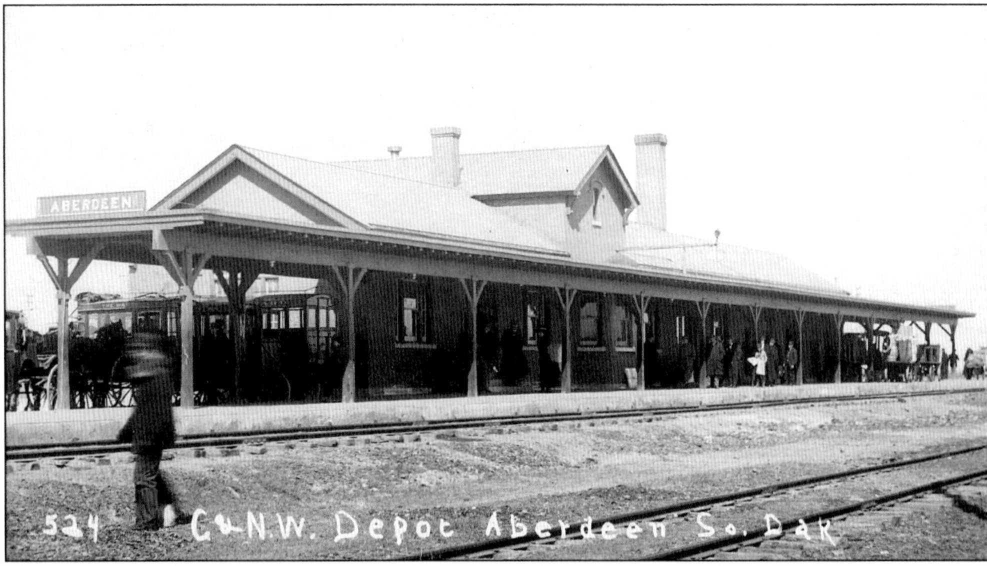

This depot was completed for the Chicago Northwestern Railroad in October of 1910 and replaced the lines small depot that was moved to Crandon, South Dakota. The canopy of this new depot was 250 feet long and 10 feet wide and sheltered a block-long brick platform. This depot welcomed President Taft's special train on Monday, October 23, 1911. In 1937, another presidential train arrived at the C.N.W. depot carrying President Franklin Roosevelt in his private rail car, the "Pioneer." Roosevelt's train cars also included a diner, sleeping cars, a baggage car, and special cars for the Secret Service, the White House staff, and the press.

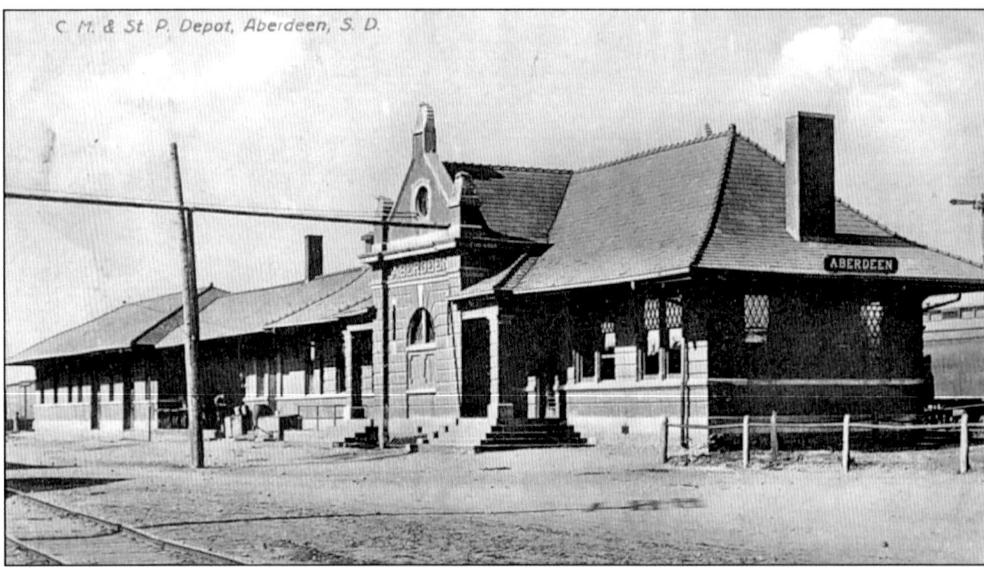

This is a southern view of Aberdeen's Chicago, Milwaukee, and St. Paul depot that opened to the public on February 2, 1904. There was no interruption in the services provided to travelers during the construction of this new depot as the old wood-frame depot was moved east to Main Street from this site and used until this structure was complete. After the new depot opened, the old depot was moved once again to a location southwest of the new depot and converted into office space for the railroad officials.

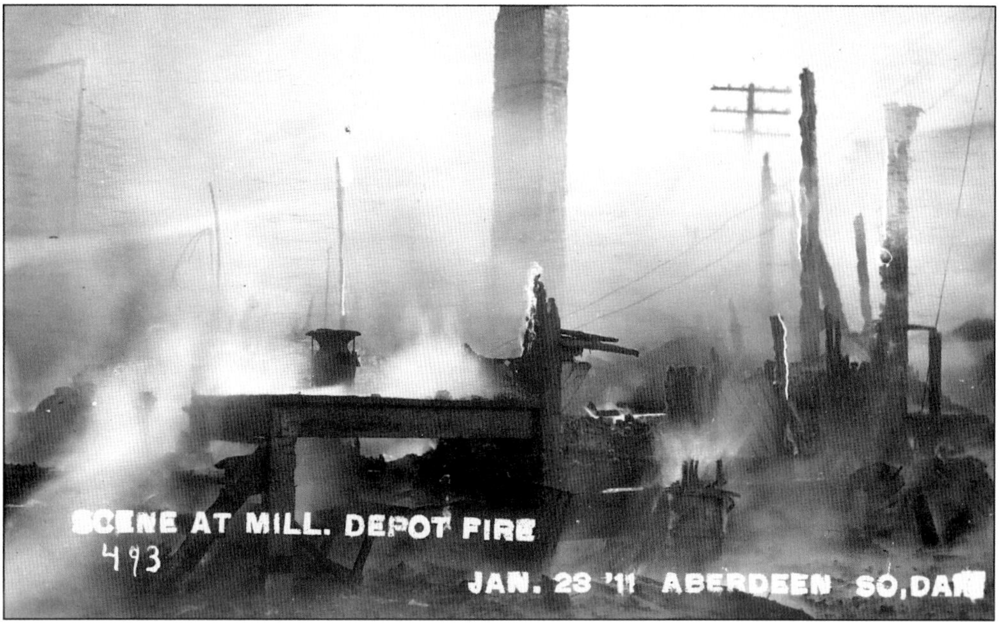

Disaster struck the Milwaukee Railroad on January 23, 1911, when fire destroyed its Aberdeen Depot. Oil stoves were being used in the 1904 depot building to provide extra heat in the dead of winter, and at 8:00 a.m. on January 23, one stove exploded in the freight house starting a fire that quickly spread to the main depot building. Losses due to this fire carried an estimated value of $250,000.

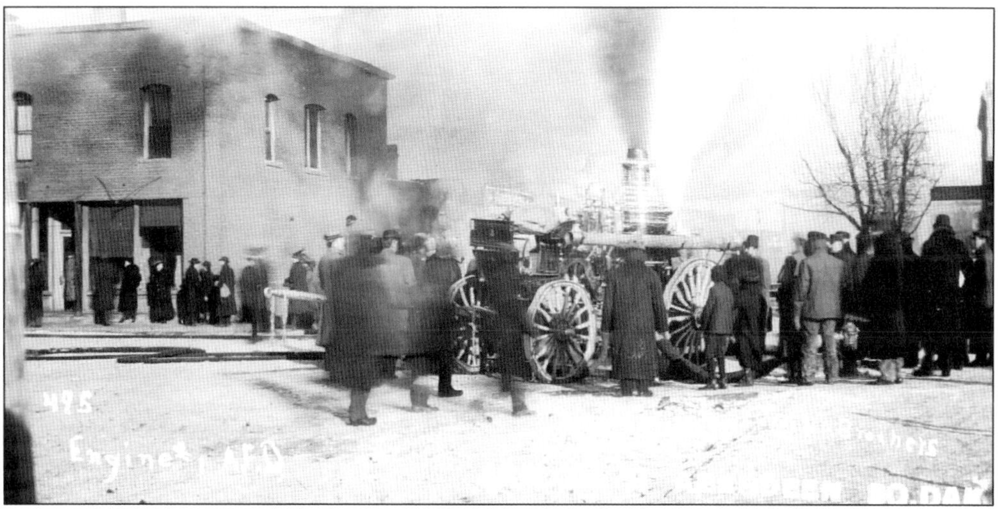

While firemen were working on the depot fire, another alarm sounded, this one at a furniture store on southwest Third Avenue. It was also on fire. One fire wagon was sent and an engine followed shortly after. Aberdeen's water supply proved to be insufficient to simultaneously fight two fires of such magnitude. At the Milwaukee fire, there was not adequate pressure for the running of two lines of hose, even with the engine working at its peak, which should have easily run three hoses wide open. The hydrant pressure at the depot fire would not throw a water stream farther than 15 feet. There was also not a ladder in the department long enough to reach the gable window of the depot.

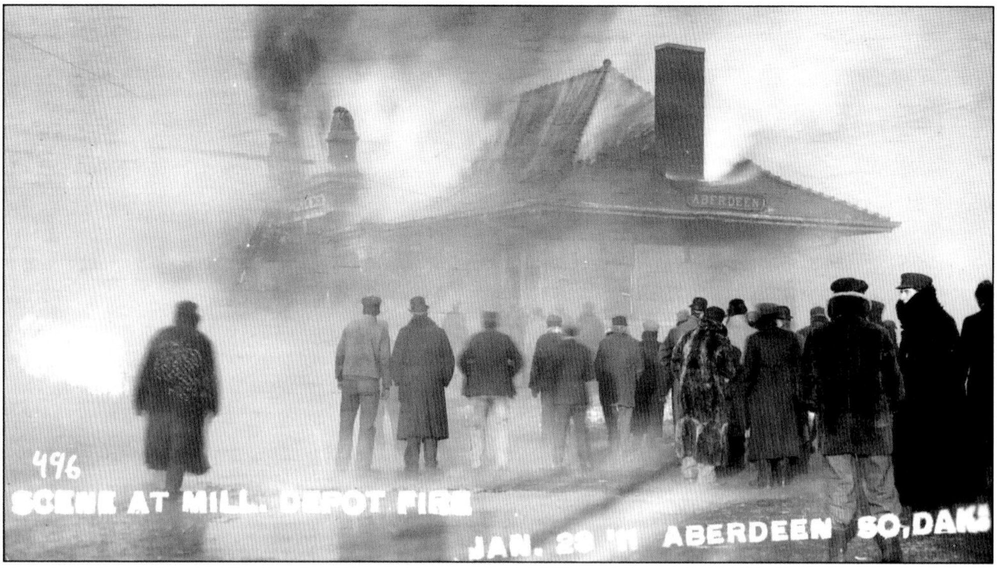

Shortly after the explosion of the oil stove in the freight house, the offices and the freight house were completely filed with dense smoke. Practically all the fixtures, office supplies, etc. were destroyed. One or two of the office men were able to save their typewriters. A claims clerk actually went back into the burning building to rescue his typewriter. He retrieved the machine but suffered severe burns on his face and hands in the process. Despite the fact that the freight house was almost completely destroyed, the small section that remained witnessed a flurry of activity after the fire as all the perishable freight was accepted and processed without a delay anywhere along the line.

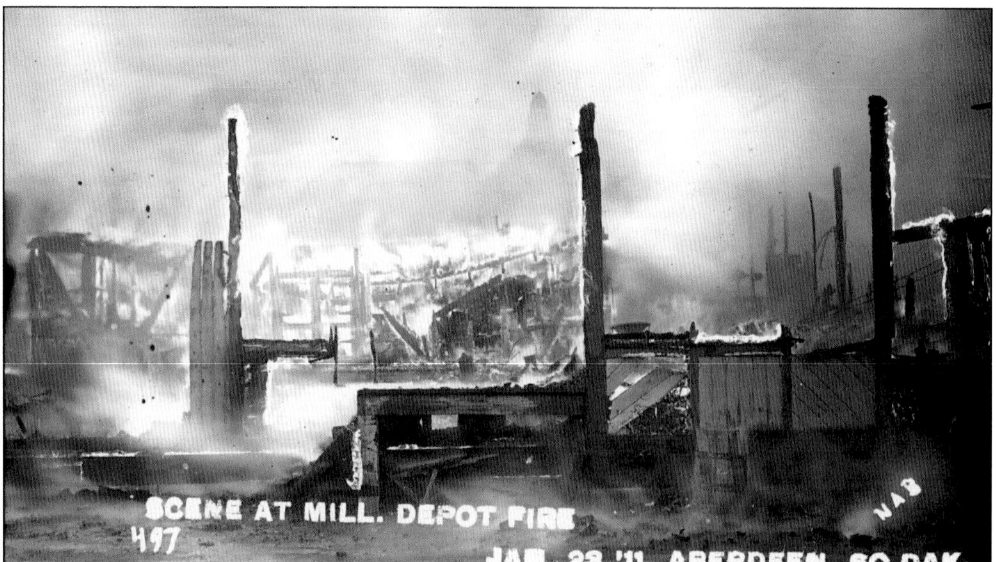

The flames in the freight house were extinguished, but not before sufficient heat traveled to the slate roof of the depot to ignite the interior woodwork. Within a very short time the roof of the depot building collapsed taking pieces of the surrounding brick walls with it. There was enough time before the walls themselves caved in to remove valuables from the depot and ticket office.

Railroad officials were quick to act once it became obvious their depot would be completely destroyed. Fifteen carloads of laborers were brought into the city at noon the day of the fire and by 6:00 p.m. that same day, six carloads of brick and other debris had been removed from the site. Lumber was ordered and delivered within an hour for a temporary ticket office and depot. Work on the frame structure began by noon on January 23 and was ready for use by noon the next day.

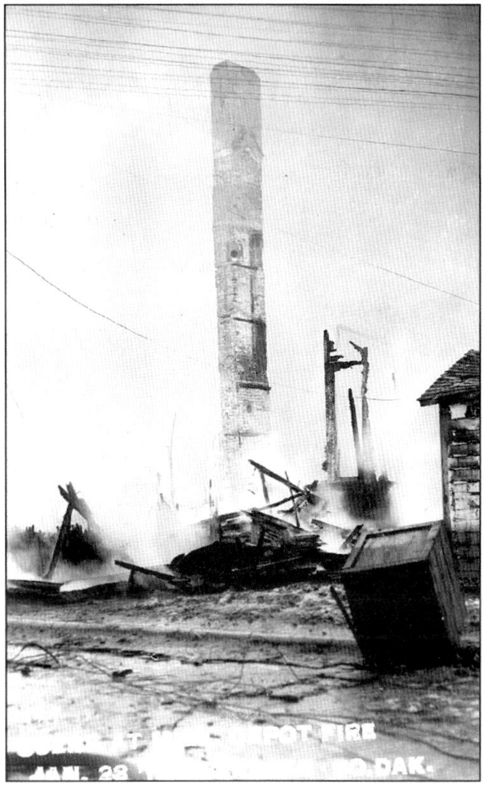

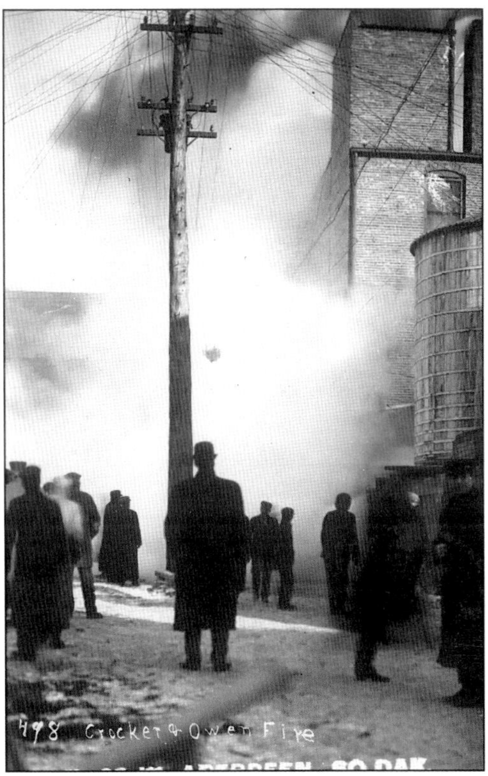

This is the scene at a second fire that broke out shortly after crews reached the Milwaukee Depot blaze. The Crocker & Owen Furniture Company fire was suspected to have started due to faulty wiring in the basement of the building. Firemen were able to save the building, but the stock, valued at $12,000, was heavily damaged by smoke and water. The business reopened shortly after the fire once the owners had a chance to travel east to replenish their stock and remove the charred debris from the building. After the two fires of January 23, 1911, fire chief Kingsley said of his crew: "The boys in the department certainly deserve a great deal of credit for the excellent work and daring they displayed, several of them risking their lives and working like wild men throughout the entire evening."

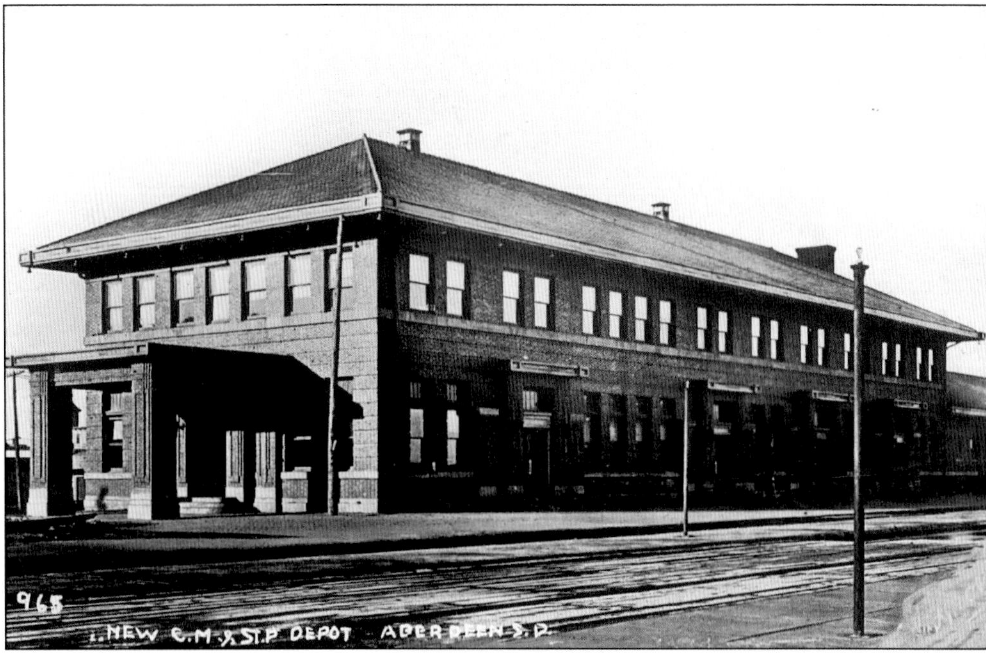

This new depot was built and in service to the public by December of 1911 to replace the depot destroyed by fire on January 23 of that same year! Building costs included $66,000 for the depot, $33,000 for the freight house, $45,000 for the roundhouse, and $24,000 for the coaling station. The two-story passenger station was billed as a semi-fireproof structure with concrete foundations and floors. The first floor contained the lobby, waiting room, ticket office, women's resting room, smoking room, newsstand, dining room, and kitchen, while the upstairs housed the offices.

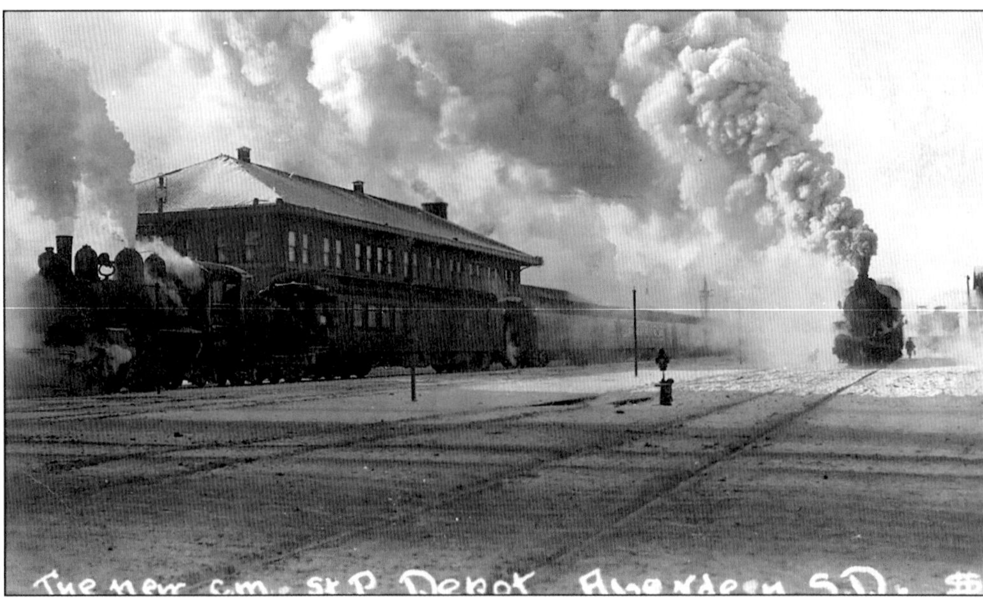

This is a picture of the same depot as above, but in the cold of winter as evidenced by all of the steam. This is dated February 1, 1912, just after it opened.

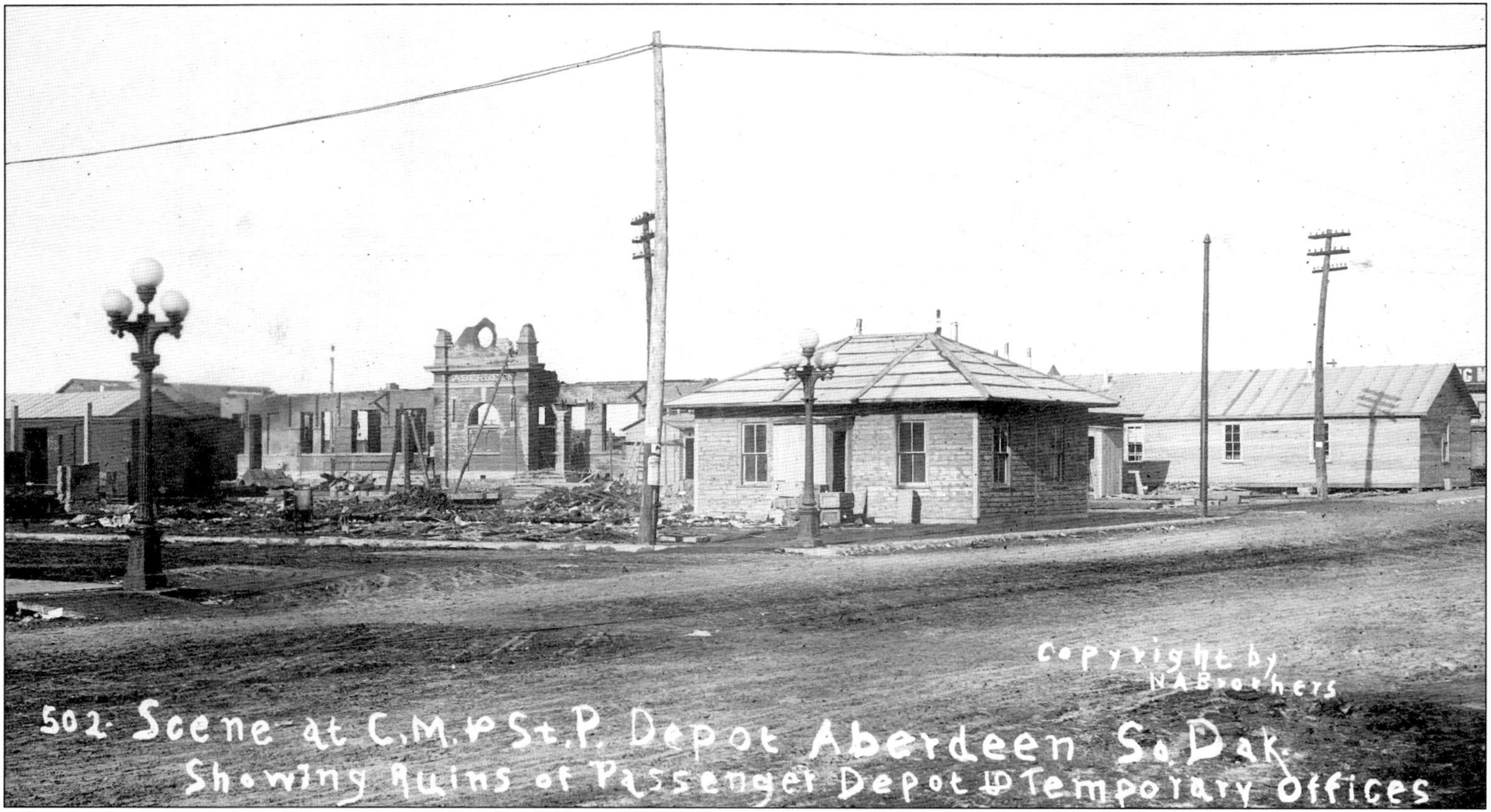

After the fire, temporary offices were set up in the Advance Thresher building at Railroad Avenue and Second Street. A temporary ticket office and passenger headquarters building was erected and in full service the day after the fire. The ticket counter was a door resting on a keg of nails and a set of desk drawers. The dispatcher's office was set up in a rail car that was fitted with the necessary wiring and parked on the siding opposite the Advance building. Section houses were brought in and located on the grounds near the old depot to be used as additional waiting room space.

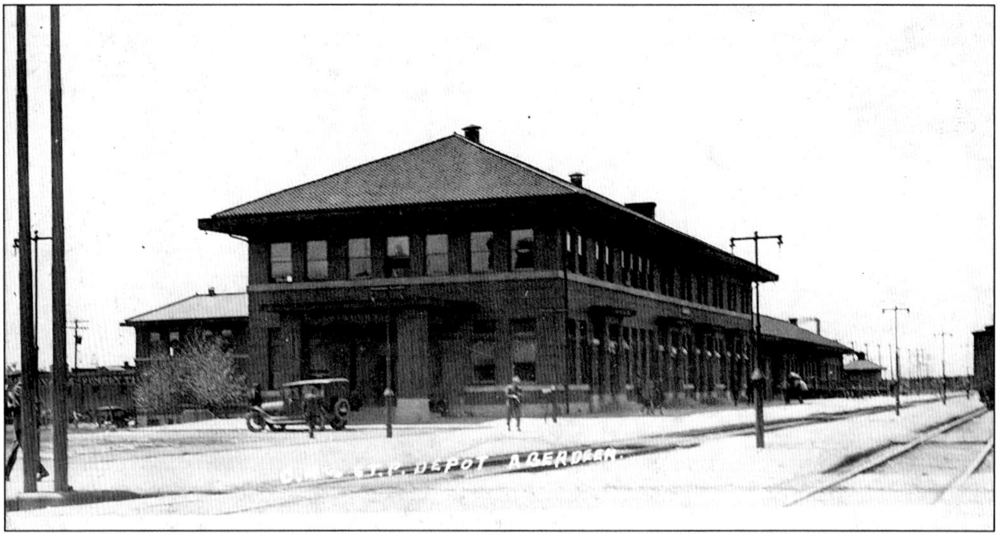

Aberdeen's Milwaukee depot also served as a mail sorting and distribution station. There were two 60-foot mail cars located on sidetracks that became the clearing center for all incoming South Dakota mail as well as all outgoing packages. During the holiday season, up to 700 bags of mail were processed daily at this depot by thirty full time postal employees and thirty college students hired for the season. It was not uncommon for all these employees to work 12 to 16 hour days to ensure mail was processed in a timely fashion. The cost of mailing a first class letter was 2 cents and a postcard was 1 cent, at this time.

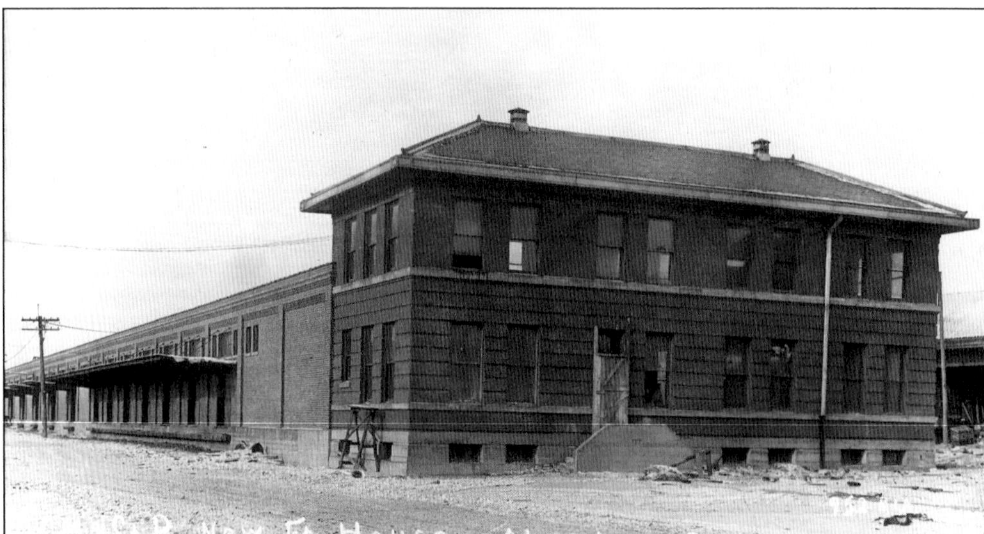

This large (24 foot x 66 foot) two-story freight house was built to the south of the passenger depot in 1911. It had a full basement that housed the company's fireproof vault. The freight agents had offices on the main floor while the clerical workers occupied the upstairs offices. A 28- by 400-foot warehouse with a 24- by 55-foot loading dock was added to this building. Tracks to the freight house were six deep and each had a 25-car capacity. Only one year after the completion of these new facilities, a 550-foot extension was added to the freight house platform to enable workers to service 150 cars simultaneously.

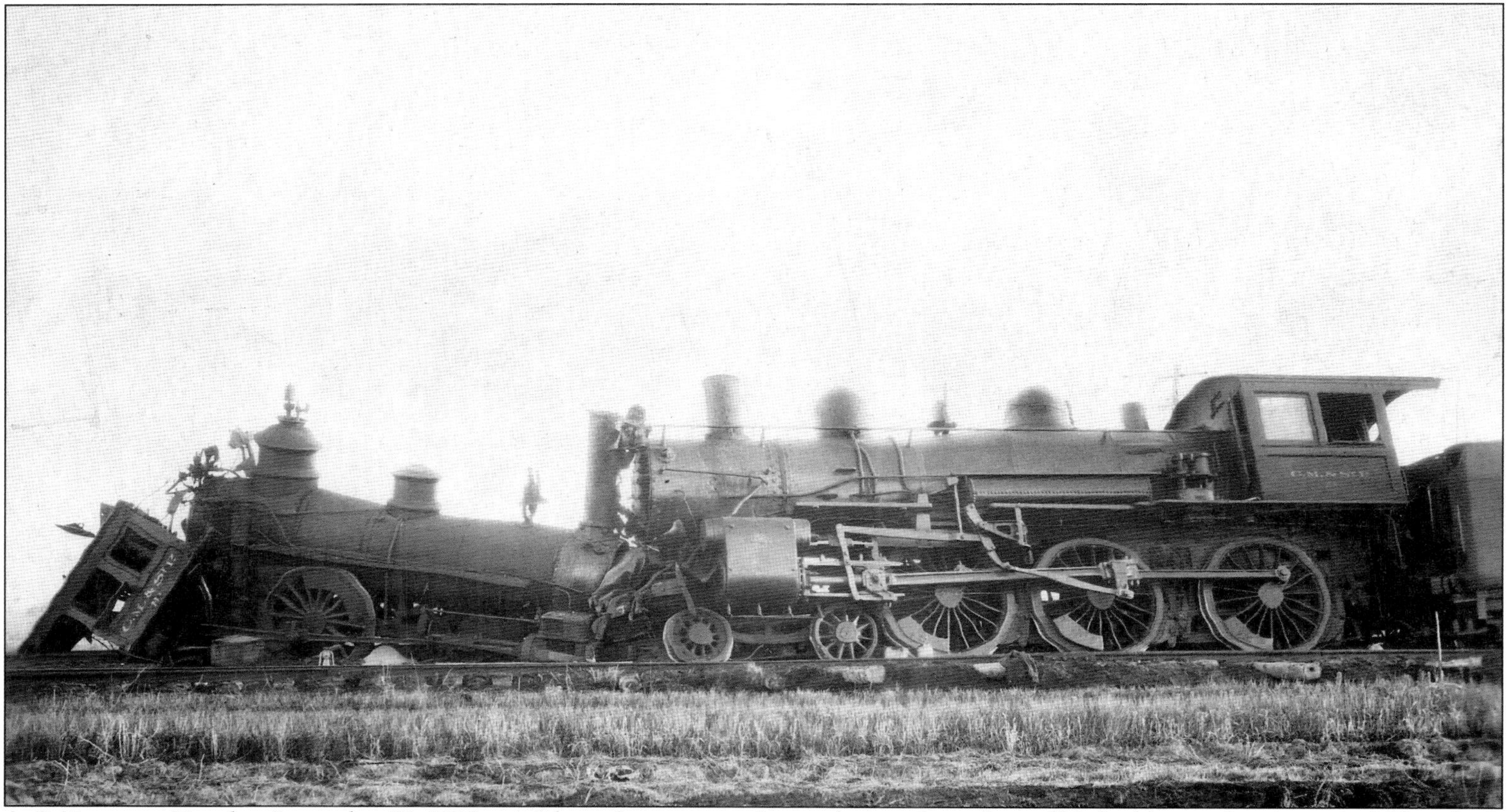

At 8:45 a.m. on Tuesday, September 27, 1910, a westbound passenger train running two hours late collided with a work train on the Milwaukee's main line near Bath, South Dakota. The work train (whose headlight had burned out) had come from Groton and missed the east switching station at Bath. Realizing the mistake, the engineer backed up and was stopped waiting for the switch to open when the passenger train struck. The engine of the work train tipped over, and the passenger train's engine was badly caved in. A temporary track was built around the wreckage and used until the main track was cleared late the following day. There were no fatalities in the pile up.

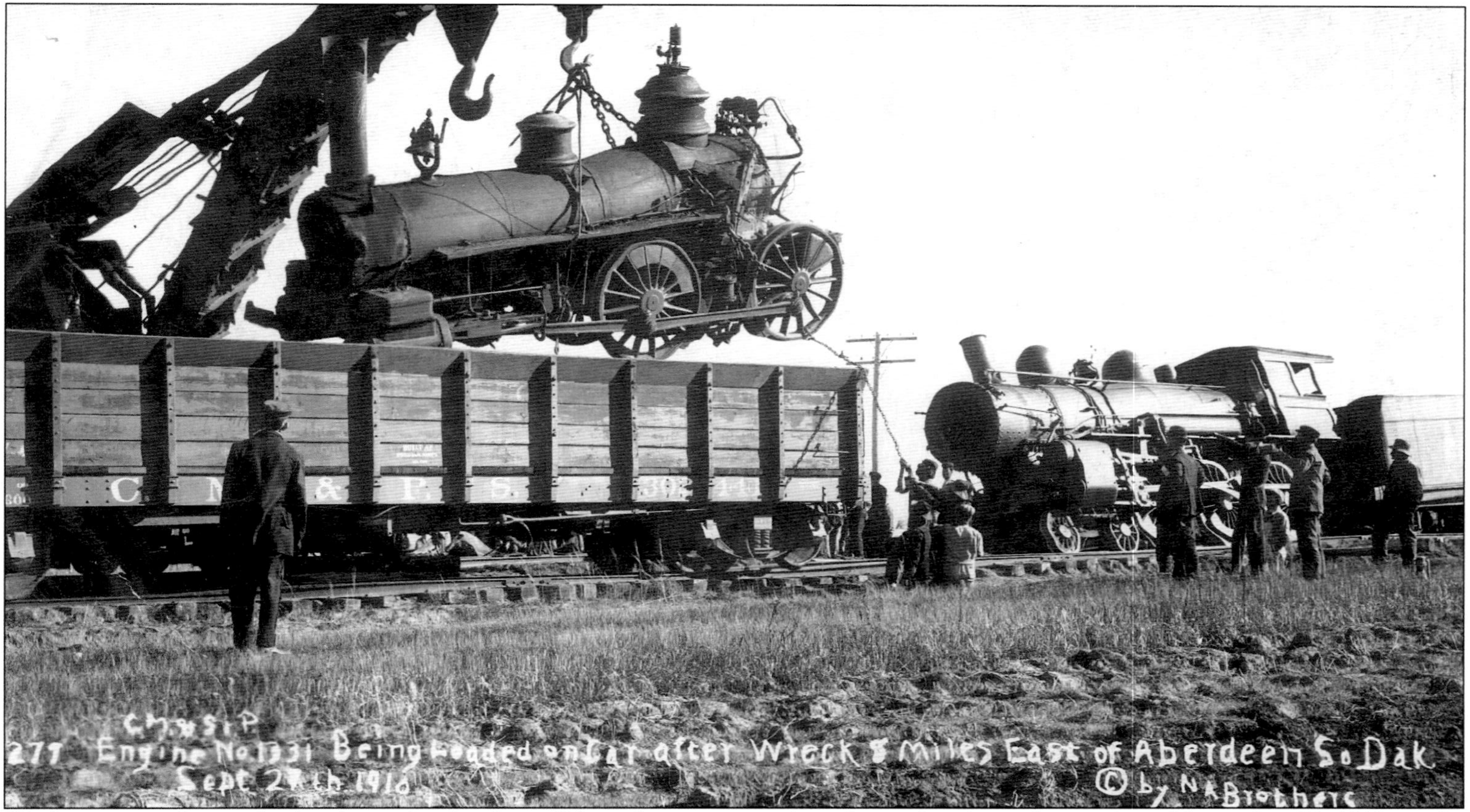

Work crews are shown clearing the tracks after the collision of a passenger train and a work train on the evening of September 27, 1910, on the Milwaukee's main line east of Aberdeen. Engine No. 1331 pulling the work train tipped over and was badly damaged. The light engine and load of the work train prevented a worse mishap because its caboose and cars broke loose upon impact. The engine crews of both trains jumped before impact, but not before the engineer of the passenger train set his emergency brakes. Two trainmen were rushed to St. Luke's Hospital in Aberdeen by Dr. Murdy who was called to the scene. Their injuries proved not to be life-threatening.

Eight

EVENTS

With healthy home town pride during its early days, many social and fraternal events were organized and held in Aberdeen. The Dakota Territorial Fair was held in Aberdeen, Dakota Territory, in 1889. In the early 1890s, the state fair was held here before the Inter-State Grain Palace was opened. Over the years many conventions were held and usually included parades. We have been entertained with good baseball teams, high school and college sporting events, the annual college Gypsy Day Parade and Shrine football game, the Shrine circus, and many carnivals.

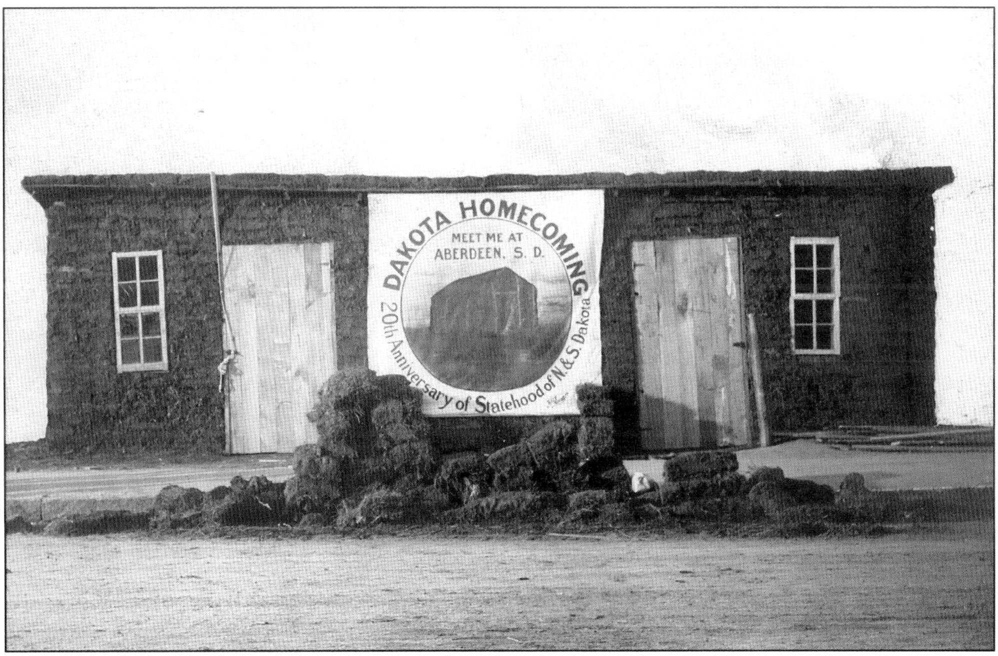

This representative "sod house" was built at the corner of Sixth Avenue and Main Street as the registration building for the 20th anniversary of statehood, which was held in Aberdeen from June 16th to the 18th, 1909. A special supplement to the *Aberdeen Newspaper* was issued that is probably the best recorded early history of Aberdeen.

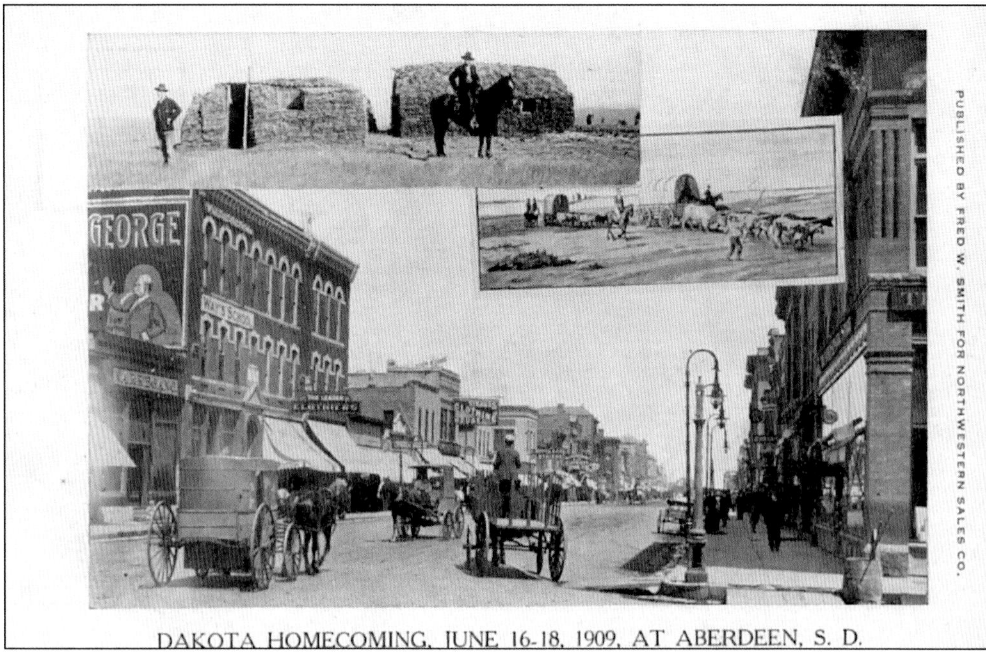

This postcard shows the changes to Aberdeen in its first 28 years of existence—from settlers arriving, then building the temporary sod houses, to the bustle of a thriving town on the prairie, complete with modern street lamps on Main Street.

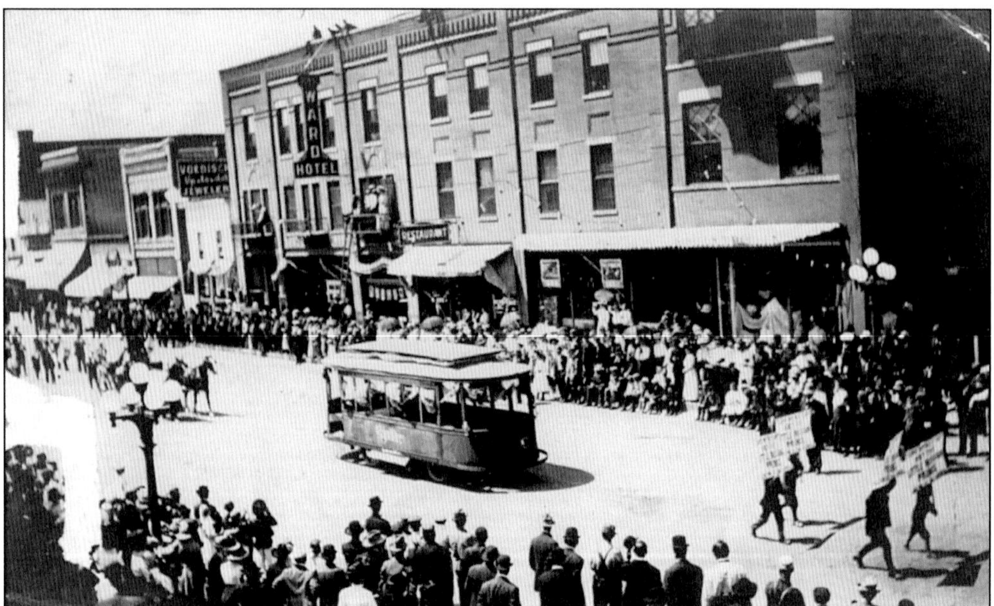

This real photo postcard postmarked on June 18, 1909, from Aberdeen was mailed just after the parade was held during the 20th anniversary parade.

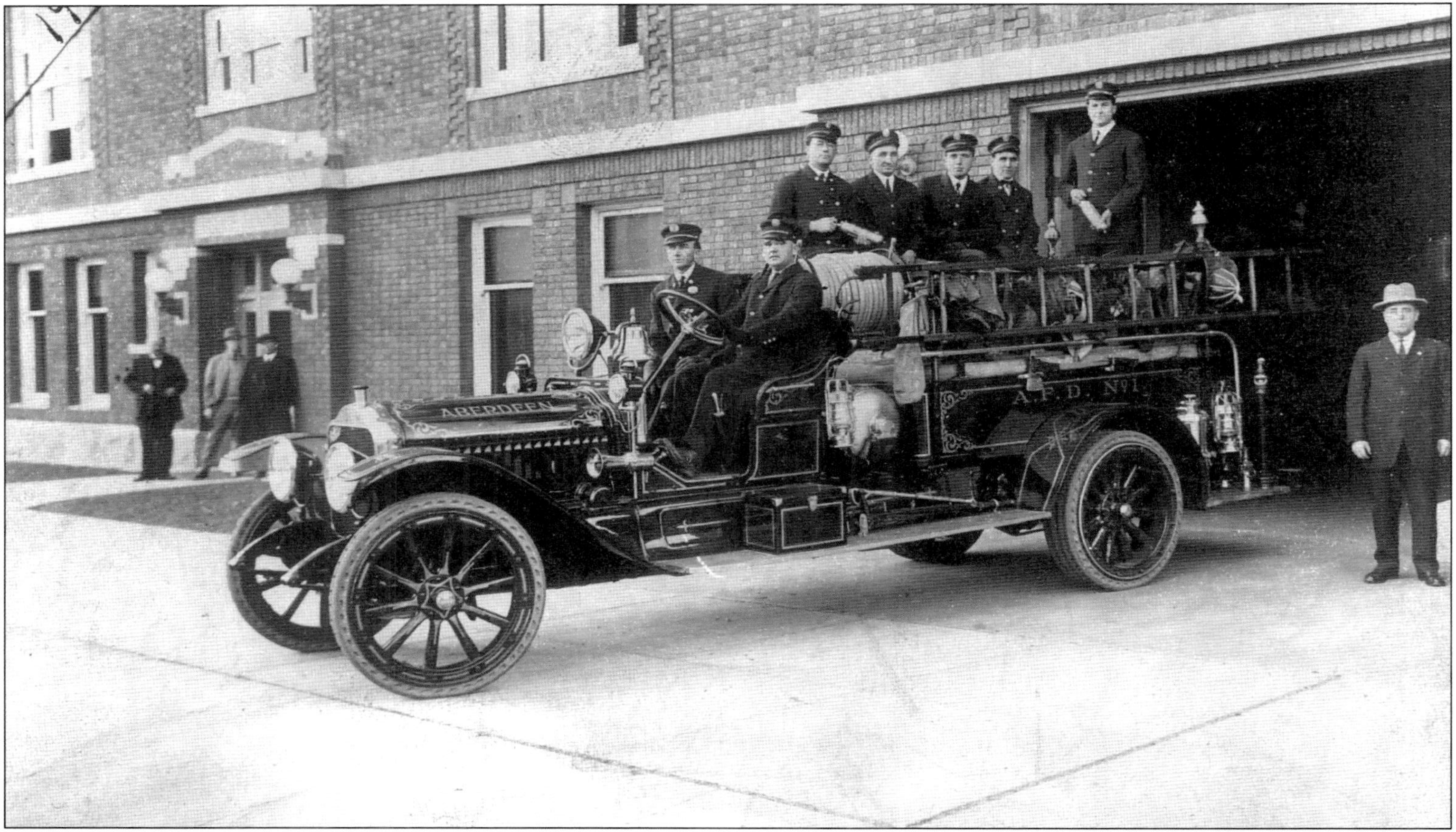

This is a 5- by 7-inch cabinet photo of Aberdeen's first non-horse drawn fire truck, dated 1914, taken in front of the fire department and the new municipal building that had just opened that year. At this time the city commissioner for fire and police was Elmer Rasmussen. The fire chief was E.I. Kingsley and there was a total of 11 Firemen.

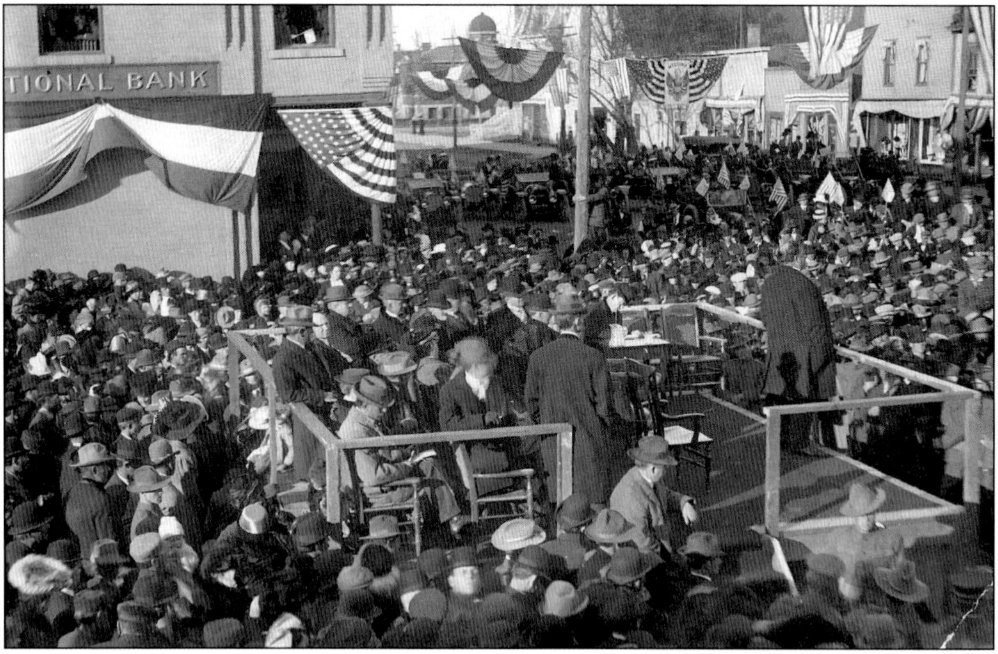

The big man on the right speaking to the crowd is President Taft during his visit to Aberdeen on October 23, 1911. There was a huge crowd and all the buildings are draped in banners and flags.

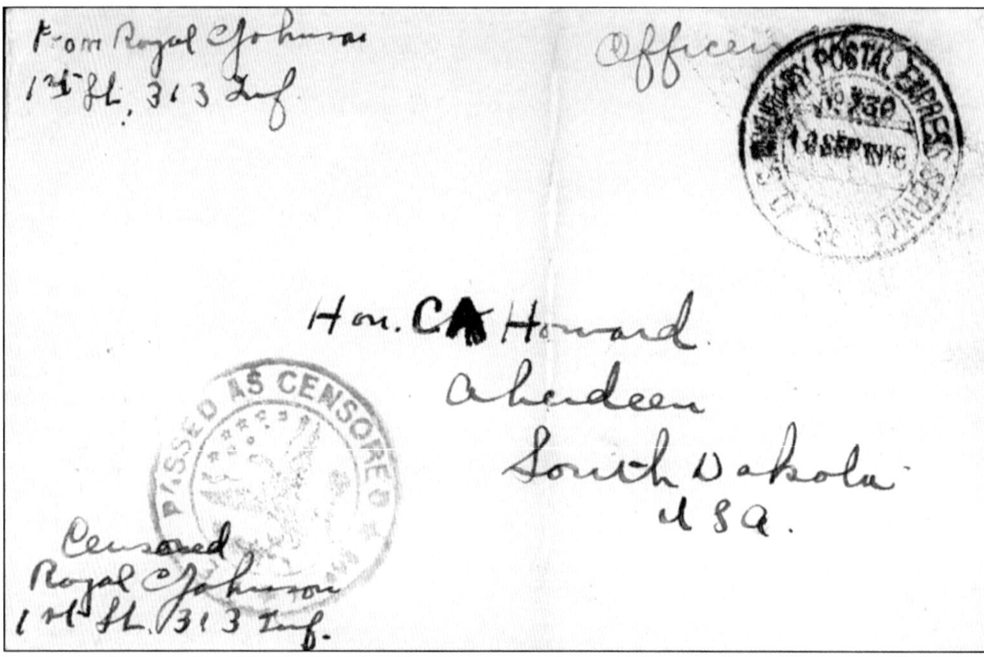

This is a World War I soldier's letter with a September 10, 1918, military cancel from Europe with the proper military censor markings. It is from 1st Lt. Royal C. Johnson while serving in the U.S. Army. He also served as a congressman from South Dakota and was a resident of Aberdeen. The letter is addressed to Charles A. Howard [Sr] who was a captain of the South Dakota Infantry and served in the Philippines during the Spanish-American War.

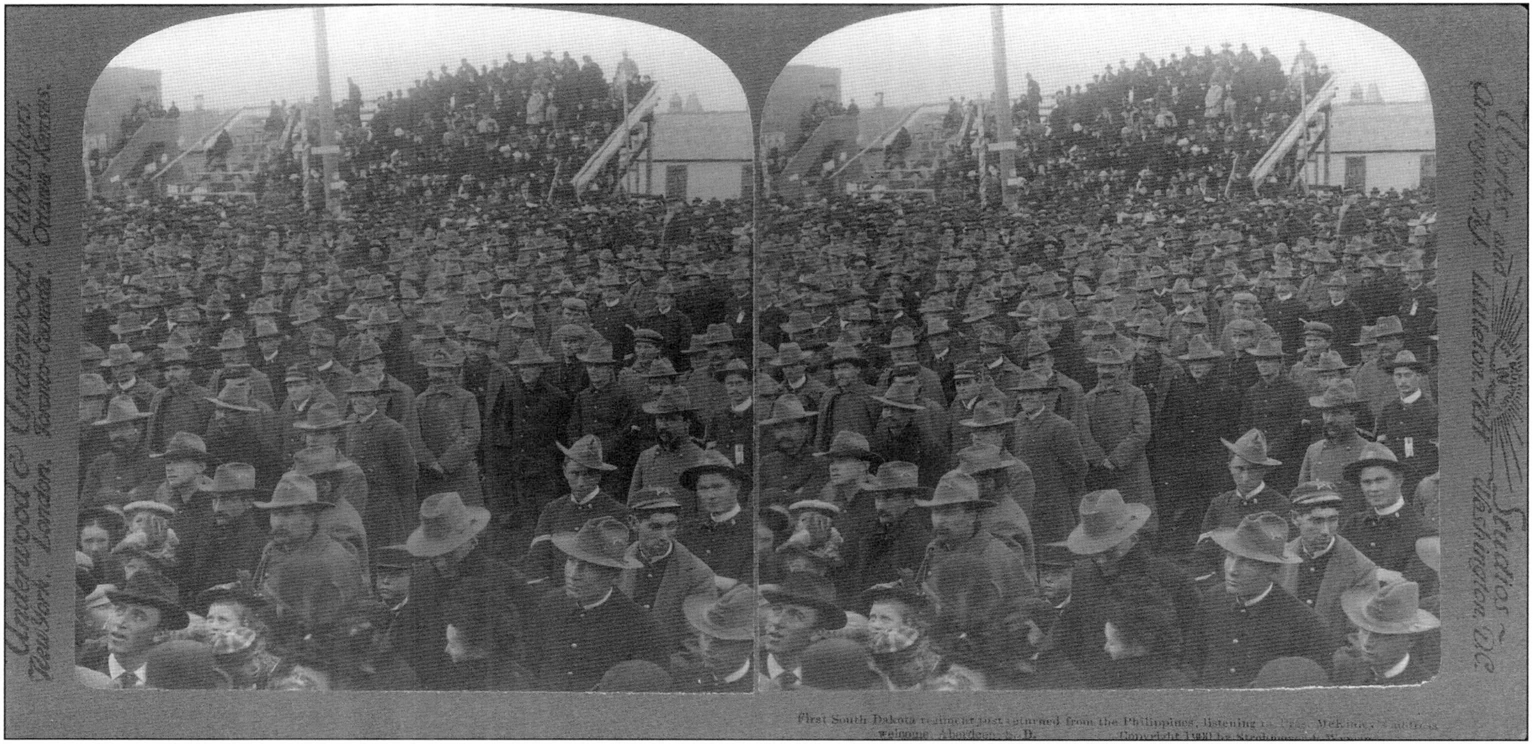

This 1898 stereo-view of President McKinley shows him welcoming home the First South Dakota Regiment from the Philippines and the Spanish-American War. Festivities honoring the president and the returning soldiers were held in the Grain Palace. McKinley was the only president to visit the Grain Palace.

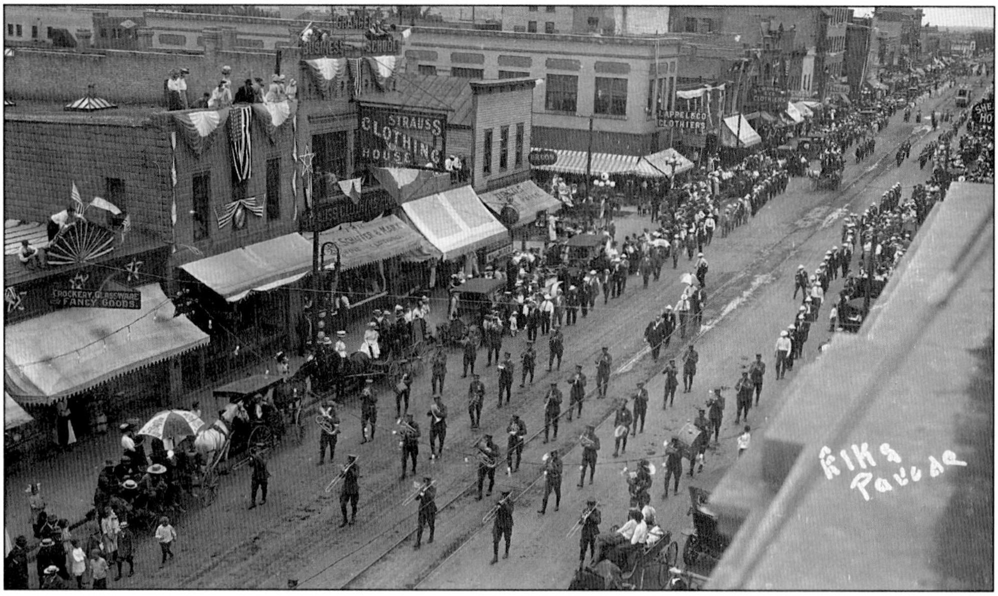

The June 7-8, 1911, Elks Convention in Aberdeen was a huge affair. A parade rivaling any other parade was held by Elks Lodges from all over the state. This picture was taken on the 400 block looking north on Main Street.

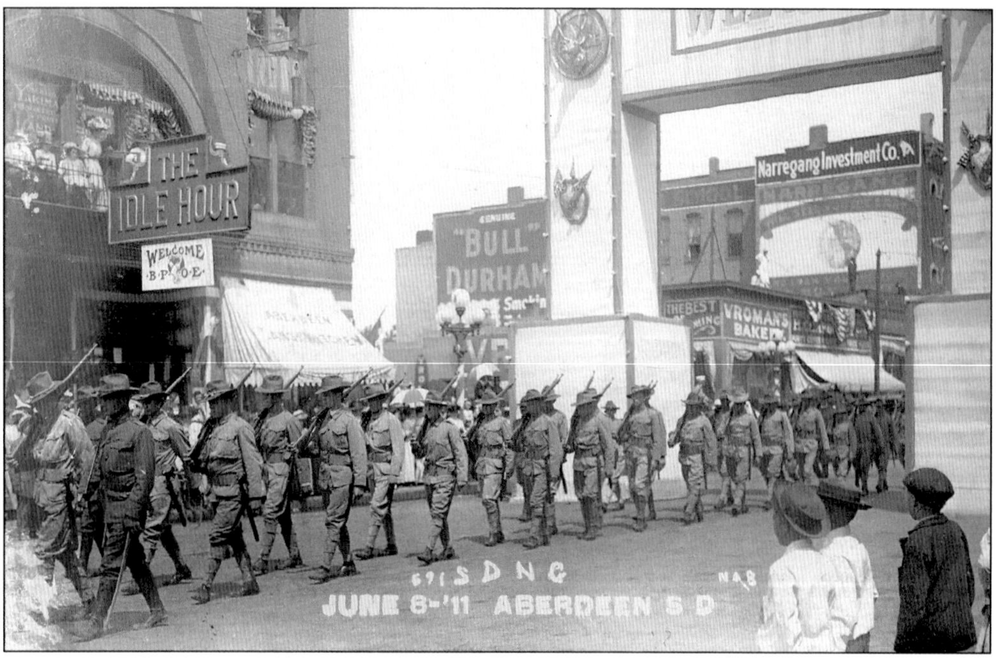

This real photo postcard is of the Elks Parade on June 7, 1911, showing the South Dakota National Guard. The NAB stands for N.A. Brothers, Photographer.

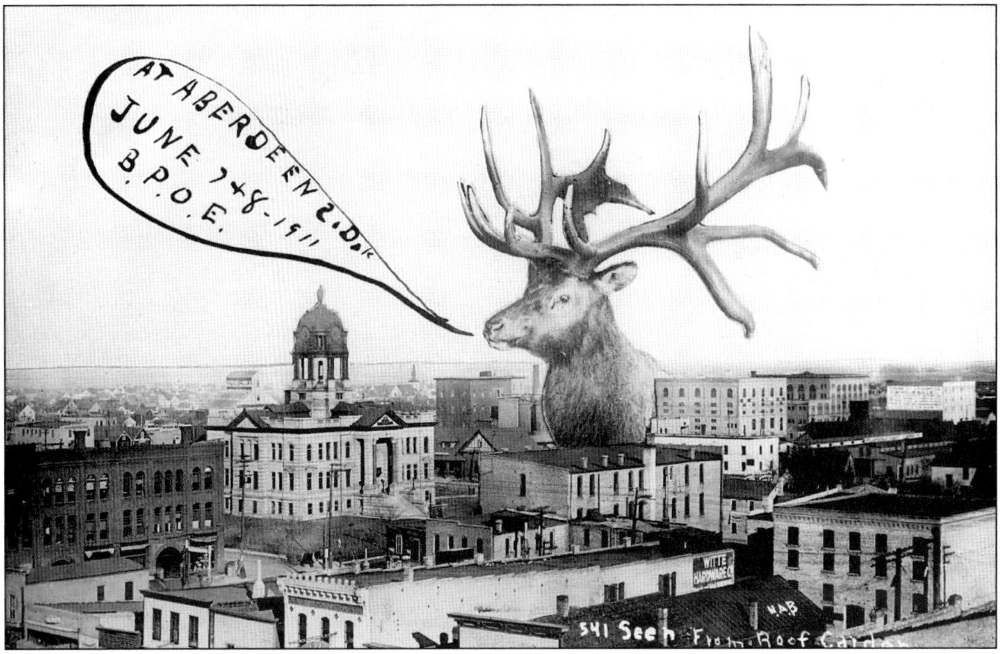

This photo postcard was taken from the Roof Garden atop the Citizens Building, looking northeast, as an advertisement for the Elks Convention. It was mailed on the first day of the convention, June 7, 1911, from Aberdeen.

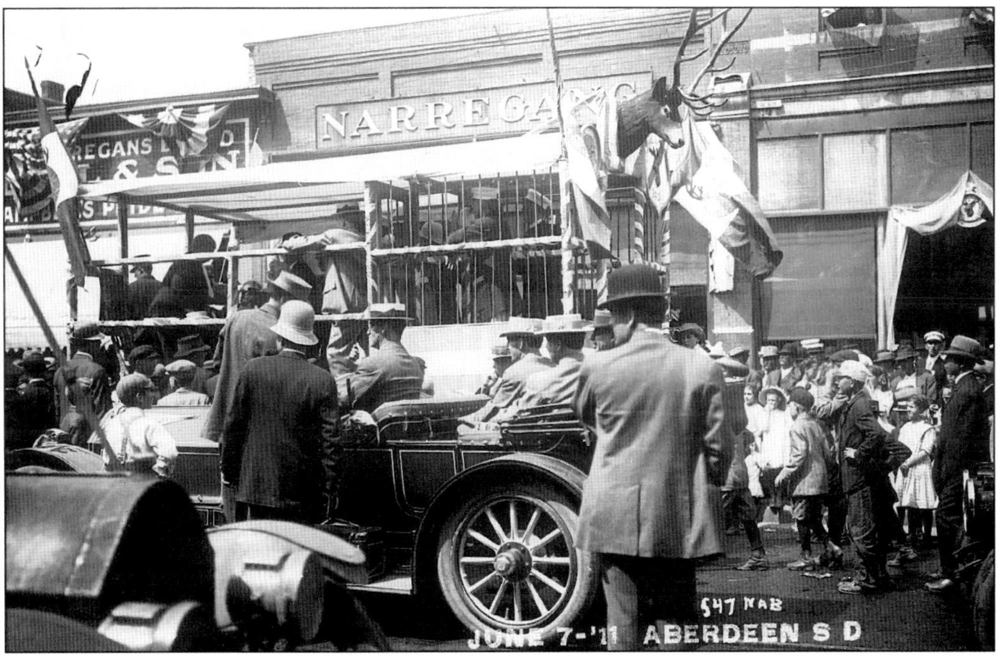

I wonder why the men on the float are behind bars? Something symbolic to the Elks I wonder? Also note that all of the men are wearing hats, something one never sees today.

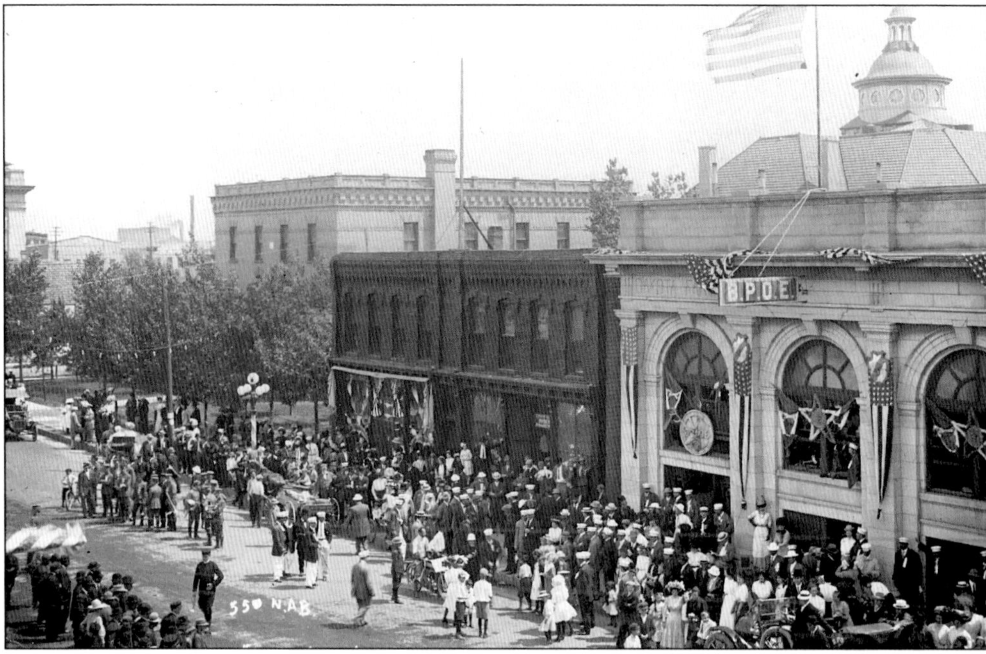

Taken from the corner of Sixth Avenue and Main Street looking northeast, you can see the parade crowd in front of the new Elks Building. From 1906 to 1910, this building housed the *Dakota Farmer.*

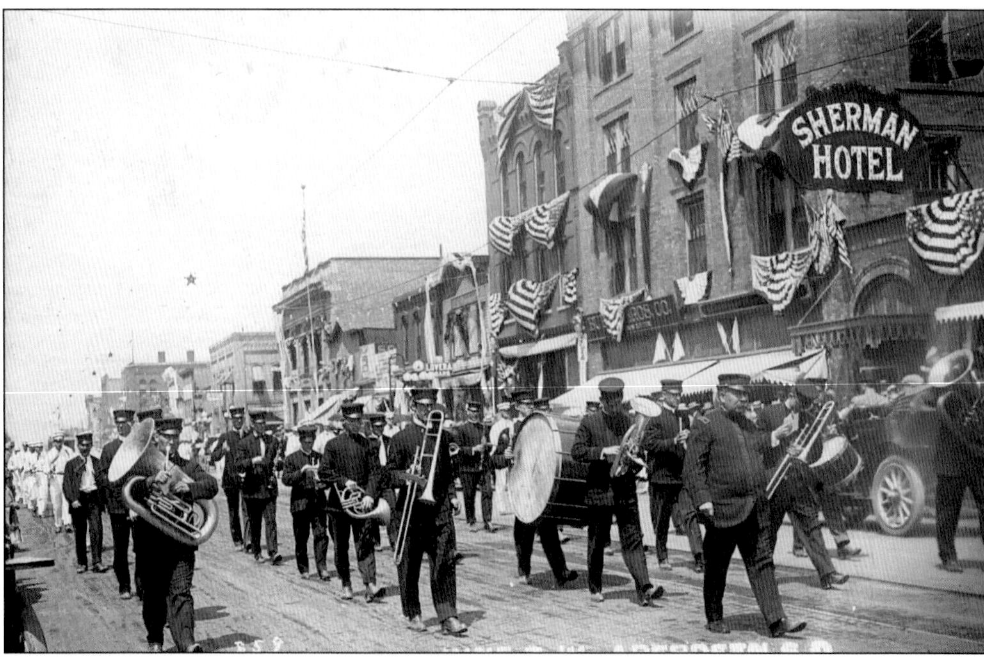

From Third Avenue and Main Street looking northeast marches an unidentified band in the Elks Parade. Note that in 1911 this section of Main Street was still dirt and one can also see the electric trolley car power lines.

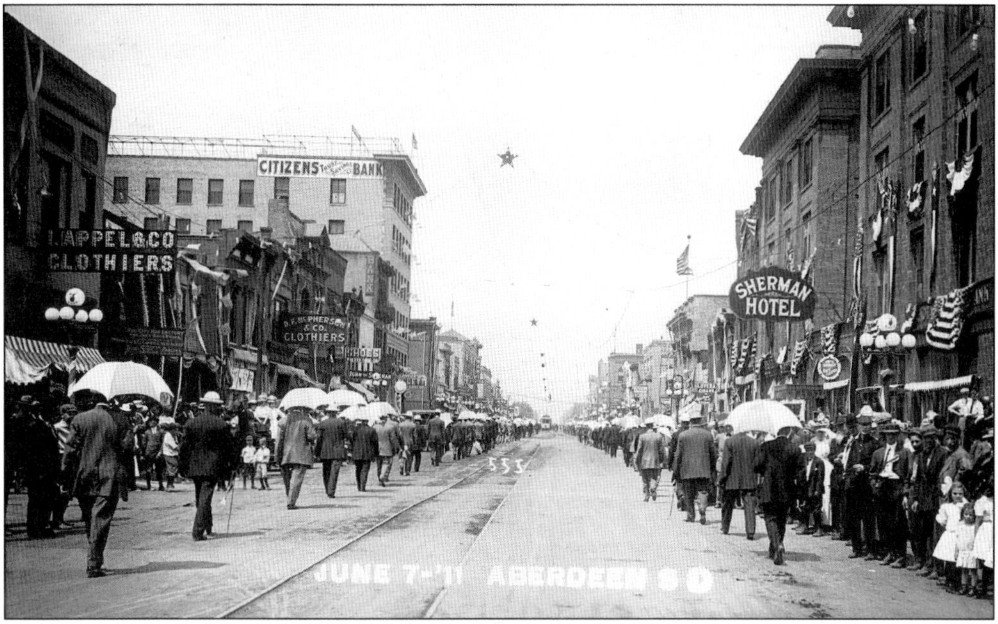

Looking north from Third Avenue and Main Street, I am surprised that there is no one atop the Citizens Bank Building on the Roof Gardens. It was not raining that day, but the umbrellas seem to be symbolic to the Elks Parade.

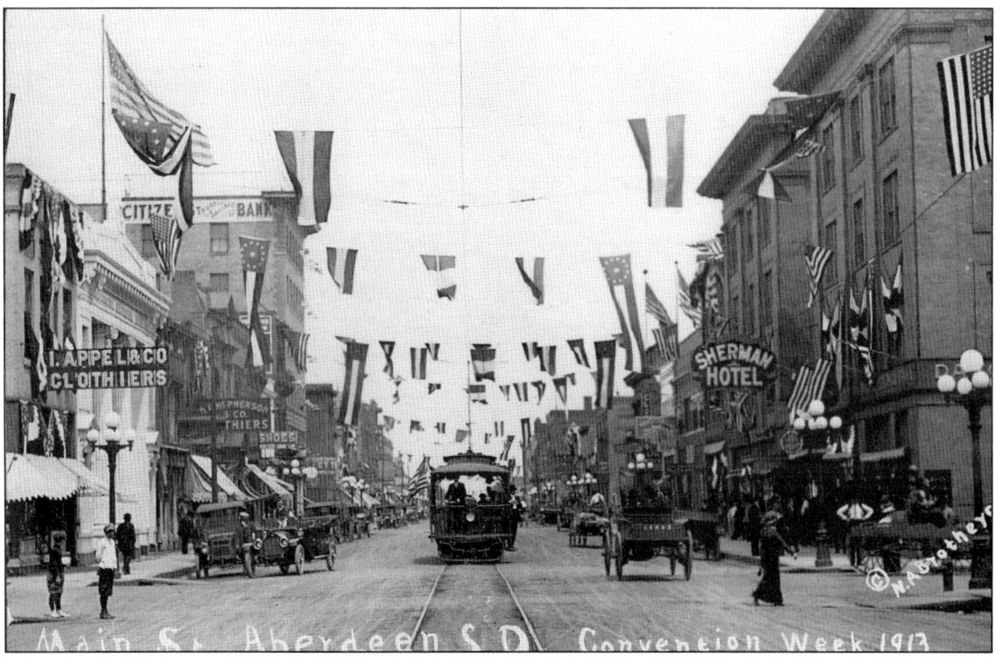

This lovely real photo postcard of the 1913 Convention Week in Aberdeen shows all of the decorations and the electric trolley. By 1913, there is not a single horse drawn vehicle in sight.

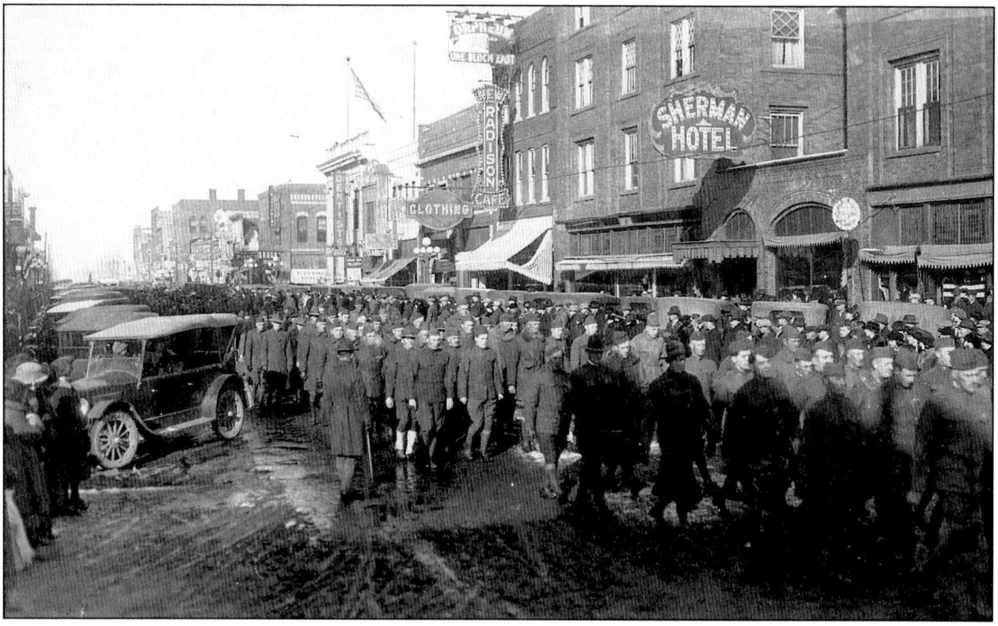

Here are two real photo postcards taken only minutes apart of the 1921 Armistice Day Parade on November 11th. I am amazed that there are only two American Flags evident in both pictures. And it also appears that it had rained earlier that day.

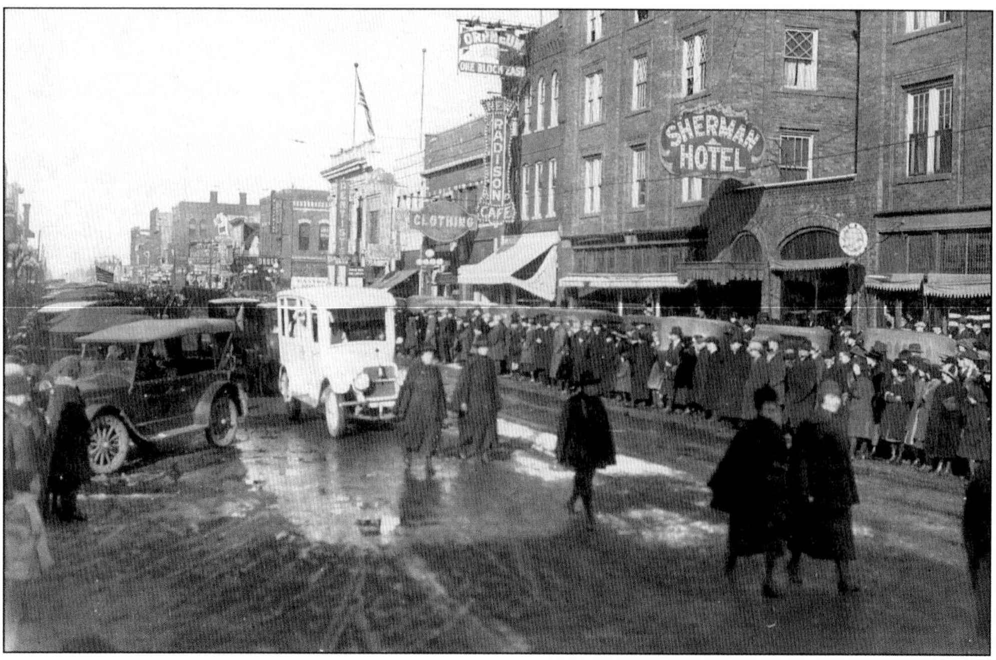